PRIVACY

PRIVACY

How to Protect
What's Left of It

———————

Robert Ellis Smith

Anchor Press/Doubleday
GARDEN CITY, NEW YORK
1979

Library of Congress Cataloging in Publication Data

Smith, Robert Ellis.
    Privacy, how to protect what's left of it.
    Includes bibliographical references.
    1. Privacy, Right of—United States. I. Title.
JC599.U5S56   323.44
ISBN: 0-385-14288-9
Library of Congress Catalog Card Number: 78-55857

ACKNOWLEDGMENTS

Many of the ideas and the facts in this book have come to
me from readers of *Privacy Journal*, the monthly newsletter I
publish in Washington, D.C. I hope that readers of this book
will send me accounts of their experiences with information
gathering and invasions of privacy. The address is *Privacy Journal*, P.O. Box 8844, Washington, D.C. 20003. The following
have been of indirect assistance: Lawrence M. Baskir, former
counsel of the Senate Subcommittee on Constitutional Rights;
David H. Flaherty of the University of Western Ontario; Paul
M. Freund of Harvard Law School; John L. Frewing of Portland, Oregon; Anthony L. Harvey of the Senate Subcommittee on Computer Services; Michael J. Hershman, chief investigator of the former National Wiretap Commission; Tony Hiss
of *The New Yorker*; Ralph Keyes, author of *We the Lonely
People*; S. Douglass Lea of the U. S. Department of Commerce; Warren Leech of Sunnyvale, California; William J.
Orme, executive member of the privacy committee in New
South Wales, Australia; Joseph Overton of the House of Representatives staff; Ronald L. Plesser, general counsel of the former Privacy Protection Study Commission; David J. Seipp of
Harvard's Program on Information Resources Policy; David P.
Weinberger of West Miami, Florida; and Alan F. Westin of
Columbia University.

The following persons have been of direct help: David Berry,
Elaine Chubb, Virginia F. Durr, Robin L. Emerson, Mary
Ellen Gale, Joan Kass, Ronald B. Lewis, David Smith, Mark
Smith, Terry Smith, Keith D. Snyder, and Mary F. Vincent.

To my mother and father

Contents

Introduction

It used to be easy to protect your privacy. You simply had to build a fence around your place and let the word get around that you "valued your privacy." I remember my parents telling me that a man who lived down the street "valued his privacy." As a youngster I knew that that meant not to bother him, to leave him alone.

But in an age of computers and other sophisticated devices, it's no longer easy to protect your privacy. That fence you build can be permeated, most likely without your ever knowing it, by wiretaps, laser beams, microwaves, or long-range cameras that see in the dark. Even if your living space were impregnable, you couldn't very well build your life around yourself, without lots of contact with the outside world. None of us can survive without some sort of government benefit these days, whether it's a driver's license, Medicaid, Social Security, tax deductions, veteran's benefits, student loans, public education. And when we apply for those benefits we have to give up a bit of ourselves, a bit of our personal privacy. Government needs personal information about ourselves to determine who's eligible for various programs and to evaluate how the programs are working.

Private business is demanding more and more personal information as well. More than 55 per cent of all retail sales are made on credit now. More than 35 per cent of us Americans no longer live in the community where we were born and where we—or at least our families—are known to the merchants in town. Most states require auto insurance now, all smart drivers have it, and nearly eight out of ten Americans carry health insurance to meet soaring medical expenses. All of these trends mean that businesses require increased amounts of personal information about each of us, to determine our eligibility for insurance, credit, employment, housing, bank accounts, and other necessities of our modern life in the United States.

Our planet has become more crowded and more complex. And information is the new "fuel" that makes it go. More than half of all labor income in the United States is now earned by workers involved, not in agriculture, manufacturing, or services, but in the production, processing, and distribution of *information*.[1]

To store and retrieve all of these pieces of information, we have the computer. The machine has made masses of information easier and cheaper to store, easier and cheaper to retrieve even at long distances, easier and cheaper to use for labeling and categorizing people. The data can now be linked from one machine to another, putting the facts out of control not only of the person who provided them, but also of the person and agency who collected them in the first place. There used to be some assurance of privacy in the fact that information collected about you might rest in a dusty manila folder at the bottom of a file drawer somewhere. That assurance has disappeared. Information about you stored in a computer system is as current as the push of a button, whether or not it's still accurate or relevant or fair. A computer record also appears more credible, because it's machine-produced, although it deserves no more credibility than the hand-scribbled notes with which it originated before it was fed into the machine.

Let there be no doubt about the dominance of computers in our lives. The industry estimates that by 1990 one out of five American workers will need some knowledge of data processing to do their jobs and six out of ten will have jobs dependent on computers.

At least two buildings that I know of in the New York City area use the tremendous amount of heat that computers generate to warm their offices in the winter cold. I have visions of workers frantically shoveling all of our personal information into massive computer systems, as the shortage of traditional fuels becomes more acute, just to keep the place warm.

Along with the need for more personal information and the machinery with which to collect it, our complex society has also produced other values that compete with the individual's right to privacy. For instance, to exercise its constitutionally protected responsibility, a free press needs to invade the privacy of individuals and publish what many consider private facts about newsworthy persons. Further, we are encouraged to be more open with friends and neighbors, more candid about ourselves. This conflicts with our desire to preserve our privacy. We are told to conserve space and resources. The more we must do that, of course, the more we must live closer together, with less living space—and thus less physical privacy—for each of us. The more we must conserve resources, of course, the more we must allow the government or some other arbiter to scrutinize our personal lives to make sure we do not use more than our share of water, fuel, electricity, or other resources. The right to privacy also conflicts with the need for efficient law enforcement and efficient government as we insist on denying information about ourselves to agencies with those responsibilities. The trend toward increased openness in government has also conflicted with our right to privacy, as some information about us held by the government has had to be released to other people who request access to it.

In other words, with the need for more personal information by government and business came an easier way to gather, store, and organize it: computers. And with them came increased concern about the personal privacy of the individual who was the subject of those computer records. We soon discovered that the right of the individual to preserve his or her privacy competed with other needs and values held dear by us as a society. With the new concern and the conflict in values came new laws and principles to supplement the traditional American protections of privacy. They are laws and principles that every American citizen must learn in order to cope effectively in today's electronic age.

PART I

Traditional Privacy Protections

1

Background

Back in 1890, Mrs. Samuel D. Warren was outraged at the press coverage of parties and dances in the city of Boston. This prompted her husband, a professor of law at Harvard University, to join a colleague, Louis D. Brandeis, in devising "the right of the individual to be let alone." A Warren-Brandeis law journal article on the right to privacy became the fountainhead of later law and social policy in the United States, a relatively new and roomy nation where privacy had not previously been a prime concern.[2]

In Warren's and Brandeis' day, the telegraph, the camera, the high-speed printing press, and the telephone were regarded by many as threats to individual liberties. Surely they altered the balance between the individual interested in preserving personal autonomy and a society hungry for news, communications, and commerce. What Warren and Brandeis said in 1890 sounds like a complaint of the 1970s: "Recent inventions and business methods call attention to the next step which must be taken for the protection of the person, and for securing to the individual . . . the right 'to be let alone.' Instantaneous photographs and newspaper enterprise have invaded the sacred precincts of private and domestic life; and numerous mechanical devices threaten to make good the prediction that 'what is whispered in the closet shall be pro-

claimed from the house-tops.' For years there has been a feeling
that the law must afford some remedy.

"Gossip is no longer the resource of the idle and of the vicious," they said, "but has become a trade, which is pursued
with industry as well as effrontery." And so the two professors
developed a legal theory of privacy to meet the threat of new
technology. Since then, the Warren-Brandeis *Harvard Law Review* article has been cited by judges as the rationalization for
an American theory of the right to privacy.

Later, after becoming a Supreme Court justice, Brandeis
called the right to be let alone "the most comprehensive of
rights and the right most valued by civilized men." When he
wrote that, Brandeis was dissenting to a court opinion holding
that government wiretaps did not violate the Fourth Amendment prohibition against unreasonable searches and seizures;
his viewpoint was later upheld by the Supreme Court, although
Congress promptly reversed national policy in 1968 and permitted certain government wiretaps.

Courts have come to recognize the right of an individual to
recover damages when his or her privacy is invaded in the following ways:

1. Intrusion upon an individual's solitude.
2. Public disclosure of embarrassing private facts
   about an individual.
3. Publicity that places the individual in a "false
   light" in the eyes of the public.
4. The use by another of a person's name or image for
   the other's profit.

Jacqueline Kennedy Onassis and Ralph Nader, both newsworthy individuals, have won court protection against intrusions upon their solitude. Mrs. Onassis' problem involved a
photographer named Ronald Galella who practices his journal-
ism like the *paparazzi* of Europe who pursue a famous subject
so relentlessly as to provoke the person into a startled pose that
can be captured on film. For this, Marlon Brando once gave
Galella a broken jaw. The Secret Service sought to keep Galella
at a distance from Mrs. Onassis and her children. He sued her,

and she countersued, claiming an invasion of her privacy. The photographer replied that he was immune from such suits because he was exercising his First Amendment right to gather the news. A court in 1973 ordered him to stay at least twenty-five feet away from Mrs. Onassis and her two children, even when she walked the streets of New York City. The court ruled that the President's widow, though a newsworthy personality, retains a "reasonable expectation of privacy and freedom from harassment."[3]

Nader, the consumer advocate who severely criticized the safety and design of American automobiles, was angered by General Motors Corporation's attempts to learn all it could about his private life. Nader sued the corporation for invasion of privacy and won. His claim said that GM agents questioned Nader's friends about his political, social, and religious views and his sexual activities; shadowed him around town; sent women to try to seduce him into illicit relationships; made harassing telephone calls to his home at all hours of the day; and installed wiretaps and eavesdropping devices to overhear his private conversations. Snooping around someone's friends and neighbors is not necessarily an invasion of privacy (although it may be actionable on other grounds), said the appeals court, nor is observing a person in a public place. But when the surveillance is so "overzealous" as to allow a GM agent to look over Nader's shoulder to scrutinize his bank withdrawal, then Nader was entitled to sue for damages. The wiretapping and eavesdropping, of course, were also intrusions upon his solitude.[4]

Examples of a public disclosure of private facts that violates privacy are a motion picture that depicts a woman as a scandalous prostitute even though years later she is leading a conventional and respectable life or a newspaper photograph of a newborn deformed baby published without the consent of the parents. A newspaper article with intimate details of one's home by a reporter who came uninvited to a party would be another example.

People would be cast in a false light, and therefore entitled to the protection of the courts, if, for instance, they were pho-

tographed embracing, even in a public place, and then the picture were used under the headline "The Wrong Kind of Love,"
or if an unauthorized fictionalized biography used facts about
them to depict them as vastly different from what they really
are.

The fourth aspect of invasion of privacy often doesn't involve private or embarrassing facts at all. It is a way courts have
used to reimburse persons whose likenesses or personalities have
been "ripped off" by commercial appropriation. A recent case
involved a "human cannonball" who asked a television news
team not to tape his act, which consisted of being shot from a
cannon onto a net 200 feet away. The news team felt that the
act was newsworthy; the entertainer felt that if the television
station showed his complete act, there would be no need for
people to pay money and come to see it. The U. S. Supreme
Court agreed that he was being "ripped off," even though no
"privacy," as we generally know it, was involved. This "right to
publicity" in the facts and circumstances concerning one's own
personhood is nonetheless regarded as part of the individual's
right to privacy. In 1978 television actor Edward Asner sued
the producers of a special show he had taped. He had appeared
without charge only because he was told the show would
benefit a charity. When he discovered that the show was not to
benefit a charity, he felt "ripped off." He sued for "invasion of
privacy," even though his professional, not his personal, life was
involved.

An absolute defense to any of these lawsuits for invasion of
privacy would have been that the individual had *consented* to
whatever occurred. The consent must be informed, but it need
not be explicit. A person may not complain later about an invasion of privacy if he or she gave implied consent. Granting an
interview to a news reporter, for instance, implies your consent
for the publication of whatever you reveal. If the tone of the article is totally different from the tone of the interview, however,
your implied consent was not informed consent. Whenever you
are asked to sign a "waiver" or an "authorization" for use of
your photograph or information about you, you are giving your
consent. This generally prevents you from complaining in court

later about the use of the picture or facts about you. Courts have said that a person may revoke consent before the damage is done.

All of these wrongs committed against individuals are what lawyers call *torts*. This aspect of the law allows you to recover damages when another party commits a wrong against you, not in violation of a contractual agreement you have and not necessarily in violation of some law, but in violation of some duty the person or organization owes you. The four-pronged analysis of the invasion-of-privacy tort has been effectively criticized by others who argue that what all of these cases have in common is simply an affront to the dignity of the individual. Courts provide a remedy for invasions of privacy as society's way of vindicating the human spirit.

Since 1965 courts have recognized that the right to privacy is entitled to protection not only through tort law, but also under the United States Constitution. You will not find the right to privacy mentioned in the Constitution, but the U. S. Supreme Court has determined that a constitutional right to privacy is implied by the wording of several constitutional guarantees: the right to free speech and assembly in the First Amendment to the Constitution is one. You can't very well exercise freedom in political expression and association unless you have a right to think what you wish and to meet with whomever you wish, free of governmental intrusion. The Fourth Amendment is the most explicit privacy guarantee in the Constitution; it ensures "the right of the people to be secure in their persons, houses, papers, and effects, against unreasonable searches and seizures." The Fifth Amendment says that no individual "shall be compelled in any criminal case to be a witness against himself." This constitutional "right to remain silent" implies that there are aspects of a person's mind that are inviolable against intrusion by the government, regardless of how important is the public interest at stake. Then there is the Ninth Amendment, which states that rights not specifically mentioned in the Constitution are retained by the people. The Third Amendment to the Constitution, one of the least known of all, protects the ancient principle that "a man's home is his castle." That amendment states: "No soldier shall, in time of peace be quartered in any house, without the consent of the Owner." This amendment was about the only one not violated in the Watergate era, and you don't hear many complaints about it these days. But it clearly implies that the authors of the Bill of Rights wanted to ensure the sanctity of one's dwelling place against governmental intrusion. As William Pitt argued to the British Parliament twenty-five years before the Third Amendment was added to our Constitution: "The poorest man may, in his cottage, bid defiance to all the forces of the Crown. It may be frail; its roof may shake; the wind may blow through it; the storm may enter; the rain may enter; but the King of England may not enter; all his force dares not cross the threshold of the ruined tenement."[5]

There are exceptions, of course, as when police are pursuing a fleeing suspect into a home or when police have a detailed search warrant based on probable cause of criminal activities, just as there are exceptions to the constitutional right to privacy. The U. S. Supreme Court now recognizes privacy as a constitutional right only in "matters relating to marriage, procreation, contraception, family relationships, and child rearing and education."[6]

The Supreme Court decisions legalizing the right of a woman to have an abortion were based on a privacy theory, as were decisions allowing an individual to possess pornographic movies in the privacy of his home and allowing people to use and distribute contraceptive devices.

The courts will recognize this constitutional right to privacy except when it conflicts with a specific constitutional right of another (a newsworthy family's privacy right does not prevail over a news organ's right to publish) or others' privacy rights (your right to use your home as you wish will not prevail over your neighbors' desire for orderly zoning in the community).

In addition to the protection in tort law and in constitutional law, there is also protection by what's called statutory law. In 1902 the highest court in the state of New York refused to award damages to a young woman whose picture was displayed on 25,000 advertisements for Franklin Mills Flour, without her permission. In quick order, the state legislature passed a privacy law allowing for a person victimized in that way to collect damages. The best-known example of an invasion of privacy prohibited by statute is the federal ban against telephone wiretapping unless one party to the conversation has given consent or the government has secured a warrant. It is a crime in all states to trespass on another's turf, and it is a crime in some states to be a "Peeping Tom." New York State regulates snowmobiles to ensure the privacy of rural residents. Wisconsin requires that a mother's right to privacy be considered before the required public announcements about custody of children. Federal law allows you to prohibit material you consider erotically arousing or sexually provocative from being mailed to your address.

These laws have been passed because lawmakers felt that the privacy protections developed by courts through the years have not been adequate for particular situations. This is especially true in a computer age, when citizens are seeking to regain some measure of control over personal information they have provided to government or business in exchange for some benefit or service. The old principles are probably not adequate when such information is stored in massive automated systems that can exchange and transmit data across long distances to thousands of recipients. Some of the information may not seem very sensitive to most people, but to one individual it may be extremely sensitive. Or the information may be innocuous in the context in which it was provided, but harmful in a different context. Generally a woman will not object if the whole world knows she is pregnant, but some woman somewhere may object a great deal if she wants to choose the time and place to break the news to her in-laws, yet meanwhile unsolicited mail sent to all pregnant women starts arriving at the house. Who among us cares whether a hospital keeps a record of our age, whether or not it's accurate? But who among us would not yell and scream if an insurance company started making assumptions about us without our knowledge based on the same information?

These problems don't fit neatly into the tort or constitutional categories of privacy rights. And besides, as someone else has noted, where three or more legal doctrines overlap to provide protection it is likely that none is very effective. That is often true in the area of privacy.

With the increased collection of personal information in the 1960s and the temptations to link it together, government study groups set out to draft new principles to cover the new situation. One effort by the U. S. Department of Health, Education, and Welfare in 1973 came up with a code of fair information practices. Those principles are:

1. There must be no personal-data record-keeping systems whose very existence is secret.

2. There must be a way for an individual to find out what information about him or her is in a record and how it is used.

3. There must be a way for an individual to prevent information about him or her obtained for one purpose from being used or made available for other purposes without consent.

4. There must be a way for an individual to correct or amend a record of identifiable information about him or her.

5. Any organization using records identifiable to a person must ensure the reliability of the data for their intended use and must take reasonable precautions to prevent misuse of the data.

To this, other study groups have added a further principle that all data banks must have a purpose that is socially desirable and that only relevant information shall be collected.

At any rate, the five elements of the code of fair information practices, or variations on them, appear again and again in laws that have been passed in the 1970s. They first appeared in the Fair Credit Reporting Act of 1970, which regulates credit bureaus and consumer investigative firms. The Swedish Data Act of 1973, including virtually the same principles, became a model. Shortly after came the U.S. Privacy Act of 1974, which regulates the federal government's own collection and use of personal information about us, and the Family Educational Rights and Privacy Act of 1974, which covers colleges, universities, and public school systems. Nearly a dozen states passed their own versions of the federal Privacy Act in the mid-1970s.

The world's largest manufacturer of general-purpose computers, International Business Machines Corporation, sponsored a study in 1973–74 that gave its blessings to the same concepts. Nowadays, when people talk about privacy what they usually mean is not only the right to keep personal facts confidential, but also the right to know what facts about them are being kept and used by others and the right to keep that information accurate and fair.

Many of these protections, whether based on tort law, the Constitution, or new statutes, help the individual to retain some control over his or her personality, by retaining some control over facts about himself or herself. This is the essence of the right to privacy.

The best protection is what you as an individual do by yourself: using laws and court decisions where they exist, using brain power and skill where they do not; refusing demands for personal information where there is no authority or need for it; insisting that organizations keep facts about you in a secure place and use them only for the purpose for which they were originally provided; demanding to see records about yourself and correcting them if necessary; reminding others to be sensitive of your concerns about privacy. And there is another side to the coin: if we expect others to respect our own privacy, we have to be prepared to respect theirs. In our personal lives, this means affording our friends, neighbors, and family the right to be let alone. And it means talking about others—to an insurance investigator or potential employer, for instance—only when there is a clear need to do so, when we are sure of our facts, when we are sure to whom we are talking and how the information will be used, when we are able to tell the individual involved what we have said, and when we are sure that we have respected the dignity of the individual involved. In our professional lives, respecting privacy means accepting a person's desire to limit information about himself or herself, asking only for information that is necessary, finding alternative ways of establishing eligibility or identity when an individual refuses to provide certain information, realizing that we can get by with a lot less personal information, and realizing that people who are reluctant to provide personal facts are not always doing so because they have something to hide.

This book tells you how to protect your "right to be let alone" in a computer age of information overkill and in a crowded, complex environment. We'll talk about four aspects of personal privacy:

1. *Informational Privacy:* Controlling personal information about yourself in banking, law enforcement, credit, consumer investigations, employment, federal agencies, insurance, personal mail, medical services, marital and professional relations, education, Social Security numbers, state government agencies, tax agencies, and telephone use.

2. *The New Technology:* Knowing more about the machinery involved so that you can guard against intrusions by computers, wiretaps, fingerprinting devices, polygraphs ("lie detectors"), surveillance, "voice prints."

3. *Physical Privacy:* Preserving privacy in your sex activities, in the mails, in the workplace, in the community, and in your home.

4. *Psychological Aspects of Privacy:* Preserving your inner sense of privacy and autonomy regardless of how much information about you is collected, how crowded your living environment is, and how snoopy your government is.

PART II

Informational Privacy

2

Bank Records:
A Mirror of Your Life

In a computer age when more and more personal information is gathered about each of us, consumers are demanding "privacy" in their financial dealings with banks, savings and loan associations, and other fiduciary institutions. They call it privacy, but what citizens are really demanding is *fairness* in the handling of information about themselves. They want:

–The right to know what information is being stored on them.

–The right to see their own records and to correct them if necessary.

–The right to have their records kept secure.

–The right to prevent disclosure of their data for a purpose different from the one for which the information was originally gathered.

Banks generally comply with the first three of these so-called fair information practices. There are few complaints about secret information gathering by banks. And maintaining timely and accurate information is definitely in the banks' interest, as well as the customers'. Customers have regular chances to check the accuracy of information compiled about them, in the form of monthly statements (although there is information in loan files and other files that many customers will want to inspect for accuracy).

There have been abuses of the last principle: disclosure of personal information to outsiders. Banks and other institutions will readily proclaim that their policy is one of strict confidentiality, but the reality is that there are several exceptions to this general rule. The White House "plumbers" discovered that Daniel Ellsberg had a psychiatrist by prying into his bank records, without any legal process. The name of his doctor would have appeared on the face of one or more of his checks on file where he did his banking. With that information, the secret Nixon administration investigative unit was able to plan the break-in into the psychiatrist's office in search of Daniel Ellsberg's psychiatric records.

In 1970 Internal Revenue Service agents were able to wave a "John Doe summons" at a bank vice-president in Kentucky, demanding to see any of the records of depositors at his bank. A summons is a legal paper, often drafted and signed by a supervisor of the person seeking the materials, that demands that the recipient of the summons hand over documents needed in a legal action. A "John Doe summons" does not specify who is the target of the search. The Kentucky bank had submitted an unusual deposit to its Federal Reserve Bank of $40,000 in deteriorated $100 bills. The IRS suspected a tax violation but had no idea at all who might be the violator.

In another case, Richard Stark, a California artist who supported radical political causes from a trust fund he had, was shocked to discover wrapped around his canceled checks and bank statement one month the following internal bank memo, negligently placed there: "This memo is to authorize you to read checks to the FBI before sending the statement to the customer."

Federal Bureau of Investigation memoranda about actress Jane Fonda mention at least thirty-three contributions to various political and religious causes. The only source for the information was Ms. Fonda's canceled checks at her bank. The same is true of FBI memoranda about Dr. Benjamin Spock, showing a $500 check made out to him from a Vietnam peace group, and Floyd McKissick, a civil rights activist who received a $2,500 check from a foundation.

In reference to the political study group in Washington called the Institute for Policy Studies, a former FBI agent in 1971 admitted that the bureau "began monitoring the checking account of the institute to determine where its money was going."

U. S. Supreme Court Justice Lewis F. Powell, Jr., said in a 1974 case, "Financial transactions can reveal much about a person's activities, associations and beliefs. At some point, governmental intrusion upon these areas would implicate legitimate expectations of privacy." The law of the land is otherwise.[7]

A majority of the Court held in 1976, "We perceive no legitimate 'expectation of privacy' " in a person's checks or deposit slips, or in microfilm copies of the same items. "The checks are not confidential communications but negotiable instruments to be used in commercial transactions. All of the documents obtained, including financial statements and deposit slips, contain only information voluntarily conveyed to the banks and exposed to their employees in the ordinary course of business. The lack of any legitimate expectation of privacy concerning the information kept in bank records was assumed by Congress in enacting the Bank Secrecy Act, the express purpose of which is to require records to be maintained because they 'have a high degree of usefulness in criminal, tax, and regulatory investigations.' The depositor takes the risk, in revealing his affairs to another, that the information will be conveyed by that person to the government."[8] The author of the Court's opinion? Justice Powell.

The Bank Secrecy Act, a misnamed piece of legislation if ever there was one, was passed by Congress in 1970 to require banks to keep certain records and make reports as ordered by the Department of Treasury so that the department could chase after white-collar criminals who use bank accounts and large cash transactions to avoid taxes or to conceal illegitimate activities. The department has issued regulations under the law that require each bank to microfilm the front and back of every check that passes through your account and keep the microfilm on file for at least five years. This includes *checks that you deposit into your account* and *checks you draw on it*. It includes every deposit slip and piece of correspondence about your account, loan payment slips, and debit notices. Many business accounts that draw more than 100 checks a month are exempt from the requirement. After the public outrage that greeted its new requirements, the Treasury Department amended the rules to exempt checks of $100 or less from the copying requirement, but just about all banks find it easier to copy all checks automatically, regardless of amount.⁹

What about access to this tempting library of information? The law is silent on that.

In originally passing the Bank Secrecy Act, the Senate said in the report that it issues with each piece of major legislation, "Access by law enforcement officials to bank records required to be kept under this title would, of course, be only pursuant to a subpoena or other lawful process as is presently the case. The legislation in no way authorizes unlimited fishing expeditions into a bank's records on part of law enforcement officials." It hasn't worked that way. Many bank officers will tell you that they have to co-operate with the FBI and local law enforcement and will make customer information available to them on an informal basis. After all, if they don't co-operate, whom will they call for help when their bank gets held up—a U.S. senator? An officer of Wells Fargo Bank in California once said, "Sometimes if a guy flashes a badge, they'll come right through here. No employee is going to run to those thick memos to see if they can talk with him."

There is also the possibility that not just law enforcement, but also commercial organizations like credit bureaus, consumer investigative firms, bill collectors, and executive recruiting services will find this sort of five-year archive of your personal life too tempting to ignore. I was surprised to discover when I exercised my right to inspect my credit bureau file that my bank in Washington, D.C., had informed the Credit Bureau, Inc., of Washington about a line of credit I have in my checking account, including the amount of the outstanding loan each month and the fact that one of my payments in the previous two years had been delinquent. I had assumed that the fact of the loan would be reported to the credit bureau, but not a blow-by-blow account each month. I wrote to the bank requesting that this information not be released and the bank agreed, saying that, because the transfer was done by computer, compliance with my request would take a couple of months.

Under the headline "Banks Find Gold in Their Data Base," a computer trade magazine reported a couple of years ago about an entrepreneur who takes the personal information in a bank's loan and mortgage application files, feeds it into an on-line central computer system, and then provides the bank with instant lists of various individuals who, on the basis of the financial data analyzed, should be coaxed into using the bank's other services. The computer company also feeds U.S. Census data into its computer analysis. Through test mailings, it can determine which personal characteristics in the loan application—checking account balance over $200, savings account over $4,000, or loan more than two years old, for instance—will result in higher response to a solicitation for a bank credit card. The same company links fifty banks in Connecticut to exchange, by instantaneous computer network, information from the credit card, installment loan, commercial loan, student loan, checking and savings account, credit, and mortgage files of the customers at each of the member banks.

Most banks now transfer funds to other banks by way of computer link-up with the Federal Reserve Communications System, called Fed Wire. This system transmits debits and credits among banks at the end of a business day. It is a wholesale electronic transfer of funds, intended, of course, to speed up the slow transfer of money by paper, in the form of checks or currency. There are other electronic transfers of funds, usually on the retail level, that raise serious concerns for the consumer. One transfer, already in operation, allows the customer to authorize his or her depository institution automatically to pay a recurring obligation, like a utility or mortgage payment. It matters little to the customer whether that payment is made by paper or electronic impulse as long as the payment gets made properly. Another form of transfer allows an employer to deposit payroll payments directly into the account of the employee. Once again, it matters little to the bank customer whether the transfer is done by paper, carrier pigeon, or electronics as long as it is done properly. Electronic funds transfer (EFT) systems can also serve the consumer in retail locations—department stores, supermarkets, or even out-of-town restaurants and hotels. By way of a computer terminal, you can withdraw directly from your account enough money to cover your purchase. Or the withdrawal can be made electronically through the cash register, at the point of sale.

For a few years, merchants have used such computer terminals at the point of sale to check with automated check authorization services. The computer matches the magnetic numbers on your check with the numbers on a checking account that, according to some other merchant, has produced a bounced check recently. The next step, of course, is to make a computer check with a local credit bureau, to eliminate the need for the consumer to fill out credit forms before opening a credit account. This could be done right at the cash register.

All of this, of course, will generate new kinds of records about our financial transactions and will centralize that tempting information in a system to which access may be gained by the push of a button, not a cumbersome in-person or mail request. More institutions will thus be linked in a joint electronic funds transfer system—banks, retail stores, employers, credit bureaus, computer service firms. It is difficult to keep information secure in such a network. It's hard to decide whether we are better off with government or with business running this system.

All of the computerized records about us, whether in banks, credit card companies, or credit bureaus and the like, can now be used to reconstruct a profile of where we *spent* our money and how we *spent* our time in a given period. If someone cared enough to find out, it can be done. An electronic system operates in the present tense (what the computer people call "real time"), not in the past tense. It can be used to tell where we *are spending* our money and how we *are currently spending* our time. This is true if someone cares enough to discover all of this about us, but clearly in a direct, nationwide electronic system the effort and expense to discover this would be considerably less than with the former paper system.

Academic experts in technology and information were once shut up in a room for a day and asked to devise the most effective surveillance system imaginable for a tyrannical regime to keep tabs on its citizens. What they devised in this experiment was exactly what the bankers want to develop nationwide in the United States—a real-time electronic funds transfer system. That should tell us something about the dangers inherent in a system that, if operated correctly, could be a great boon to each of us.

The scary part of all this is that privacy safeguards in our current paper system of banking are hardly adequate. Meanwhile, bankers are building an automated system with even more dangers to our privacy.

A fairly typical bank policy on confidentiality reads as follows: "No officer or employee shall disclose to any person other than to directors, officers, and members of local advisory committees the amounts of loans made, the state of the bank and its funds, or any of its business transactions that are not of a public nature, except information to persons inquiring about their own affairs, except ordinary credit information, and except information required to be disclosed by law or as directed by the Board of Directors."

The problems with the policy are that its thrust is to protect the bank's interests, not the customers', that it is full of loopholes, and that it is usually ignored when it really matters.

You have nothing to hide? Your canceled checks, remember, record virtually everything about your activities and they often include your physical description, your Social Security number, your telephone number, and, if you're unfortunate enough to shop in some places, your fingerprints.

A glance at the canceled checks in my account for the past three months shows the following: TV repair payment (including date of birth, Social Security number, telephone, height, weight, sex, hair color), loan payment, appliance repair (including the location of my office), name of my liquor store and amount paid, child's sports activity, amount of monthly pharmacy bill, auto insurance amount and company, electricity use, association membership, tax bill, department store bill, parking violation, gasoline use, out-of-town travel, loan to a friend, name of my children's school, purchase of books, repair of a musical instrument, use of heating fuel, name of my travel and entertainment credit card, magazine subscriptions, health insurance carrier, occupation, amount of a restaurant tip, name of my food store, physician, dentist, and—adding insult to injury —the fact that I paid four dollars to the credit bureau for a copy of my own file.

The information in your checking account can be a mirror of your whole life, a reflection you do not want to be seen by the wrong set of eyes—like those of a government or commercial investigator who adds two and two and gets five. Your checking account is, in fact, a distorted mirror of your life. The amount of money that passes through my liquor store in my personal checks, for instance, is no true reflection of the amount of liquor I consume, nor is the amount of money I pay to a major oil company a true reflection of the amount of gasoline I consume, nor is a check payable to a particular publisher evidence of my reading tastes. I often get extra cash at my liquor store and I often buy products other than gasoline with my major oil credit card. The magazine subscription may be a gift or a means of staying informed on both extremes of an issue. I don't want unknown strangers drawing conclusions about me based on what's reflected in my canceled checks—that I am a big drinker, that I am an owner of a gas guzzler that consumes more than my share of energy, or that my political views are identical to those of a magazine that I have paid for.

Banking services are not limited to checking accounts, of course. Safe deposit boxes are not as safe as most people believe. Under recent court decisions the Internal Revenue Service has valid access to a safe deposit box, before or after death, with or without the depositor's permission or knowledge. State laws vary widely about the procedure when a box holder dies. In some places, a joint box holder who survives is excluded from access until state tax authorities have a look. On the other hand, some states permit immediate access to your box, after your death, to relatives, your lawyer, or your executor.

WHAT CAN YOU DO?

State laws in a few localities provide some protection. Fiduciary institutions in Maryland may not disclose financial information unless you have authorized the disclosure or have been notified of an official subpoena for your records and then been given twenty-one days to challenge its legitimacy in a court. California, Illinois, and Louisiana have similar laws. So does Alaska, except that notice need not be given to the customer if a search warrant, as opposed to a subpoena, is issued.

A search warrant, incidentally, is an order signed by a judge or magistrate directing a government law enforcement official to seize materials. It must be specific in naming the materials sought, the object of the investigation, and the reasons why there is probable cause for believing that a crime has been committed. It is subject to the constitutional limitations in the Fourth Amendment. A subpoena is a legal command for papers in the control of a named individual or institution, for use in a civil or criminal legal proceeding. It is usually routinely signed by a court clerk, often before someone else fills in the details. Your protection is not in its issuance but in the fact that the paperwork exists on which you can later challenge the legality or appropriateness of the command for documents. A summons is a legal document that also directs the recipient to produce a response, but it is commonly signed by an administrative officer or attorney, often the one presenting the command for materials.

Court decisions in Alabama, California, Florida, Idaho, New York, Minnesota, North Carolina, and to a limited extent in Iowa and New Jersey, have implied that a bank is liable to the customer for unauthorized disclosure of customer information in the absence of specific legal process such as a summons or subpoena. The right to have simultaneous notice of a legal demand for your bank files is crucial so that you may go to a court and challenge the summons or subpoena on the basis of irrelevance, harassment, or your Fifth Amendment right not to be compelled to testify against yourself. Equally important is for the court to recognize that you have *standing* to raise objections, because it is generally considered that it is the Fourth Amendment rights of the record keeper, not the customer, that are at stake. Under that reasoning, the customer would have no right to object in court to the seizure of someone else's possessions, namely, the bank's.

You should know that the Tax Reform Act of 1976 protects your bank records from Internal Revenue Service snooping without your knowledge.[10] This new law limits only federal tax agents in their investigations, not the FBI, other federal enforcement officers, local police, or private businesses seeking bank information. You are entitled to notification whenever the Internal Revenue Service demands your records, and the IRS must have a summons to see your bank files. The requirement applies equally when the IRS goes to any other third-party keeper of financial records on you, like a credit card company, a credit bureau, an employer, or the telephone company. You must be notified by the IRS within fourteen days of the due date of the summons so that you have an opportunity to challenge the validity of the demand. A court may allow the tax service to waive the notification requirement if exceptional circumstances apply.

You are entitled automatically to suspend your bank's compliance with the summons if you act within the fourteen-day period, and then a federal judge will decide whether the summons must be obeyed by your bank. The 1976 law also requires the tax agents to notify a court when it seeks the financial records of a class of persons under a "John Doe summons" without specific names.

In the fall of 1978, Congress passed a law limiting, in a similar way, access to bank records by other federal investigators (not local or private investigators). Now, the bank customer is entitled to notice whenever a federal agent seeks a copy of his or her financial records held by a bank, savings association, or credit card company.

A person with a sense of privacy can negotiate a contract with his or her own bank to set down the ground rules for release of information to strangers. Insist that the bank notify you whenever a third party asks to see your records. (Only federal agents are covered by the 1978 law.) List the kind of information you feel is fair for your bank to store about yourself. Reserve the right to see and correct your records in the future. Instruct the bank not to exchange data about you between one operation in the bank and another (the tax preparation office and the personal loan department, for instance; or the trust department and the marketing section). And instruct your bank not to exchange information about you with outside marketing firms or computer service companies without your consent. List the types of information whose routine disclosure you have no objection to.

Responsible banks should agree to such terms, and many have. A bank that refuses is telling you something about how it regards you as a customer. A bank that refuses may reveal to you a great deal about the disclosures it regularly makes about its customers. The contract language need not be legalistic. Draw up the agreement by yourself, sign it, and send it to a bank officer for his or her signature. If the bank violates the agreement, it may be liable for a breach of contract.

Here is some sample language:

1. The bank recognizes a responsibility to protect the privacy of information and records relating to the financial transactions of its customers, and adopts and promotes a general policy of nondisclosure of identifiable records to all third parties.

2. The bank pledges specifically that none of its employees will, on a mere demand or request unsupported by legal process or the written consent of the customer, provide any government or nongovernment

party with access to any identifiable records or information concerning the undersigned customer.

3. The bank further pledges that before complying with any formal subpoena, court order, or statutory duty to disclose such information it shall make a reasonable effort to communicate such demand to the customer within two days of its receipt by the bank. Within legal limits, the bank shall not comply with such a demand until the customer involved has had an opportunity to respond, within fourteen days of receiving notice. The mailing of a copy of the subpoena, court order, or statutory duty to the customer's current address shall constitute a reasonable effort to communicate the demand to the customer.

4. The bank and customer hereby agree to the above declaration and will uphold it to the fullest extent possible.

5. This agreement shall not extend to the examination and audit of the operation of the bank in accordance with applicable state and federal banking laws, provided that no auditing or examining agency shall use the records or information for any purpose other than regulatory or statistical purposes. Nor shall the auditing or regulatory agency disclose to third parties any identifiable records about the customer, except under the terms of this agreement.

6. The customer will not be treated in any manner different from other customers, because of this agreement, in bank services, charges, or rates of interest.

_____   _____
Date   Customer

_____
Bank Officer

People who feel especially strongly about this have some alternatives. You can try to do without a checking account, by using cash, money orders, cashier's checks, traveler's checks, and other devices. Or you can use checks that are resistant to microfilming. The dark red paper on which they are printed is supposed to make photoreproduction impossible.

Or you can open a Swiss bank account. Bankers in Switzerland are famous for providing "numbered accounts," in which the name of the depositor is known only to the bank. The banking industry in Switzerland has been criticized by law enforcement agencies around the world for providing a shelter for tax-free or otherwise illicit financial dealings, but the Swiss point out that the service began so that Jews and others persecuted by the Nazi regime in Germany would have a depository for their funds free from the reach of an oppressive government. In addition, the Swiss regard tax evasion as an administrative, not a criminal, matter and will not co-operate with foreign governments seeking to enforce criminal tax laws. Numbered accounts are also available in Lebanon, Uruguay, Hong Kong, Singapore, and the Bahamas.

A bank customer should be cautious about giving his or her Social Security number to anyone who asks. Knowing your number, another person can pose as you and discover all sorts of personal information. The number is the most likely means by which computer data banks in different organizations may be linked together—to talk behind our backs—making automated decisions about us without our knowledge or involvement. A customer should be especially careful that the Social Security number not be used as a bank account number or be printed on his or her checks or on mailing labels.

A request for the Social Security number in connection with its original purpose is, of course, authorized. This applies to any bank account that produces interest, dividends, or other income that must be reported by the bank to the Internal Revenue Service. The need for obtaining a Social Security number from customers who have non-interest-bearing checking accounts is not as clear. Just about all banks ask for it; many will do without it if you object. They are then supposed to keep a file on their efforts to ask you to give your number. Treasury Department regulations under the Bank Secrecy Act require the bank to "secure and maintain a record of the taxpayer identification number of the person maintaining the account; or in the case of an account of one or more individuals, such bank shall secure and maintain record of the social security number of an individual having a financial interest in that account." That means that on a joint checking account only one of you need provide a Social Security number. Don't be deceived if a bank agrees to your request not to provide your Social Security number; it can probably get it easily through its membership in the local credit bureau. Remember that the Bank Secrecy Act regulation is an obligation of the bank, not of you as a customer. And remember that the act seems to cover only deposit or share accounts, not safe deposit boxes, loans, trusts, and other bank services. There is no need to provide a Social Security number when you receive these services.

Don't think that you are the only person who has troubles with bank records and worries about disclosure of financial information. A man who formerly lived in Alexandria, Virginia, tells the following story: "Computers often make mistakes. About two weeks ago, we got a letter from a family in Florida who used to live in Virginia. They had received my daughter's bank statement. The computer made a mistake. Now it wasn't significant, because the amount of money was inconsequential; but it might have been if it had been somebody in a different circumstance." That happened to Gerald R. Ford one month before he became President of the United States.

3

Criminal Records:
How to Beat a Bum
Rap Sheet

On the night of July 15, 1974, Warren Hudson was stopped by
police as he walked along New York Avenue in Washington,
D.C. He was charged with putting a gun to the side of a man's
head and pulling the trigger. A deaf-mute had informed police
by signs and writings on a piece of paper that Hudson was the
gunman. He was arrested, booked on a charge of assault, and
confined in lieu of $10,000 bond. When the victim died, Hud-
son was charged with murder.

After reading newspaper accounts of the incident, an eyewitness came forward to police and said that she and a friend saw
the victim shoot himself. An autopsy verified that this was a suicide. The deaf-mute changed his story, Hudson was released,
and the charge was dropped—all within three days of the arrest.
But the murder charge against Warren Hudson did not disap-
pear. It remained on file with the District of Columbia police
department and probably with the Federal Bureau of Investigation. The District of Columbia police, like most police departments, have an agreement to send the FBI arrest records
involving major offenses.

Warren Hudson is black and a Vietnam veteran. At the time he was unemployed, twenty-three years old. He petitioned the court to destroy the record, arguing that his chances of getting a job were severely limited with an arrest record involving homicide. The judge agreed with that, noting that a survey of New York employment agencies, for instance, showed that three quarters of them would refuse to refer an applicant with an arrest record. The judge added further, "A prior arrest record will often determine how the person will fare in subsequent encounters with the police, prosecutors and the courts."

To the extent that someone like Hudson is limited in job opportunities and in his ability to walk the streets free of police suspicion, that person's freedom and autonomy have been diminished. His privacy has been invaded, whether you define privacy as the right to do what you wish without offending others or the right to control information about yourself. The retention and disclosure of criminal information, then, becomes a matter of privacy, although many people fail to see the connection. Notions of privacy are interwoven with the idea that the government may not single out an individual for punishment outside the judicial process, without due process of law.

According to the FBI, law enforcement agencies make about 10 million arrests a year for all criminal offenses, except traffic violations. Of those arrested, more than 1.7 million are never prosecuted, and an additional 3.9 million are acquitted or have the charges against them dismissed. The chances of being arrested are six out of ten for a white man living in a urban area and more than eight out of ten for a black man in the city, according to the 1967 report of the President's Commission on Law Enforcement and Administration of Justice. Fully half of the persons arrested in a given year are never convicted of any crime, and 75 per cent are never convicted of the charge on which they were arrested.

"Negroes nationally comprise some 11 per cent of the population and account for 27 per cent of reported arrests and 45 per cent of arrests reported as 'suspicion arrests,'" said a federal court in California in 1970 in a landmark case. "Thus, any pol-

icy that disqualifies prospective employees because of having
been arrested once, or more than once, discriminates in fact
against Negro applicants." At another point, the same court
said, "There is no evidence to support a claim that persons who
have suffered no criminal convictions but have been arrested on
a number of occasions can be expected, when employed, to perform less efficiently or less honestly than other employees. . . .
Thus, information concerning a prospective employee's record
of arrests without convictions is irrelevant to his suitability or
qualification for employment."[11]

Simple, isn't it? Or is it?

A man with a conviction for armed robbery was hired by a
moving company in Silver Spring, Maryland. Subsequently he
raped and murdered a young woman living in an apartment
building where he was working. The surviving husband sued
the moving company, among others, and collected several million dollars in a 1975 settlement. The lawyer for the husband
argued, however, not that the moving company should have
known about the criminal record and rejected the man for employment, but that, once discovering the record, it should have
given him very close supervision. The moving company did not,
in fact, do that; all three members of the moving crew on the
day of the attack were inexperienced and had been drinking.

That situation involved a *conviction*, which is a finding of
guilt, unlike an *arrest*, which is no more than an indication that
a police officer had adequate suspicion to make a detention.
What if the man had been arrested twice or more on charges
of rape, but never convicted? It would not be rare for an individual not to be tried on a rape charge, because rape victims are
often reluctant to testify in open court, or there is no corrobo-
ration, or the charges are dropped because the individual is convicted of another offense. Is an employer entitled to know
about the arrest record and to consider it in the hiring decision? There is disagreement about this.

To me it's clear that employers hiring for positions of special sensitivity should be able to take that information into account: this would include employment involving large sums of
money, direct involvement with unattended children, entry

into private residences unsupervised, the handling of drugs, or special relationships of trust. The nature and frequency of the charges, the duration of time since they occurred, the nature of the job and its supervision, countervailing character references, and the pattern of the individual's past conduct are important factors in the hiring decision.

The existence of an arrest record ought not to deny employment itself. And the law in most places says so. An employer that as a matter of policy denies jobs to anyone with an arrest record is clearly violating the law.

Arrest and conviction information is used by credit bureaus, landlords, journalists, licensing boards, insurance investigators, professional associations, college and military recruiters, and others, as well as by employers. So it should not be surprising that a person arrested wants to make sure that the information is accurate, that the disposition of the event is included in the arrest record (whether it was dismissal, acquittal, or another finding equivalent to not guilty), and that the dissemination of the record, however accurate and timely, is limited to those with a legitimate need to know and to those of whom the individual is aware. An arrested person wants his or her record expunged (destroyed) where local law permits this, or at least sealed (segregated in police files so that it is accessible only in particular circumstances with high-level approval). The person convicted of a crime likewise has an interest in seeing that his or her record is kept timely and accurate (including parole or pardon) and that after a reasonable time it is expunged where local law permits.

The person on the current Supreme Court who takes the most interest in the right to privacy (and has a very restrictive view of it) is William H. Rehnquist. He takes a dim view of the idea that a citizen's right to privacy allows him or her to alter the records of a police jurisdiction that made an arrest, regardless of whether the arrest was valid or not. "An encounter between law enforcement authorities and a citizen is ordinarily a matter of public record, and by the very definition of the term it involves an intrusion into a person's bodily integrity," Rehnquist has said (in the Stephens Lectures at the University of Kansas Law School, in 1974). "To speak of an arrest as a private occurrence seems to me to stretch even the broadest definitions of the idea of privacy beyond the breaking point. . . .

"It might better serve the goals of those who dislike the consequences of open access to arrest information to conduct an educational campaign against the visitation of such harsh consequences in the employment market upon one who has a past record of arrests, rather than attempting to seal up only one possible source of such information."

A Virginia man has been trying to conduct an educational campaign of his own for some twenty-five years since he was arrested for a nonviolent offense in Pennsylvania. Several years ago he successfully petitioned Pennsylvania authorities to expunge the record and he has a letter to prove it. But in the meantime, he revealed the fact of the arrest when he applied for federal government employment. (The federal government no longer asks about arrests, only convictions, on its application forms.) The Civil Service Commission, the federal government's personnel office, refuses to delete the reference to the ancient arrest from his personnel folder because it says that the man voluntarily disclosed the information when he applied for a job. The man has been haunted by the arrest record for all of these twenty-five years, attributing to it various failures to get promoted and to become fully accepted by his co-workers. Who is to say whether the arrest record or the man's obsession with it has caused his problems?

Edward Charles Davis III, of Louisville, Kentucky, was gainfully employed as a news photographer in 1971 when a security guard in a downtown store detained him on suspicion of shoplifting. The charges against him were allowed to lapse after his not-guilty plea. A year and a half later, Louisville and Jefferson County police circulated flyers to 800 merchants with the mug shots of "ACTIVE SHOPLIFTERS." Davis was among those pictured. Shortly after that, his boss called him in to warn him to be careful about his conduct. "It did not take long for everyone in the department to know that I was on an active shoplifters' list; and at that time I was the only black working in the department, which made it extremely difficult to function," recalls Davis. Within seven months he felt compelled to quit. And yet "the jokes and questions still persisted. I found myself not doing simple things, like not going downtown, not wanting to go shopping with friends."

Who would deny that Davis' freedom to work, live, and move in and around Louisville had been limited, that his privacy had been diminished? Justice Rehnquist would deny it, and did so when Davis' lawsuit came to the Supreme Court in 1976. Davis was seeking money damages and a cessation of distribution of the flyer. Davis' claim, Rehnquist said, is "far afield" from the Supreme Court's prior constitutional decisions concerning privacy. "His claim is based not upon any challenge to the State's ability to restrict his freedom of action in a sphere contended to be 'private' but instead on a claim that the State may not publicize a record of an official act such as an arrest. None of our substantive privacy decisions hold this or anything like this."

People like Davis would have problems enough trying to prevent the distribution of 800 flyers or one police folder with misleading personal information, but their task is made just about impossible with the introduction of computers into criminal justice record keeping. Arrest records, regardless of their validity and importance, take on a computer life of their own, multiplying like rabbits from one computer system to another. There is rarely a check for accuracy or timeliness.

Christopher North knows. He was arrested in 1974 after he approached the Secretary of Transportation when the cabinet member was touring San Francisco's new subway. "Do you think the President should be impeached?" he wanted to know. North got no answer. As he was pulled away by subway police, he repeated his question with increasing volume. He was arrested for assault and resisting arrest. He was charged, fingerprinted, and scheduled for trial. Federal charges of assaulting a cabinet officer were dropped. The trial judge in county court found the other charges a waste of time and successfully urged the prosecution to drop them. By this time, however, the record and fingerprints of North, a schoolteacher temporarily employed by the Postal Service, had been provided to the State

Board of Education. And he discovered that an arrest and fingerprint file on him ended up at the subway police, the Berkeley police, the state police, the Postal Service, the FBI in San Francisco, the FBI in Washington, and probably the Secret Service.

The Federal Bureau of Investigation operates a massive computer data bank of criminal information in Washington, D.C., called the National Crime Information Center (NCIC). It includes descriptions of about 1 million vehicles or vehicle parts stolen or involved in felonies in the past four years; 400,000 stolen license tags; 20,000 boats stolen in the past four years; 1.3 million stolen or recovered guns; 2 million stolen securities; and 1.4 million other stolen articles. It also includes records about people: 150,000 wanted persons, 20,000 missing persons, and 1.3 million "computerized criminal histories"—arrest and conviction data on multistate offenders. FBI rules say that state police departments and federal agencies that submit these records to the computer system are responsible for updating the records—to show that a charge has been dismissed or a stolen automobile recovered—but it doesn't always work that way.

The NCIC is linked by electronic network to each of the state police departments and most of the major city police departments. Police in all states may query the system, although only twelve states and the federal agencies are currently in a position to submit computer data to the system. A cop on the beat, either by radio or by minicomputer, may query the NCIC whenever he confronts an individual to see whether he can get what's called "a hit." That's a response by computer—usually within seconds—that the individual described by the cop on the beat matches the description of a wanted or missing person in the NCIC computer in Washington. The importance of this kind of active library of wanted persons for law enforcement is obvious. With the use of federal law enforcement money that flowed from the Department of Justice in the 1960s, just about all large police departments have built their own local counterparts to the NCIC, so that the cop on the beat may simultaneously query a computer data bank of persons with involvement in the cop's locale, as well as the NCIC data bank with multistate offenders. Some of these local police data banks include the names of persons who have complained about crimes.

The acronyms for these so-called criminal justice information systems combine local pride and visions of an all-knowing electronic dragnet.

San Francisco area police call their computer system CABLE (Computer Assisted Bay Area Law Enforcement), and in Missouri, of course, it's MULES (Missouri Uniform Law Enforcement System). Connecticut has CONNECT (Connecticut On-Line Enforcement Communications and Teleprocessing).

In Los Angeles, there's ORACLE (Optimum Records Automation for Courts and Law Enforcement). In Berkeley, California, it's Miracode. In Washington, D.C., it's WALES (Washington Area Law Enforcement System). The Kansas City police, who pioneered the whole business, named their system ALERT II (Automated Law Enforcement Response Team). Iowa catches criminals with TRACIS (Traffic Records and Criminal Justice Information System). Lowell, Massachusetts, has a BEAT (Breaking, Entering, and Auto Theft) program.

It all began with a theoretical prototype in 1970 called SEARCH (System for Electronic Analysis and Retrieval of Criminal Histories). For a long time the FBI insisted that these criminal records systems be kept separate from a community's other noncriminal computer records. It said there had to be "a cop at the top," to preserve the integrity of the records. But localities convinced the federal officials that this was unnecessarily expensive and that shared computer systems could be designed so that nonpolice agencies did not have access to criminal information in a shared system, and vice versa.

Using a hand-held computer terminal, a police officer can usually get a hit or no-hit within three seconds. No probable cause or even suspicion is necessary to make an inquiry. On a slow day, cops have been known to feed NCIC the names of complainants and the registration numbers of automobiles passing through a toll booth—even the numbers on cars used in television shows. There have been notable "hits" in which fleeing suspects or drivers of stolen automobiles have been apprehended. In the pre-computer era they would have escaped detection.

There have also been mistakes, as when a California couple spent the night in jail because the computer system reported that they were driving a stolen car. They were. The car had been stolen a year earlier and returned to the rightful owners. And a Maryland couple had to pay police to get back their automobile, after a cop fed NCIC the wrong serial number, got a hit, and confiscated the auto. A man in Florida, asleep in his car at the side of the road, was shot and killed by a state trooper who misread a computer hit and thought the car was stolen.

A young man riding in an auto in Dallas was arrested and held for four hours because an NCIC report showed him absent without leave from the Marines. In fact, he had been discharged from the military three months earlier after AWOL charges were dropped. The confusion was resolved and he was released. Within six months, he was stopped while hitchhiking and detained for twenty-four hours because the NCIC still recorded him as AWOL. Four months after that, he was stopped for driving without an inspection sticker and locked up for four hours because the FBI's computer system *still* showed him AWOL.

A young man arrested on an out-of-date computer hit hung himself in his jail cell in upstate New York.

In operating NCIC, the FBI has always taken the position that it is in the role of librarian, not responsible for the content of the information it disseminates to users. If you complain to the bureau that a record about you is inaccurate, it will send you to the local police that originated the entry in the computer system. However, in some instances, courts have pinned the responsibility for accuracy and confidentiality squarely on the bureau.

In addition to its computerized National Crime Information Center, the FBI maintains an even more massive collection of personal information in its Identification Bureau. The division has more than 160 million sets of fingerprints on file. They include prints submitted by local police after an arrest, as well as prints from tourists who traipse through the bureau's head-quarters in Washington. There are prints of employees submit-ted by the security guards at private businesses, and prints from applicants for federal jobs. The division also files information on some 60 million arrests of approximately 19 million identifiable persons. The FBI receives thousands of requests a day from local police agencies and others to check a fingerprint or a name for a criminal record. The Civil Service Commission, the military, and occasionally a member of Congress may re-quest a check on an individual, but the FBI rarely provided a copy of what it had on file to the individual involved, until re-cent laws and court decisions changed that.

"In short," said District of Columbia federal judge Gerhard A. Gesell in 1971, "with the increasing availability of finger-prints, technological developments, and the enormous increase in population, the system is out of effective control. . . . The bureau cannot prevent improper dissemination and use of the material it supplies to hundreds of local agencies." Still, the judge would not order the FBI to expunge the arrest record of a man picked up in Los Angeles on a suspicion that later proved to be erroneous. Instead, the judge ordered the FBI to make sure that records of that sort do not get distributed out-side the law enforcement community.

At a time when none of us is safe from the terrors of violent crime, it may be hard to accept the idea that an individual has a right to be liberated from a prior arrest record or, especially, that a person should have the right to start afresh, with a clean slate, after reasonable time has passed since a conviction. But the alternative is to label forever each individual with his or her criminal record and exclude that person from meaningful em-ployment. That leaves only one choice for the person to sur-vive: more criminal involvement. I would much prefer to have a man with prior criminal involvement employed by a store where I shop than to have him unemployed, waiting for me on the street when I leave the store.

"When a releasee is denied the means of making an honest living, every sentence becomes a life sentence." John N. Mitchell said that when he was Attorney General of the United States, in 1971, four years before he became a convicted felon.

Back in 1910 Winston Churchill said this in the British House of Commons:

> The mood and temper of the public with regard to the treatment of crime and criminals is one of the most unfailing tests of the civilization of any country. A calm, dispassionate recognition of the rights of the accused . . . a constant heart-searching by all [who are] charged with the duty of punishment—a desire and eagerness to rehabilitate in the world of industry those who have paid their due; tireless efforts toward the discovery of curative and regenerate processes; unfailing faith that there is a treasure if you can find it, in the heart of every man. These are the symbols which in the treatment of crime and criminals, mark and measure the stored up strength of a nation, and are sign and proof of the living virtue in it.

WHAT CAN YOU DO?

Courts have agreed that to deny you a job because you have been arrested violates the Civil Rights Act of 1964, which covers companies and agencies employing more than fifteen persons. If you are asked about arrests not leading to a conviction in a pre-employment inquiry you should protest that the inquiry itself violates your civil rights. Some state laws flatly prohibit such an inquiry, whether written or oral. Illinois is one such state, although it permits inquiries about convictions. Some states are not as explicit, but regard inquiries into arrests as a violation of their fair employment laws, unless the inquiry can be shown by the company to be necessary to business or have no disparate impact on minority applicants.

If you have a *conviction* on your record, state law may still allow you to answer in the negative when asked whether you have been convicted. Employers must tell you in Massachusetts, for instance, that you may respond "no record" if your record includes only misdemeanor convictions more than five years old. This law applies also to university admissions. Oregon law allows you to petition a court to set aside a conviction, if it is your first offense, so that it is "deemed not to have occurred." Or state law may allow you to expunge (destroy) the record after the passage of a reasonable period of time. This is often true of drug offenses and other nonviolent crimes.

Ironically, expunging an *arrest record* that did not result in a conviction can be more difficult because only recently have state legislatures come to realize the harm that can come to individuals whose arrest records are widely disseminated. Usually you must hire an attorney and petition a court for elimination of the record; state laws usually permit, but do not require, a court to order expunction.

Some states allow a judge to order "sealing" of an arrest record. This is a process of segregating the arrest record so that only certain police officers may see it under certain conditions. In New Jersey, when a record is sealed law enforcement agencies must answer "no record" to inquiries about the individual, and not allow the record to be used outside the agency that originated it. Missouri and other states entitle you to receive your record, fingerprints, and related materials as soon as you are acquitted or charges are dropped. If the offense is minor or the arrest was clearly a mistake, some police departments may return the record of the arrest to you or destroy it on the spot. There may remain a report about the incident on the police blotter, a chronological report of the day's arrests, but there would be no report accessible alphabetically by your name.

Even if there is no state law specifically permitting destruction or sealing of a criminal file, courts possess *equitable powers* to order it anyway, because it's fair and ought to be done. Persons faced with such a situation can argue to a state court that the existence of the record violates their right to privacy, and many courts accept this argument. Or the individual may argue in state or federal court that the existence of the record violates the Civil Rights Act of 1964 by providing a means for an employer to discover an arrest record about an individual, or that it violates another federal law against government officers depriving you of your rights under the Constitution.[12]

The FBI's computer system and—because they are funded by the federal government—the states' counterparts are covered by federal law. It states: "An individual who believes that criminal history information concerning him contained in an automated system is inaccurate, incomplete or maintained in violation of the [law], shall, upon satisfactory verification of his identity, be entitled to review such information and to obtain a copy of it for the purpose of challenge or correction."[13]

The FBI will ask for fingerprints to verify your identity, but a nonfederal law enforcement agency will often accept alternative identification. You should go to the police department or sheriff's department that you believe has computer access to a criminal justice information system and request an appointment to see a copy of your record. There may be a fee of ten dollars or less. You should then return at the appointed time, with an attorney if you wish, to review the record about yourself. If there are errors, you should notify the police department. If you request, you are entitled to a list of the law enforcement agencies that have received inaccurate reports about you in the past. The local police department is then obligated to disseminate the correction to all agencies that received the erroneous or incomplete data. Any record that does not include the disposition of an arrest is incomplete, except for dispositions that occurred within ninety days. and you are entitled to have that information included in your record.

If the keeper of the record refuses to correct the record to your satisfaction, you have a right to appeal within the state law enforcement system. If you are not satisfied with the appeal decision, you may then file a civil lawsuit in a court.

This right of access does not extend to intelligence and investigatory files, although you may have rights of access under other state or federal law.

There are no limits on the outside disclosure of *conviction* information in these federally funded computer systems. *Arrests* (and accompanying information) in which there has been no conviction may be released to outsiders only if a state law, court decision, or municipal ordinance allows disclosures of that type. Some employers require an applicant to obtain from the police an official certification of no criminal record. Federal regulations are clear that you cannot be forced to do this, unless your employer is entitled by state or local law to see your whole record.[14] Some state laws are more restrictive about dissemination of information from criminal justice information systems and from manual files.

If you have ever been arrested or accused of shoplifting, you should discover whether stores in your city check with a screening service before they hire. These services keep a record of any accusations of shoplifting reported by stores in the area. The stores then check to see whether your name is on the list before they hire or when they detain a suspicious shopper. These agencies are subject to the federal law covering credit reporting companies, and so you are entitled to know what the agencies are keeping on you and to correct it if necessary. The companies often do not abide by all of the requirements of the federal law and they are difficult to locate.

4

Consumer Credit Bureaus:
The Switchboard in the
Personal Information Network

In the extensive network of personal information held by different organizations, the credit bureau is the switchboard. Typically, the credit bureau in your community—many communities have more than one—is a highly mechanized operation, linked with affiliates in all parts of the country, keeping very current information on your bill paying and on your financial obligations. It relies on financial institutions, department stores, local government, and credit card companies for its information. It provides information to financial institutions, department stores, employers, landlords, lawyers, government agencies, academic researchers, credit card companies, mailing list companies, insurance companies, law enforcement, and other credit bureaus—all by high-speed computers.

Unlike many collections of information, its vast library of personal information is not dormant. It is invigorated each month with computer "input" from any and all of the credit bureau's clients and others. When I saw my own credit bureau file I was surprised to see the latest status of my bank loan and the present outstanding balance owed to each of the local department stores come out of the computer.

In most communities, the credit bureau was started by the leading retail merchants so that each store would not separately have to check out applicants for charge cards. As we have seen earlier, two simultaneous trends changed the nature of the personal-information business. First, Americans began to move away to different communities more frequently. This meant that the whole process of checking on an individual's credit standing had to begin again, unless there was some way for the credit bureau in your former home town to forward its report on you. The credit bureaus began to form affiliations for these exchanges. At the same time came the introduction of computers, which provided an ideal way to keep track of the thousands of bits of constantly changing information in credit bureau files. The Associated Credit Bureaus, Inc., the principal trade association, began to offer a computer plan (called "software") for its members, but the cost of the machines was high. The Credit Bureau, Inc., of Washington, D.C., figured it needed $1 million in 1969 to convert its files on 2 million shoppers to computers. That was nearly half the credit bureau's yearly revenue from consumer reports. The merchants were unwilling to make the investment, and so they sold the credit bureau in Washington to the Credit Bureau, Inc., of Georgia (CBI), an affiliate of Retail Credit Co., in Atlanta. CBI already owned thirty-five credit bureaus throughout the South and several in the New York area. CBI has also acquired the bureaus in San Francisco, Washington State, Oregon, and Idaho.

In Detroit, a biophysicist named Dr. Harry C. Jordan inherited a credit bureau from his family in the 1950s. He saw the potential of computers in this business in the 1960s and convinced banks in California to finance his conversion to computers and to use his reports on credit applicants.

His Credit Data Corporation then established a New York City computer facility and hooked Buffalo, Syracuse, Chicago, and Detroit into the network. In 1968 the company was bought by TRW, Inc., a conglomerate involved in aerospace work. It became known as TRW-Credit Data Corporation.

TRW-Credit Data is active on the West Coast, the East Coast, and Chicago, with its local credit bureaus using the central computers in California. Retail Credit Co., now known as Equifax, Inc., owns credit bureaus throughout the Southeast, the Pacific Northwest, Canada, and the New York City area. Equifax is also the nation's dominant consumer investigative company—but more about that in the next chapter. Chilton Corporation has about forty credit bureaus in the Boston, New Orleans, and Denver areas, among others. Trans Union Systems Corporation, formerly Union Tank Car Corporation, has acquired credit bureaus in the Chicago, St. Louis, Philadelphia, and Louisville areas and in Southern California. Associated Credit Services, Inc., formerly the Credit Bureau of Houston, has most of the action in Texas.

These five national companies account for most of the credit reporting in the nation, through either the credit bureaus they own or the computer services they provide other credit bureaus. Through their trade association they may query one another's computer systems and exchange information. (TRW does not participate in the trade association, however.) The bureaus provide interactive computer terminals to the merchants they serve so that the merchants may constantly update credit information on their customers and may check electronically on the credit ratings of new customers.

With their automation and regional markets, the companies can provide instant credit ratings on large numbers of people. Through their trade association, they can exchange credit information with their competitors, when, for instance, an individual moves from New York to California and wants to open charge accounts at stores there. With this co-operation, these companies can also service the *national* credit grantors—the major oil companies, book clubs, mail order houses, banks that issue national credit cards, and travel-and-entertainment credit card companies. A credit grantor, whether a department store or a major oil company, can obtain a credit report on an applicant who is residing in or has just moved from a far-off city in at least three ways. First, it may obtain the report directly from the credit bureau in that city for a fee, by way of telephone, mail, or computer teletype terminal. Second, it can ask the credit bureau in its own city to get the report. Or, third, the local credit grantor could use a broker, who will get it by computer from the credit bureau he knows services the region where the far-off city is located. Chances are there would be no more than two credit bureaus to choose from in a certain region. The national credit grantors generally use brokers.

Credit bureaus, either through brokers or directly, provide another service besides reporting on the credit ratings of a computer list of individuals. This service is called *prescreening*. The credit bureau will take a computerized mailing list that a credit card company or bank plans to use to advertise its services and run it through its computer data base of consumers in its region. The computer will either flag or delete from the list the names of persons with credit ratings below what the mailer considers adequate. Or the prescreening may single out all of those persons with characteristics that the mailer is trying to appeal to: income over a certain level, suburban residence, large family, between certain age brackets, patronage at certain prestige stores, regular users of another credit card, and so on.

With a mailing list thus prescreened, the mailer can clearly target its advertising and markedly increase the percentage of affirmative response. Or the mailer can even send an invitation to get its credit card to the addressees and be assured that their creditworthiness presents no great risk. Prescreening has become essential for many large mailers as postal rates have increased.

Many consumers are surprised when they receive unsolicited invitations to apply for credit or when a telephone salesperson says, "We already know that your credit rating qualifies you for a charge card at our store." By the way, sending you an unsolicited credit card, as opposed to an invitation, violates federal law. You have no liability unless you sign and use the card.[15]

TRW and other companies also provide computers for services that notify a merchant who telephones if your credit card is listed among those that are invalid or if your bank account number is listed among those for which bad checks have been recorded. Devices in cash registers can now read the magnetic numbers on your check and make the inquiry directly by computer with no human involvement.

What information does your local (but nationally owned) credit bureau keep on you? Name and address, age, often Social Security number, salary, employer and length of employment, prior employer, for you and your spouse; and perhaps your automobile ownership and outstanding mortgage. This information is provided by its member credit grantors, from the credit applications you filled out.

The credit bureau also keeps a running account of your credit at the department stores in town, of your mortgage and personal loan at the bank or savings and loan association, and some of your national bank credit cards. "Then, we added to these, all judgments—small claims and municipal—for the past five years, taken directly from the court records," in the words of promotional literature from the Credit Bureau of Greater Santa Cruz County in California. "We then went to the courthouse and gathered all the state and federal tax liens. Next, we went to the county banks and gathered all their installment, mortgage loan and Master Charge information. At the same time we microfilmed the derogatory and paid account information [from banks, national credit card companies, and furniture stores]." Typical files at some credit bureaus also include repossessions, bankruptcies, unsatisfactory accounts, accounts assigned for collection, news stories, and lawsuits filed against you.

The information is coded so that it may be stored and transmitted easily by computer. Each of the stores and financial institutions with which you deal is assigned a number. The computer record of your account then shows the date on which the credit grantor last reported to the credit bureau, the date your account with the credit grantor opened, the highest credit you have ever been extended on the account, the account number, the instances when the account has been thirty, sixty, or ninety days past due, a coded description of the account (open, revolving, or installment), and a code that rates the account. The Credit Bureau of Washington, for instance, codes its files 0 if the account is too new to rate, 1 if you pay within thirty days or as agreed; 2 if you pay after sixty days or have two payments past due, and so on to 5 if you are 120 days overdue. A 7 means that you are paying the bill with a deduction from your pay or under a bankruptcy; 8 means that the merchandise has been repossessed; and 9 denotes a bad debt or an abandoned account with a balance due (6 is not used).

Each of your checking accounts is listed, with the date it was established and whether the balance is "hi," "med," or "lo."

With these data each credit grantor makes a decision whether to extend you credit; the credit bureau itself does not make this decision, nor, usually, does it have one credit rating for all of your activity.

The more financial information of this sort that a department store can provide, the more popular it is with the credit bureau and perhaps the lower are its monthly charges. Information about you, then, becomes a barter commodity for credit grantors, saving them money. Credit grantors that do not disclose this financial information are charged higher rates for credit reporting services.

There are at least two "Catch-22s" in this situation. First, some credit bureaus provide financial counseling services when you get in over your head, or before you establish credit. The credit bureau usually records this fact in its files, unbeknownst to the consumer who uses the counseling. Who knows whether a credit grantor interprets that as an adverse factor or not?

Second, federal law allows you to know the contents of your record without charge if you have been denied credit or employment because of it (otherwise the bureau is allowed to charge a small fee; most bureaus do so only if you want a copy or if you come back too many times). Trouble is, the credit bureau didn't know that you were turned down for credit until you told it. That information, then, is added to your record. The same may be true of information you provide to establish your identity when you want to inspect your files, like your Social Security number or driver's license number.

Most consumers accept the need for credit bureaus. They may be surprised to learn that the credit bureau keeps such detailed records on them, but they rarely object to the information gathering as an invasion of privacy. What they do object to is inaccuracy in files about them, whether or not it results in decisions adverse to them. My experience has been that much of the industry takes a nonchalant attitude toward accuracy. Its standards are certainly far more lax than those I was accustomed to in the newspaper business. Mistakes in news reporting become known immediately. Responsible newspapers correct them responsibly, and even if they don't, readers are able to evaluate the credibility of the newspaper generally by its rate of accuracy. The same is not true in the subterranean credit reporting industry. Mistakes are never discovered until they cause you harm, or until you take the initiative to inspect your file, which is your right under federal law. Until this law was passed in 1970, consumers knew nothing about credit reporting and were turned away when they tried to track down an error.

When I went to see my own credit file, I discovered on the computer "printout" an account with Sears, Roebuck and Co. that I have never had. There was an account number listed with it. As is my right, I asked that the information be reinvestigated or deleted. I was told that the photocopy machine was broken and so a copy of my file (four dollars) would be sent to me. Thirteen days later it arrived, listing instead of the Sears account a BankAmericard account that I do not have.

I cannot say I have met anyone who has inspected his or her own credit file without finding at least one mistake. Of course, the errors were generally not serious enough to result in adverse decisions, except for a delinquent balance that the person felt should be explained because it involved a dispute with a store or financial institution.

When Richard Brudzynski of Cleveland checked his file he was surprised to learn that the credit report listed him as a stock clerk, previously employed as an attorney. In fact, Brudzynski worked as a stock clerk before he became a lawyer. A bachelor, he was even more surprised to learn that the credit file listed him as married—to, of all people, his own mother.

Philip Meyer, a newspaper reporter in Washington, wrote in the Washington *Star* in 1974, "The credit bureau had my age, number of dependents and salary wrong and listed me as having no account at a department store where I have maintained an active account since 1962. And it indicated a credit card account which I do not have."

On the other hand, credit bureaus in different parts of the country have been victimized by schemes in which people pay $1,000 or more to have credit files doctored in their favor. Sometimes a dummy company is established to report highly favorable information to the credit bureau about the individual, or employees of the credit bureau are bribed to alter a record.

Some credit bureaus will not provide government agencies with information at all; others do a lot of work for the government. Some will not provide information to debt collectors; others will. Some are careful about the sources of their information; others will take it any way they can get it.

Several years ago, a credit bureau in the nation's capital ran a service called Welcome Newcomer (not to be confused with Welcome Wagon). The nice lady from Welcome Newcomer would call on new residents of the neighborhood, perhaps with samples in hand, to welcome the woman of the house, and recommend schools, libraries, and shopping. A housewife in Arlington, Virginia, described how the "service" worked:

> She asked me where my husband worked and when he was born and what our bank was. When she started asking about our bank, I said I didn't want to give out that information. She was writing everything down. She explained it by saying something about how stores in the area like to know about new people so they can send them advertising or invitations for credit cards or whatever. I found out she was from the credit bureau about two thirds of the way through the interview when she gave me a letter saying "Dear Newcomer" and I noticed up in the corner there was a seal that said, "A service of the Credit Bureau."

The Federal Bureau of Investigation's COINTELPRO counterintelligence program of dirty tricks against dissident groups and individuals in the 1960s included "notifying credit bureaus [and others] of [group] members' illegal, immoral, radical and Communist Party activities in order to affect adversely their credit standing or employment status." This was done in fifty to one hundred instances, according to FBI Director Clarence M. Kelley.

Out of all of this, one thing is clear: each citizen should inspect his or her own file to protect his or her interests.

WHAT CAN YOU DO?

The federal Fair Credit Reporting Act of 1970 says that your credit bureau "shall, upon request and proper identification of any consumer, clearly and accurately disclose to the consumer the nature and substance of all information (except medical information) in its files on the consumer at the time of the request, . . . the sources of the information, [and] the recipients of any consumer report on the consumer which it has furnished within the six-months period preceding the request [or two years prior in the case of reports to employers]."[16]

"Nature and substance" does not mean that you are entitled to see, feel, caress, and carry away your report, although some companies allow this as a matter of voluntary policy. Many consumer representatives feel that the law should be amended to require visual inspection by the individual.

You should locate the credit bureau in the classified section of the telephone book. (It may be listed as a credit reporting agency, but not as a credit union, collection agency, or credit card company. You may also find companies that report on the creditworthiness of commercial businesses—like Dun & Bradstreet—but these are not presently covered by the Fair Credit Reporting Act.)

The law says that you may go by in person, accompanied by an adviser if you wish, or may write in advance verifying your identity and have disclosure made over the telephone at your expense. If you dispute the information, the credit bureau must reinvestigate it promptly and, if it cannot verify the data, must delete them from the files. If a dispute remains, you are entitled to a statement (up to one hundred words) with your side of the story in the file. Make sure a reference to your statement is included in the computer file, if not the statement itself. The law says that you may also request that the corrected or amended file be sent to recipients who received the original report on you.

Whenever you are denied credit or any other benefit, the credit grantor must send you the name and address of the credit bureau whose report did you in. You are also entitled to know what information the credit grantor used in denying you credit. There's one more important element of this consumer protection legislation: credit bureaus must not disclose information about bankruptcies after fourteen years and any other *adverse* information after seven years, including lawsuits (unless the report is to someone who is going to loan you $50,000 or more).

If you feel that a credit bureau has not complied with the act in any respect, you may hire a lawyer and sue, or you may complain to the Bureau of Consumer Protection, Federal Trade Commission, Washington, D.C. 20580, or its offices in Atlanta, Boston, Charlotte (North Carolina), Chicago, Cleveland, Dallas, Denver, Honolulu, Kansas City (Missouri), Los Angeles, Miami, New Orleans, New York City, Oak Ridge (Tennessee), Philadelphia, San Antonio, San Francisco, and Seattle. The commission does not pursue individual complaints. But it has the power to order a company to comply with the act, and your complaint may bring about reform.

The following states have laws similar to the federal Fair Credit Reporting Act: Arizona, California, Connecticut, Kansas, Maine, Maryland, Massachusetts, Montana, New Hampshire, New Mexico, New York, and Oklahoma; so also does Dade County, Florida. In Maine and New York, credit reporting companies must receive authorization from the consumer before furnishing a report. In Oklahoma, you're entitled to a copy of your report before the retail store sees it. Companies in Kentucky may report convictions, not arrests.

The federal Equal Credit Opportunity Act prohibits credit discrimination on the basis of race, color, religion, national origin, sex, marital status, or age (unless you're not old enough to enter into a binding contract), or discrimination because you receive welfare assistance or because you exercise your rights under federal consumer credit laws, including your right to correct a file. Married people may have credit information listed in each of the husband's and wife's names if both use the credit accounts. This means that a credit history will be available for each person if he or she is divorced or widowed. If you wish credit information to be reported by credit grantors to the credit bureau in your own name as well as your spouse's, you should notify each of the credit grantors individually. By law, credit bureaus must be equipped to maintain separate credit files for each spouse.[17]

The Fair Credit Billing Act, a 1975 amendment to the Truth in Lending Act, provides a procedure for settling disputes over bills, so that the consumer does not feel that he is helpless in dealing with an unresponsive machine.[18] If you send a written notice of a billing error to the company within sixty days of when it first appeared on your bill, you preserve your rights under the law. At that point, you may withhold payment of the disputed amount, but only that amount. You must receive an acknowledgment within thirty days and a correction or explanation within ninety days. During this time, you may not be threatened with damage to your credit rating, or sued for the amount, nor can the disputed amount be reported to a credit bureau or others as delinquent. If you are not satisfied with the explanation and say so by letter within ten days, the creditor must tell credit bureaus and others that you feel you do not owe the money. If the creditor fails to follow these rules, you're entitled to forget the first fifty dollars of the amount in dispute, even if it turns out to be correct. Remember, the law applies only to complaints about the *accuracy* of a bill (including a charge for something you did not receive) but not to complaints about the *quality* of goods and services. In some cases you may withhold payment from a credit card bill, however, if you are unsatisfied with the goods or services you received and have gotten no satisfaction from the seller directly. The law doesn't cover installment credit or commercial loans.

Several states have laws similar to the federal law, restricting the creditor from telling someone else about your unpaid bill if it is in dispute. These states include California, Connecticut, New Jersey, New York, Utah, and Virginia.

There is, then, a complex of state and federal laws that provide you with consumer rights to ensure that credit bureau reports are accurate, timely, and fair; that there is a procedure for resolving billing disputes; that credit is not denied on discriminatory grounds; and that bill collectors maintain fair standards.

If you are an apartment dweller, you should know that the Fair Credit Reporting Act gives you the right to challenge information gathered about you by a bureau that reports to landlords what sort of tenant you are. These bureaus operate in many large communities. One in Charlotte, North Carolina, called Tenant Reference Guide Inc. (TRG), works this way: a landlord who subscribes may call the bureau with the name of an applicant for housing and receive a report on whether the person has previously bounced a rent check, damaged property, skipped out on a lease, or been the subject of a serious complaint (loud parties, barking dogs, and so on). TRG checks with previous landlords, banks, and sometimes the police, as well as its card files on 150,000 renters in the area. Anybody who's curious may have a copy of TRG's report about him- or herself. The Federal Trade Commission regards the circulation of "blacklists" among creditors—or landlords—as a violation of the act. TRG says it agrees and does not provide such lists. The Charlotte company also shuns computers, although many companies have offered to automate the bureau's files. "I think people do better work than computers, at least in our line of work," says the manager.

5

Consumer Investigations:
The Gossip Trade

The story of consumer investigations is the story of one company, Retail Credit Co., of Atlanta, Georgia. Because of the company's name and because the company also owns several credit bureaus around the country, consumer investigations have often erroneously been called credit reports or credit investigations. The law regulating both credit bureaus and consumer investigative companies is known as the Fair Credit Reporting Act, because of this popular misconception.

In fact, the difference is that a consumer investigative firm collects subjective information about life-styles, usually from neighbors and the individual himself or herself, to determine eligibility for insurance or employment. These files are rarely computerized, and they are not used for credit decisions. By comparison, credit bureaus gather objective information about your bill-paying and credit activity from merchants and lenders. This sort of information lends itself to computerization. It is transmitted to merchants and other credit grantors to determine eligibility for credit (and occasionally for employment).

The Retail Credit Co., which since 1976 has been known as Equifax, Inc., conducts more than 80 per cent of the investigations of individuals done for automobile, health, and life insurance companies. The company conducts nearly half of all

the investigations of individuals done for employers making decisions about applicants. It is the largest company in the sale of
these employment investigations and by far the dominant company in insurance investigations, according to the Federal
Trade Commission, the federal agency that regulates this industry. Equifax also controls about 75 per cent of sales among
companies that conduct investigations for fire and casualty insurers.

"Investigation" is a misnomer, because Equifax does not at
all conduct a methodical inquiry into facts, using several persons with diverse investigatory skills. What it does typically is
send a young man in his twenties, who will stay with the company for five years or so, to talk to the individual involved and
as many neighbors as possible in twenty minutes or less. He
may make inquiries by telephone, or if pressed draw conclusions based on an individual's zip code, neighborhood, last
name, or age. You can see the consequences to you if the
Equifax man picks the wrong neighbor to ask about your character, habits, finances, medical condition, and driving abilities.
The notes of his talks with neighbors are typed up, in crude
English, and shipped off to the insurance underwriter who ordered the report—at ten dollars or more per report, depending
on the value of the insurance policy. An underwriter is an employee of the insurance company who decides whether you are
a worthy risk for the company to insure. Equifax also does comparable work to verify claims for insurers and to snoop around
before an insurance company participates in a lawsuit.

A New Bedford, Massachusetts, florist told the Federal
Trade Commission that in December 1973 she was approached
by a representative from Equifax who said that the company
wanted to update its credit report on her. "I was afraid if I
didn't co-operate, it would be a mark against my credit," the
woman said later. She had no reason to doubt the man's purpose, because he identified himself as a representative of Retail
Credit Co.

The man asked her about creditors, the number of children,
and her sources of income. In responding, the florist revealed
that she received funds for a partial disability since suffering a

"nervous breakdown" when her husband died. When the woman became hesitant about providing further information, the representative referred her to his Retail Credit Co. supervisor.

The woman called the supervisor and found him at first vague about the investigator's purpose. Then he blurted out, "Look, lady, you are going after a contractor in New Bedford." Then it became clear to the woman. She had tripped on a brick and injured her knee not long before at a construction site and was seeking reimbursement for her medical expenses from the responsible contractor. The Equifax visitor, in fact, was trying to dig up useful information about the widow for the contractor, not "updating" his credit files. "If I had known," said the widow later, "I would have told him to see my attorney."

The case illustrates—for those who have "nothing to hide"— how information that is innocent in one context can be crucial, or even derogatory, in another context. The case also shows that Equifax gets into trouble mainly through its own carelessness. One North Carolina man got a letter from the company denying him information about his file and erroneously enclosing a copy of it with the letter. A Pittsburgh sales manager discovered incorrect information in his Equifax file after a friend at the company volunteered to show him the file. A New Hampshire man discovered his incorrect file when it was inadvertently mailed to him, apparently because he was in the insurance business. (The insurance man was also a state legislator, and he successfully set out to pass a tough state law regulating the consumer investigation industry.)

Equifax has more than its share of disgruntled employees who have leaked evidence of company practices to me and to other crusaders over the years. Based on the reports I have seen, I would call this one about a Mississippi woman fairly typical:

> EDUCATION: Extent of her education is not known, but sources report that she appears to be well educated as she seems intelligent and leaves the impression of being an educated person by her speech, etc.
> FINANCES: She has a good financial reputation. She

seems to be successful in the insurance business and
has been known to be a good manager of her finances.
She seems to be thrifty and she pays her bills. Her
worth is made of equity in home by both she and the
husband. They have insurance and personal effects
and cash. He has a good income from the sell of bonds
and securities as learned. No criticism of her finances.

TRAITS: Mrs. ___ is regarded as an aggressive type person and in stable [*sic*] in her work. She is also known
to be a "straight forward" person. She says what she
feels like saying. Sources state that she is an odd sort
of person.

Insurance underwriters tell me that drivel of this sort helps
them to make decisions on issuing policies. Can you imagine
this sort of "reporting" being acceptable to a Hollywood gossip
columnist, a small county sheriff's department, or a junior high
school newspaper? Yet Equifax reports are far more influential.
It has 7,000 persons running around the country writing such
reports on 22 million citizens a year. Its reports often result in
insurance rejected, rates increased, jobs lost, or simply gross invasions of privacy that are offensive and embarrassing even if
they do not result in monetary loss.

Here's an employment report:

EMPLOYMENT: 9/65–9/67—Mr. Van Vleck was fired
for mouthing off at his superior. He was not a good
salesman, did not relate well and sources here really
have no good things to say about the subject. We are
advised that there is some question of his drinking
and his finances while here. Definitely not eligible for
rehire.

HEALTH-HABITS: No health problems. No drug or narcotic uses known. He is stated to be a steady user of
intoxicants, about a daily user and there were some
suspicions that he drank to excess but we could not
verify these.

FINANCES: He is stated to have been in extremely
modest financial circumstances here and sources state

that his wife was extremely poorly dressed and that she wore clothes some 15 or 20 years old. We also learn that the subject had a financial problem of sorts although we learn of no outstanding debts. He had hoped to get back on the financial ladder by collecting several hundred thousand dollar payments from [insurance] because of a bad accident that his wife had had. He went back to [the West Coast] with the expectation of getting a large payment but as best known to sources this large payment did not materialize. We are unable to learn of any creditors and sources feel that he may have been just living on a very low income but living on a high scale as his apartment was over $300 a month rent.

PERSONAL REPUTATION: He had been divorced in the past from his 1st wife, Susan, but was remarried when he arrived [on the East Coast] in 1965. We learn that his given name was actually von Vleck but that he changed his name during World War II by changing the von to van apparently because of the German situation. At time he also dropped the prefix entirely. At any rate while he was in this area he was known as Van Vleck and lived first in a rented apartment at ____. He signed a long term lease here, 2 or 3 years for rent over $300 and had considerable difficulty meeting these payments. However, these payments were met apparently at the expense of his wife's dressing well. . . . His wife accompanied him back to [the West Coast] and although inquiry states separated the couple was married here. His wife supplemented the income of the family by working at a local travel agency. There were no children. He was not well liked here, stated to be very argumentative, unruly, surly type of individual.

SPECIAL ATTENTION TO SALES ABILITY: Our sources cannot say anything favorable about the subject on any of these factors.

POLICE RECORDS: Not available, court records checked and none found.

After reading this, I knew what Warren and Brandeis meant when they wrote in the historical article on privacy mentioned in the introduction: "Gossip is no longer the resource of the idle and of the vicious, but has become a trade, which is pursued with industry as well as effrontery." The subject of the report agreed, and put a response into his Equifax file. His college degree had been omitted in a description of his education, and his net worth at that time was understated. He wrote:

> My x-wife is an extremely attractive woman, who never dressed poorly. This is a joke! She was secretary to the president of [the travel agency] and she was entrusted to escort tours to Europe for the company. Does this sound like a woman in shabby attire? I am not aware of any slow-pay situation, although it may have occurred at one time or another but certainly not chronic. The informant is incorrect about the accident settlement expectations. My wife's case was settled for $12,000 (not several hundred thousand). And the settlement was made prior to my return to [the West Coast]. (This part of the report is all wet.)
>
> Traits: If the interviewer had spoken to anyone at [my university] where I was involved in many functions, my wife included, he would find if anything I was very popular (any number of influential references can be provided). At one point due I suspect to office difficulties I did drink more than was usual for me but by no estimate could it have been called problem drinking. I was once married before and her name was Ella (not Susan). Susan is my mother's and sister's name. I remarried in 1962 (not 1965). My name was never von Vleck nor was the name of anyone else in my family. The family name had been van Vleck and the VAN was dropped in the 19th Century (all that reference to WW II is nonsense). I had the VAN reinstated in 1961 by court order stating under

oath that that had been the proper family name. I had a three-year lease. I tried to break the lease to move to a better and less expensive apartment. I settled with the landlord by paying him $1200 to break the lease. The rent may have been late a few times. That comment about paying the rent at the expense of my wife's appearance is ridiculous. [The names in this report have been changed to protect the identity of individuals.]

An Equifax report a half dozen years ago said that a woman and her daughter in a South Dakota town of 1,200 persons practiced "moral standards and habits which may not be accepted standards of society." It said they entertained disreputable men. The woman had just purchased a new Chevrolet and an insurance company ordered the report when reviewing her policy. The mother and daughter received welfare payments, and so the Equifax investigator jumped to conclusions about how the woman could afford a new car. On the basis of the report, three companies rejected her for auto insurance. She proved to them that she paid for the Chevrolet with a $6,000 inheritance. She later received a cash settlement from Equifax.

A Vancouver, Washington, woman was rejected for auto insurance because of a report that she was living with a man to whom she was not married. "People in your age group tend to lie about their living conditions if they're not socially acceptable," she said she was told by an Equifax examiner. In the end, Equifax interviewed the assistant manager of the woman's apartment complex and was told that she was not living with a man, but Equifax would not convey this new evidence to the auto insurance company.

Often it is true that a man and woman are living together without being married, and often this information is included in insurance reports, usually with derogatory overtones from the investigator. Some insurance underwriters ignore the information. Others say it is relevant to know which other persons in the household will be driving an automobile or to anticipate a potential squabble over life insurance proceeds. Still, too often, it is used to deny coverage to women (rarely to men). Equifax often reports the same information to potential employers, and the woman loses the job. The practice of living together is no longer rare in the United States (although it's illegal in some states). The number of unmarried people living together under age forty-five has increased fivefold in this decade. About 1 per cent of all American households have an unmarried woman and man living together.

Many Equifax staffers have a pretty narrow, orthodox view of how folks ought to conduct their lives. In 1972 a San Francisco man went by the local Equifax office to inspect a report done on him for a life insurance policy. One item in his file was not revealed to him at that time. His file included a comment that he used "his hands in an effeminate manner, also talks in an effeminate manner."

Automobile insurance companies thrive on these sorts of comments about habits, in their pursuit of drivers who live "stable" lives. One large company instructs its underwriters: "The stable person lives at peace with his family, his neighbors, his boss, and himself. He recognizes and accepts his obligations and responsibilities as a citizen of the community, lives within his means and does not frequently change either his job, his residence, or his spouse. . . . Any variation from the normal conventional mode of living usually has an adverse influence on a risk." In case you wondered, the company feels "marriage is the normal state for mature adults."

Pursuing claims to which you are entitled is considered unconventional. "Special attention has been given to past losses due to subject being well known in this area, as being extremely 'claim conscious' and has submitted several minor claims with several different insurance companies. We did develop through outside sources that the subject has had his insurance cancelled on several occasions due to excessive claims. Subject is known to be the type person that will submit any claim and usually has a full knowledge of what is covered and what is not. This information was verified through outside sources as well as the local claims adjuster who has worked with the subject in settling claims." A North Carolina man had his insurance policy canceled because of this Equifax report.

Can there be any doubt that the consumer must have a way of confronting such information so that he or she may correct it if necessary or at least put an explanation into the record? That is exactly what Congress provided in the Fair Credit Reporting Act of 1970 (although, in the two cases just mentioned, the law was violated when the men were not told fully what was in their files).

WHAT CAN YOU DO?

Your rights to individual access and challenge under the law, as described in the previous chapter on credit bureaus, apply equally to investigative consumer reports, which are described in the law as "information on a consumer's character, general reputation, personal characteristics, or mode of living . . . obtained through personal interviews with neighbors, friends, or associates of the consumer." The law requires that you be told about *all* information about you held by the investigative company, not just the basic report prepared when you apply for a job or insurance. "Claims reports" and investigations of the claims that you submit for insurance payment, reports made to state licensing boards, reports made to a lawyer in a lawsuit, and special reports must also be disclosed to you. The following are not covered by the law: reports on commercial businesses, reports related to commercial credit, a report for "key man" insurance taken out by a company on an executive, social service agency reports on adoptive parents and similar reports, investigations conducted "in house" by your employer, and notifications to a retailer not to accept certain credit cards. Motor vehicle departments are covered by the law when they report driving information to insurance companies and others.

As with credit bureaus, you must be notified when a report is ordered and, if the decision of an employer or insurance company is adverse, you must be told where you may go to see your record (unless the report was for a job for which you had not applied). That ends the responsibility under the law of the insurer or employer; the responsibility lies next with the consumer investigative firm to tell you "the nature and substance" of its reports on you and the names of whoever has seen it in the past six months (or two years in employment situations).

Medical information need not be disclosed (except in Arizona, California, and New York). The names of investigative sources need not be disclosed (except in Arizona and New Hampshire). Visual inspection need not be made (except in Arizona, California, Maine, Maryland, and New York). The federal law *allows* all of these to be done, but they're not required. For straightforward help, write to the Federal Trade Commission, Washington, D.C. 20580, or its district offices listed in the previous chapter for the free *Consumer Booklet No. 7, The Fair Credit Reporting Act, A Checklist for Consumers.*

If you have not been denied a job or insurance or credit, you are still entitled to know what's in your file. Look for Equifax, Inc., in the white pages of your telephone book (or perhaps under Credit Reporting Agencies or Consumer Reporting Agencies in the classified section). Or write to Equifax, Inc., Box 4081, Atlanta, Georgia 30302; telephone (404) 875-8321. The company has related affiliates that may be listed in your local directory, if Equifax is not: Gay and Taylor, Inc. (insurance adjusters); Atwell, Vogel & Sterling, Inc. (inspections for property insurers); Physical Measurements, Inc. (reporting on blood pressure, height, weight, and so on, for insurance companies); Retailers Commercial Agency, Inc. (telephone reports on mortgage borrowers); Credit Bureau, Inc., of Georgia; Credit Bureau of Montreal Ltd.; Credit Marketing Services, Inc. (promotions for credit card companies); Market Information Service (market research); Retrieval Services (retrieval of lost or stolen credit cards); and Dataflo Systems Division (computerized motor vehicle reports). These affiliates can direct you to one of the 1,300 offices of Equifax Services, Inc., the affiliate that conducts consumer investigations.

Equifax's primary competitors in insurance reports are:

–Hooper Holmes, Inc.. 170 Mount Airy Road, Basking Ridge, New Jersey 07920; telephone (201) 766-5000

–O'Hanlon Reports, Inc., 59 John Street, New York, New York 10038; telephone (212) 349-6550

–American Service Bureau, Inc., 211 East Chicago Avenue, Chicago, Illinois 60611; telephone (312) 440-5100

In addition to Equifax, these are the major companies that prepare employment reports:

–Burns International Security Services, Inc., 320 Old Briarcliff Road, Briarcliff Manor, New York 10510; telephone (914) 762-1000

–Dun & Bradstreet Inc., 99 Church Street, New York, New York 10007; telephone (212) 285-7000

–Edris Service Corp., 161 William Street, New York, New York 10038; telephone (212) 349-2330

–Fidelifacts/Metropolitan New York, Inc., 25 Broad Street, New York, New York 10004 telephone (212) 425-1520

–Hooper Holmes, Inc., 170 Mount Airy Road, Basking Ridge, New Jersey 07920; telephone (201) 766-5000

–Informative Research, Inc., P.O. Box 3430, Anaheim, California 92803; telephone (213) 225-5604

–Pinkerton's, Inc., 100 Church Street, New York, New York 10007; telephone (212) 285-4800

–Wackenhut Corp., 3280 Ponce de Leon Boulevard, Coral Gables, Florida 33134; telephone (305) 445-1481

Dun & Bradstreet is principally known for commercial credit reports, which are not covered by the Fair Credit Reporting Act. Most of these companies would be pleased if they never heard from consumers; so know your rights before you call or write.

If you go to one of these firms and discover something in your file that is inaccurate, you may have it reinvestigated without charge. Possibly you would want to sue for libel. If you discover something in your file that is true (and therefore not libelous) but that you feel invades your privacy because it holds you in a false light or discloses private facts about you, you may want to sue for an invasion of privacy. The law says you can't. That's a compromise inserted in the original congressional bill to relieve some of the industry's intense lobbying against it. That process is called quid pro quo—you give us something, we'll give you something—but my translation is "Screw the Consumer." That's right, the law gives the investigative firm immunity from privacy (and defamation and most forms of negligence) lawsuits, based on information disclosed under the act. That immunity extends to your neighbors who provided information that you feel invaded your privacy and to any company that uses the information. It does not extend to "false information furnished with malice or willful intent to injure."

In its fair credit reporting laws, the state of California deleted this immunity for consumer investigative agencies (but it remains for credit bureaus). New York and Maine have also deleted immunity in their laws. Twelve states and Dade County, Florida, have passed their own fair credit reporting acts that in some cases afford greater consumer protection than federal law. In Maine and New York, for instance, you have the right to authorize an investigation before it is conducted— that is, the company may not have you investigated without your authorization. Under federal law, the company must simply notify you of a pending investigation.

It's possible you will be asked to sign a waiver of your rights to sue when you ask to inspect your file. If the waiver is worded identically to the law, don't worry about signing it. The law says you may also be asked to sign permission for a person of your choice to accompany you. Beyond that, watch what you sign. Don't sign something like the following: "I hereby authorize the company to make necessary investigation of any item which I may dispute and to transmit the results of such investigation to any person to whom it has previously reported such disputed information. I authorize any business, organization, professional person, or anyone else to give full information and records about me." This is a blank check to investigate you any time, anywhere. Wait to see whether you want to ask for a reinvestigation; some inaccuracies may be corrected on the spot. You have a right to have corrected information sent to whoever got the original report, but you may decide to do this selectively. In any case, there's no need to authorize another investigation of you. Still, you may want to write your own authorization to reinvestigate a particular event or fact and to do so for a very limited period of time.

Remember, you do not need permission from your insurance company. You do not need a written request. You do not need an appointment. You have a right of access even though you have not suffered from an adverse decision. You do not need to pay if you have been victimized by an adverse decision. (It may be to your benefit to pay the nominal fee and not reveal that you have been rejected for a job or insurance; that fact will find its way into your record.) You don't have to make specific requests to see every fact in the file; all of it must be told to you. You don't have to disprove information specifically in order to get a reinvestigation. Simply assert what is inaccurate.

Beyond inspecting and correcting your own file, there are other things you can do. When you are told that an investigation of this type will be conducted (as required by law), alert your neighbors, even the ones you do not know well. Tell them not to co-operate if you wish; it will not hurt you. Tell your insurance company that you do not think these "investigations" are very reliable, and provide alternative means to verify your reputation. Tell an employer who wants to order such a report that you prefer to see it before he makes a decision based on it, or that you prefer he use alternative means to check you out. Some insurance companies. like the Equitable Life Assurance Society, use their own staff investigators, not Equifax; others, like Allstate Insurance Cos. and State Farm Insurance Cos., order consumer reports on only one out of five or one out of ten applicants. Shop around for the companies whose policies are more responsible than the others.

By joining group policies, you eliminate the need for such investigations, because the company is insuring all members of the group, regardless of the results of a background check. The rates may be higher for group policies.

Anticipate problems in a consumer report. If you have a disgruntled neighbor, or if you are "cohabiting," or if your neighbors have seen you intoxicated or behind in your bills or both, tell the insurance company and explain the circumstances. Tell the insurer that you're a good risk anyway, and offer evidence.

Watch what you say if an investigator asks you for information about a neighbor. Ask for identification, check with your neighbor first. Don't pretend to be an expert on your neighbor's finances, health, drinking, or smoking. Don't worry about hurting your neighbor if you simply say you don't feel that such interviews are proper or fair. Don't leave the impression ever that there is adverse information that you can't or won't talk about. If you are told that the investigator is "from ____ insurance company," ask for proof. Chances are he or she is from a consumer reporting firm. One Equifax investigator told me his common trick was to go to a pay telephone at the local post office, call a number, and say, "This is Mr. Jones at the post office. We need the forwarding address for ____." Another told the Federal Trade Commission, "I would go to the claimant's home and say that I was looking for a person I believe that resided in the neighborhood and had they ever heard of that person." One consumer complained that Equifax sent a young girl to the home posing as a high school student writing a paper on highway safety (a pretext for asking about a neighbor's driving habits).

In Australia, one insurance snooper would even let the air out of the tires of a person who had filed a claim for injuries to his back. The snooper would then hope to catch the injured person changing the tire. An investigator in this country told a government commission that he would call women with similar claims and ask what kind of detergent they used. Regardless of the answer, he would ask whether a photographer could take pictures of her for an advertisement. When she agreed, the snooper would then hope to trap the woman into lifting laundry despite her back injury and take a photograph of her.

Whether as the source of information or as the subject of a report, remember two things about the dominant company in this field. First it argued to the Federal Trade Commission that it should have to meet a lesser standard of care (and accuracy) in its lower-priced reports for the usual insurance policy than it does for policies in the millions of dollars. And second, the official Equifax company policy on privacy, as expressed in its 1973 annual report, is as follows:

> Can modern man find complete privacy? "Yes," is the answer most commonly given, "but only if he is willing to live in a mountaintop cave with an immovable boulder."

6

Employment Records: The Tools of the Boss's Tyranny

Alexander Solzhenitsyn wrote in *Cancer Ward:*

> As every man goes through life he fills in a number of
> forms for the record, each containing a number of
> questions. . . . There are thus hundreds of little
> threads radiating from every man, millions of threads
> in all. If these threads were suddenly to become visi-
> ble, the whole sky would look like a spider's web, and
> if they materialized as rubber bands—buses, trams and
> even people would all lose the ability to move, and
> the wind would be unable to carry torn-up newspapers
> or autumn leaves along the streets of the city. They
> are not visible, they are not material, but every man is
> constantly aware of their existence. . . . Every man,
> permanently aware of his own invisible threads, natu-
> rally develops a respect for the people who manipulate
> the threads.

In American society the most significant "people who manipulate the threads" are the federal government and an individual's employer. American law has developed protections against

governmental abuses—the concepts of constitutional rights, due process, equal opportunity, and individual liberties. Governmental functions are subject to constant scrutiny by the press. New laws give each citizen the right to obtain documents about the government's decision making and to attend most of its meetings. Its record keeping about citizens is now subject to legal restrictions.

The same is not true of the private employer.

Unless you work for the government itself, there is no body of constitutional law to protect you if your employer chooses to deny your right of free speech, freedom against unreasonable searches, right to remain silent, right to confront the witnesses against you, right to a fair trial and an appeals process, or right to privacy. Nor do you even have the power of a vote to use as leverage.

Can there be any doubt that the employer exercises powers of life and death over each of us at least as great as the power of government? The power to deprive us of our livelihood, often with no notice. The power to terminate our health insurance coverage, our pensions, the possibilities for education. The power to lay off, to transfer to an undesirable community, to reassign to an unhappy job. The power to make us miserable. The power to strip us of our identity, to the extent that our vocation is our identity.

The tools by which the employer exercises its dominion over us are the records it keeps on us—the "little threads" that Solzhenitsyn wrote about. And there are currently no controls over this record keeping. Virtually no legal limits on the information that an employer may gather. No limits on the disclosure of that information to others. No limits on the method of storage or dissemination. No requirement (except in four states) that an employee may inspect his or her own files. No requirement that an employer correct inaccurate or unfair records about an individual.

Most companies have always wanted to know everything about everybody who works there or applies for work. Henry Ford's "Social Department," as he called it, sent fifty investigators around to the homes of assembly-line workers to find out their marital situation, number of children, religious and ethnic backgrounds, and more. "How much money had he saved, and where did he keep it? His social outlook and mode of living also came under scrutiny. His health? His doctor? His recreations? The investigator meanwhile looked about sharply, if unobtrusively, so that he could report on 'habits,' 'home condition,' and 'neighborhood.' All this information and more was placed on blue and white forms," according to *Ford*, a biography by Allan Nevins.[19]

Things have not changed much at the Ford Motor Company. The company requires most nonunionized applicants to sign the following authorization:

> I understand that I shall not become an employee of Ford Motor Company or any of its subsidiaries until I have signed an employment agreement with the final approval of the Employer and that such employment will be subject to verification of previous employment, data provided in my application, and any related documents or resume; and will be contingent on my submitting to a physical examination and satisfying the physical qualifications for employment as determined by the Employer. I authorize educational institutions, employers, law enforcement authorities, organizations and individuals having relevant information concerning me to release such information and I release all concerned from any liability in connection therewith. I understand that an investigative report may be made which might include information concerning my character, general reputation, personal characteristics, and mode of living (whichever may be applicable) and that I can make a written request of the consumer reporting agency for additional information as to the nature and scope of the report if one is made. I understand that if I am employed, evidence of U.S. citizenship or U.S. resident status and a birth certificate or other evidence of date of birth is required.

When you strip away the excess language, the applicant here is authorizing any organization or person to provide any information about himself or herself to Ford Motor Co., without any liability at any time in the future for negligence or malice or inaccuracy by Ford Motor Co. or anybody who provided the information. "In actual fact, little background checking is done," according to Ford's personnel director, except for professional and supervisory positions. But *all* nonunion applicants are asked to sign the authorization, without any limits of time or scope, so that the company has this "blank check" on file, to use later when needed or simply to dangle over the worker's head like the sword over Damocles in Greek mythology.

The starting point for employment record keeping, as any personnel officer will tell you, is the employee himself or herself. The employee fills in the "number of forms for the record, each containing a number of questions. . . ." And he or she is forced to sign the authorizations to permit access to medical, credit, prior employment, law enforcement, credit card, and other data collected on the individual. No signature, no job.

There are no limits to the questions that personnel departments dream up to ask applicants. A typical application will ask for the following information, none of which is necessary until the applicant is actually hired, if then:

- —Persons to notify in case of emergency
- —Social Security number
- —Age and marital status
- —Color of eyes and hair
- —Engaged to be married?
- —Hobbies and leisure-time activities
- —Compensation received for prior injuries
- —Veteran's benefits for schooling
- —Wife's and/or mother's maiden name
- —Driver's license number and expiration date
- —Father's income
- —Spouse's employer

A woman applying for a job as a social worker in Montgomery County, Maryland, was asked the following:

Has any blood relation had tuberculosis, diabetes, cancer, or heart trouble?

Have you ever had or have you now swollen or painful joints, color blindness, frequent dizziness, history of head injury, night sweats, pain or pressure in the chest, chronic cough, cramps in your legs, frequent indigestion, dentures, venereal disease, recent gain or loss of weight, lameness, "trick" knee, foot trouble, frequent trouble sleeping, frequent or terrifying nightmares, depression or excessive worry, any drug or narcotic habit, excessive drinking use, periods of unconsciousness, fear of heights, fear of closed spaces, glasses?

Have you ever attempted suicide, been a sleepwalker, lived with anyone who had tuberculosis, coughed up blood?

Females only, have you ever been pregnant, had a vaginal discharge, been treated for a female disorder, had painful menstruation, date of last menstrual period?

The woman was persistent. After two years of court activity, she managed to get the county to delete the "females only" questions, as well as the questions about mental health, alcohol, drugs, night sweats, worry, and sleeping.

The written application forms, which sometimes run up to ten pages each, are just the beginning. Applicants are asked all manner of questions in the personal interview, and the interviewer, of course, is taking notes. "I have been told by prospective employers," said Tom Nadeau, a California writer, "to cut my hair, let my hair grow, stand up straight, shave my mustache, grow a mustache, join a union, sign a paper saying I would not join a union, that my degree was worthless, that it was unfortunate that I had a degree, that I must supply my own car and that it must be an economy model, that I ought to dress better, that I ought to buy some more 'relaxed' clothes, that I was not creative enough, that I was too hip, too square, that my previous salary was too low, that my salary history indicated I would not be happy with such a low-paying job, that I was unfortunately married and therefore too tied down, or on the other hand, that my wife and I have traveled too much. Interviewers have asked me to summarize my political views, to write my biography, to describe myself in one sentence and to rate myself according to a chart on my aggressiveness, my determination to please and my loyalty."

Nadeau's conclusion from all of this: "Generally speaking, the sleazier the job, the longer and more detailed the application."[20]

With your signed authorization in hand, the personnel office is able to gather more personal data on you from doctors and hospitals, credit bureaus and consumer investigative companies, prior employers, neighbors and co-workers, schools and colleges —even mystics, palm readers, oracles, fortunetellers, and gurus, if the company feels this is helpful. Many companies require highly intrusive personality tests. Some companies even analyze handwriting to screen applicants. Others use electrical devices that measure stress in the voice, or so-called lie detector tests. Your ability to eat lunch in an appropriately relaxed and/or stimulating manner is important to some companies. Studies have shown that none of these is an accurate predictor of job performance.

The Ford Motor Co. provides a good example of the sorts of other information that is collected on employees. A medical questionnaire and the results of a medical examination are included in the folder or kept elsewhere. There are annual evaluations by supervisors, as well as a regular survey to assess the employee, his or her place in the company structure, and possibilities for future promotion. And there are comparisons with co-workers for deciding who gets merit raises and promotions and layoffs. This latter form is not available for the individual's inspection because it includes personal information on others in the department and proposals for raises that are not final. Ford also has "a development plan" for each middle and senior manager and for minorities and women at lower grades. The first page contains name, birth date, service date, education, honors, and work experience both within the company and previously. "The second page contains management's view of the individual's potential, specific plans for development work assignments, and the names and assessments of those other employees who are considered qualified replacements," according to a 1976 study of Ford's personnel record keeping.

The personnel folder also includes letters of commendation or warning and "various forms or memoranda depending upon local practices." These can include newspaper clippings and informal notes from co-workers, information about health insurance claims, and suggestions made by the employee.

Many companies have employees submit claims for insurance reimbursement of medical expenses through the company's personnel department, and so copies end up in the employee's personnel folder. At other companies, a copy of the claim is sent by the insurance company to the personnel office. Either way, what this means is that co-workers are able to peek at sensitive information on these forms that is none of anyone else's business—the name of a psychiatrist or a cancer clinic, a consultation for marital difficulties or a payment for dentures, the name of a gynecologist or a podiatrist, the identity of a child's sickness or a checkup for gonorrhea. What this also means is that a supervisor rummaging through a personnel folder to evaluate an applicant or employee often runs across medical information that should have no bearing on the decision.

Ford Motor Co. says no insurance claims are filed in its personnel folders.

Ford's computerized files include separate payroll systems for hourly and salaried workers, including date of birth, sex, educational background, marital status, dependents, and deductions for union dues, health insurance, loans, credit union, bonds, and so on. The computerized system for salaried workers also includes the employee's position, organization, salary, and last nine positions and salaries with the company. It is this record that is most commonly used for routine inquiries from outsiders.

Just about all companies readily confirm that a person is employed and for how long; many will disclose salary without the consent of the individual. The rules of the Civil Service Commission, the federal government personnel office, state that the name, present and past position titles, grades, salaries, and duty stations of a present or former government employee are facts open to the public.

Every company's automatic response to a question about its policy on disclosing information about an employee is, "We maintain the absolute confidentiality of records about our people." Company officials may actually believe it, but the exceptions to the policy are countless. For instance, employers use consumer investigating firms or credit bureaus for background information about applicants. Agreements with these firms usually require that the employer, in turn, provide information about individuals as requested by the consumer investigating firm or credit bureau. This information is not always limited to salary, length of service, and job title. It is hard to believe that an investigating company would continue to service an employer unless the investigators, in turn, were getting the information they want with regard to reputation, life-styles, reliability, work record, dangerous activities, driving abilities, and other information about employees.

Many companies consider an application for a job with another employer as evidence that an individual has consented to the release of information about himself or herself to the second employer.

Companies provide employee information to a steady stream of researchers, and the individual is rarely consulted. And then there are the information needs of the government: equal employment opportunity agencies want to know the race, sex, age, religion, handicaps, and national origin of workers, as well as detailed data about promotions, salaries, hiring rates, and layoffs. The Occupational Safety and Health Administration wants employee medical information to assess health hazards on the job. The Internal Revenue Service and Social Security Administration want payroll data, as well as detailed information in particular inquiries. Defense agencies need security checks on employees working on defense contracts. The Department of Labor wants information on wage differentials.

The Bureau of Labor Statistics requires still more reports. Other agencies that regulate banking, communications, labor relations, transportation, health care, education, commerce, nuclear energy, or small businesses need data on identifiable persons. State government seeks information for taxes, unemployment compensation, safety, and other purposes.

Courts have regularly ruled that an *employer* may not refuse to provide personnel information of this type to the government by claiming that it is protecting the privacy of its staff. This does not mean that an *employee* is compelled to provide this information to the employer.

Local police and federal law enforcement make demands on companies for employee information. Some companies require a search warrant or formal summons. Others do not. Some companies notify the employee. Others do not.

Because public employees are paid with tax moneys, the records of state and federal employees have been subject to inspection by others. This includes state university staff in many states. States have passed recent public records—"sunshine" or "freedom of information"—statutes that require most government records to be open to inspection. The attorney general of Florida ruled in 1973 that all employee files in state government were open to the public under that state's public records law. Courts in Massachusetts have ruled that the release under the state's public disclosure law of the salaries of police officers or school district employees does not violate their privacy.

On the other hand, many "sunshine" laws, including the federal law, that require government bodies to meet in public permit closed meetings when personnel matters are discussed. "Freedom of information" acts, including the federal law, that allow public inspection of government documents permit the government to withhold from disclosure "personnel and medical files and similar files the disclosure of which would constitute a clearly unwarranted invasion of personal privacy." It's important to remember that these laws *permit* government agencies to protect individual privacy, but do not *require* it.

Record keeping, of course, is only one way that the employer keeps tabs on the employee and thereby diminishes his or her privacy. Like Henry Ford, many companies today believe that what an employee does in off hours is the business of the employer.

A senior vice-president of Manufacturers Hanover Trust Co. argues, "Banks must be aware of the personal conduct of their employees because an off-the-job reputation will have a real effect on the ability of the bank to maintain the sense of integrity that it must earn and keep. In fact, the best interests of bank employees are served through the obligation of a bank employer to minimize the temptation to steal, particularly when the staff member has both a weakness in terms of debts, gambling, alcoholism, drug addiction, or the like, and the opportunity to convert cash or securities to personal use." Bank policy requires staff members to obtain permission before acting as the official of any outside organization, except for "social, religious, philanthropic or civic organization, colleges or schools, clubs within the Corporation or a trade or professional organization associated with banking or business."

A school principal tried to fire a divorced teacher in Wyoming after he expressed concern about a light in her bedroom on evenings when her children weren't home. He also told her to lose weight. Also in Wyoming, another principal tried to fire a male teacher partly because he was dating an unmarried teacher in the same school, a practice some principals frown on. The FBI, to this day, will transfer or dismiss an agent whose private living arrangements are not acceptable to the bureau.

The Alexandria, Virginia, fire department in 1977 began a policy of not hiring applicants who smoke, even if they smoke only at home.

Many companies worry excessively about employees' behavior, political beliefs, and modes of dress when off duty. The main victims of this off-hours harassment lately have been employees of energy utilities who campaign for effective controls of nuclear energy development. The utilities have maintained surveillance of these employees' political activities and compiled separate dossiers on them that certainly can do no good for the employee at promotion time.

International Business Machines Corp., the world's largest manufacturer of the equipment that has brought about increased public concern about personal data collection, has had since the beginning of the 1970s a progressive policy respecting its employees' privacy. The chairman of the board in the 1960s, Thomas J. Watson, Jr., had a pretty good rule of thumb with regard to employees' off-duty activities: "We have a concern with an employee's off-the-job behavior only when it reduces his ability to perform regular job assignments, interferes with the job performance of other employees, or if his outside behavior affects the reputation of the company in a major way." One of the toughest decisions for a supervisor to make is determining when private behavior—whether it's alcohol or drug use, time-consuming personal projects, or physical or mental illness—affects job performance or attendance and therefore becomes the employer's concern. Until they reach that point, of course, outside activities are none of anyone else's business. Alan F. Westin, author of the landmark study on privacy and data collection, *Databanks in a Free Society*, pointed out after a later study of personnel records, "Employment raises special privacy concerns. Unlike the credit or medical area, the subject of the data has a continuous relationship with the data collector. Employment constantly involves a superior making decisions about subordinates and selecting persons for the prime opportunities in the employment hierarchy. Workers are not always in a position to challenge the policies of a company." However, armed with a little foreknowledge, the individual can improve his bargaining position when dealing with an employer.

WHAT CAN YOU DO?

Employees of government or private businesses have a right by law to see their own personnel files in California, Michigan, Oregon, and Maine. Employees in Maine are entitled to a written explanation when fired. Only Michigan's law gives an employee the right to amend the record if it is inaccurate, and there are no limits on the disclosure of employee information to outsiders. *Public* employees in the following states have rights of access and correction: Arkansas, Massachusetts, Minnesota, North Carolina, Ohio, and Virginia. *State* employees have these rights in Connecticut, Indiana, and Utah. *Federal* employees have such rights, under the Privacy Act of 1974 described in Chapter 7.

Where there is no law, employees and applicants should seek to inspect the files kept on them anyway; about 60 per cent of American companies, including General Electric Co., IBM Corp., Caterpillar Tractor, Cummins Engine, Eastman Kodak, and Koppers, say they permit individual access, at least to part of a record. Sometimes this is a matter of right under a union contract, as in many of the bargaining agreements between telephone companies and the Communications Workers of America. Under many union contracts, a member may authorize a union representative to have access to the member's personnel record, and the company must agree. In still other instances, labor arbitrators have ruled that to deny individual access is an unfair labor practice.

But even where there is no company or union policy, attempts to inspect one's files may succeed. There have been proposals in Congress to require this as a matter of law, and companies will be anxious to show that they already do this voluntarily. Personnel officers and others commonly tell legislators and others that few if any employees even care about seeing their own records. Even if it does not succeed, an employee's attempt to inspect his or her own record will show that employees do care enough to ask.

It is also possible that an employee's request to limit disclosure of information about himself or herself will be respected, as may a request to destroy obsolete information.

Under the federal Fair Credit Reporting Act, employees and applicants must be notified if an investigation about the individual's character, general reputation, personal characteristics, or mode of living is to be conducted (unless you have not specifically applied for the job in question). Upon request within five days of this notification, the employer must disclose the nature and scope of the investigation. If adverse action is taken as the result of the investigation, the employer must so notify you and give you the name and address of the company that conducted the investigation so that you have an opportunity under the law to learn the nature and substance of all information about you in the files of the consumer investigation company. You then have a right to have any disputed information reinvestigated or to have your side of the story included in your file. You are also entitled to know which employers have received reports on you in the past two years.[21]

You should remember that sometimes the employer needs you more than you need it, especially if you have skills that are in demand. If you are in a strong bargaining position and if you feel strongly about disclosure of information about yourself, you should include these considerations in your employment contract from the start. The right of access or a limitation on outside disclosures without your consent may be written into your work agreement before you sign it. By the same token, it may be possible to attach conditions to the information you supply your employer. Indicate on the application form that you wish to be notified if certain information on the form is disclosed outside of the personnel department or outside of the company. Indicate that you reserve the right to submit a new form after a few years and to destroy the current application form.

Whether or not you are in a strong bargaining position with the employer, you should not assume that you have to fill in every blank of every form put in front of you. When asked for age, you may want to respond "between 40 and 60" or "unk." By the time the personnel officer discovers your entry and learns that "unk" means "unknown," you may already have been hired.

Personnel forms are usually written to cover all classes of employment. There's no need to list your physical handicaps if you are applying for a nonphysical job; and there's no need to provide great detail about your income and dependents and housing costs if you are applying for an unskilled job and minimum pay. If you are not going to be operating a vehicle on the job, don't bother answering the question about driver's license.

If you do not fill in some of the blanks on a form, it may well be bounced back to you. Instead, scribble hieroglyphics like "n/a" (for "not available" or "not applicable"), "irr." (for "irrelevant"), or "WBSUE" (for "will be supplied upon employment"). The clerks who process your forms may be reluctant to admit that they do not know what your entries mean.

To meet federal and state equal employment opportunity requirements, companies often ask applicants and employees for information that, if used in the hiring decision, would result in illegal discrimination—race, color, religion, national origin, age, sex, or handicaps. There are laws requiring employers to compile this information as part of affirmative action plans, but there are *no* laws requiring the individual to provide it. (Affirmative action plans hardly ever involve religious groups, and so the question about religion is rarely if ever appropriate on an application form. It is conceivably appropriate once you are hired if the company wants to figure out which member of clergy to call if you die on the job. Once again, remember that no law says that you have to answer a question just because someone asks it.)

In filling out any form, your assumption should be that it will become part of a computerized network and that it will take on a life of its own, beyond your control.

An employee who finds *untrue* information in the file that tends to damage his or her reputation may be able to sue for libel. An employee who discovers true information that he or she regards as an invasion of privacy, under the principles mentioned in Chapter 1, may be able to sue for an invasion of privacy. Don't be surprised, then, if your company asks you to waive your right to sue before it lets you see your own file. That's "Catch-22." You may want to consult an attorney so that the waiver can be edited to preserve some rights for yourself.

Remember that individual access to employment files and limits on the disclosure of employment files are areas where there is no clear-cut law to help you, only bits and pieces of legal principles that, when used imaginatively, can provide some protection.

7

Federal Government Files: Computer Population Explosion

In the beginning God created the heaven and the earth.

Computers did not begin that way.

In the beginning, United States taxpayers created computers.

For the U. S. Bureau of the Census in 1890, an employee invented punch cards that could represent a person's name, age, sex, address, and other personal data and be counted electronically. Without some sort of mechanized tabulation, the nation might not have been able to count its 62 million population, as required by the Constitution. The Census Bureau and, by the 1930s, the Social Security Administration pushed the development of electronic data processing. They could not have done their jobs without the machines.

The first electronic computer, ENIAC, was developed in 1946, for the U. S. Army, at taxpayers' expense. UNIVAC I, the first computer to become well known to most Americans, was completed at the Census Bureau at taxpayers' expense. In 1955 just about all the nation's one thousand computers were owned by the federal government, at taxpayers' expense.

Today federal taxpayers are the largest single purchaser of

computer machines and services. The federal government buys one out of every twenty-two computers made, operating ten thousand machines in all.

I have proposed a program of mandatory birth control for federal computers. My plan is that before a federal agency installs a computer, it must certify to Congress that the machine has been designed so that it may not inseminate another one and produce a mini-computer. No one in Washington takes me seriously.

Government officials have had to find something to put into all of these machines to justify the exorbitant expense. Just as the Census Bureau did in 1890, federal agencies mainly put personal information into their machines. The federal government has an average of eighteen files for each man, woman, and child in the United States.

There are a total of about seven thousand data banks in the federal government with information on 3.8 billion identifiable persons, according to the Office of Management and Budget, which oversees expenditures in the federal agencies. Not all of these data banks involve computers, but three quarters of the records about people are stored in automated or partially automated systems, not manual files.

More than half of the government's information systems are operated by three agencies. The Department of Defense, with its huge work force, intelligence gathering, and contracting activity, has by far the most, 2,219, with 321 million different names. The Department of the Treasury, with its tax collection, alcohol, tobacco, and firearms registration, and Customs Service, has 910 systems, with 853 million names. The Department of Health, Education, and Welfare, which houses the Social Security Administration, as well as student loan programs, has 693, with 1.3 billion names. The Department of Commerce doesn't have nearly as many different systems of records, but with its Bureau of the Census it has records on 447 million identifiable individuals. The population of the United States in 1978 was estimated at 218 million.

About half of the government's individual records are kept to evaluate government programs and to determine who's eligible for benefits. Veterans' loans, Social Security payments, student loans, food stamps, and farm subsidies are good examples. The other half are maintained to do the government's work—collect taxes, enforce the law, defend the country, and disburse money.

The systems of records range from the Migrant Student Record Transfer System and Client Oriented Data Acquisition Process (for drug patients) and the Department of Agriculture's master list of all farmers by county to the Pentagon's list of blood donors and the Consumer Product Safety Commission's list of its employees involved in automobile accidents with government vehicles. The Privacy Act of 1974, among other things, required all agencies to make a public list of all of their systems of records. These lists are published annually by the Office of the Federal Register, which produces the government's daily compilation of regulations. The volume *Protecting Your Right to Privacy: Digest of Systems of Records* is available at major libraries or for purchase from the Superintendent of Documents, U. S. Government Printing Office, Washington, D.C. 20402. The 700-plus pages of listings are classified by government department, not by subject matter, and so there is no way to know which systems of records may hold records about you except to leaf through all of the listings.

Jean Benacchio of Long Island, New York, was unaware of one of the government's large computer systems until she was detained by U. S. Customs Service agents at an airport. Her name had been entered into the Customs computer system of suspects when a 1974 investigation by the Federal Drug Enforcement Administration recorded that she was seen with a person suspected of international drug trafficking. The investigation subsequently cleared her name, but she remained in a computer printout prison for more than a year. For eighteen months Ms. Benacchio had to undergo what she called "embarrassing and humiliating" searches each time she entered the United States. This was more than a minor inconvenience because she was engaged to a man who lived in Toronto and traveled to and from Canada often. One time in 1976, she said, she was involuntarily removed from an airplane in Toronto, forced to disrobe, and searched without explanation. As a result of the harassment, she said, her engagement was broken. Finally Ms. Benacchio succeeded in getting her name erased from the drug agency computer, but not before more strip searches at airports.

Joe Eaton of Miami was stunned to find himself listed among the targets of the Internal Revenue Service's Operation Leprechaun, which spied into the private lives of various taxpayers in Florida. Under federal law, he requested a copy of his file. The request was denied because his file remained part of a pending investigation. On appeal to the tax commissioner's office, he received his file. Joe Eaton was stunned again. He had turned up in the Internal Revenue Service files, he discovered, because a young man on trial for drug violations had Joe Eaton's name on a piece of paper in his wallet. The reason for that was obvious. Eaton is a federal judge in Miami, and the youth was one of more than five thousand who had appeared before him. That was the only connection.

Steven Heard of Seattle was glad he used the Privacy Act to see files on him at the Department of the Treasury. The Bureau of Alcohol, Tobacco, and Firearms response said that a 1970 telex message within the bureau stated, "Heard is reported to be such a radical on explosives that the only way he can get satisfaction in his mannerliness [sic] is to set off an explosive. He is reported to have a supply of explosives in his home which we understand he has converted some to bombs. He has a blasters permit. He is breaking state law." A representative of the bureau admitted in writing to Heard, "We agree that this information is false and we have expunged this early unsubstantiated record."

Naturally, efficiency experts figure that the government would save a lot of money by centralizing all of these disparate collections of information. With a centralized computer system in which information could be retrieved by an individual's name or number, each federal agency would not have to collect and store duplicate information, nor would the agency have to ask the individual to fill out a lengthy form each time he or she applied for benefits. In 1965 a study commissioned by the U. S. Bureau of the Budget proposed a Federal Data Center to centralize personal data collection. Two subsequent studies endorsed the idea.

The proposal caused a national uproar. Congressman Cornelius Gallagher of New Jersey convened hearings and said the idea would lead to "the computerized man," stripped of individual identity and privacy. "His life, his talent and his earnings would be reduced to a tape with very few alternatives available." Vance Packard, the noted author on these matters, testified that the data center (which was also referred to as National Data Center) could lead to "a depersonalization of the American way of life."[22] House and Senate hearings pretty much squelched the idea. Americans have an immediate distaste for centralization, computerization, and demands for personal information. When the three are combined in a proposal for a National Data Center, the public reaction is immediately negative.

The temptation to consolidate federal record keeping is also a strong one. In spite of the negative reaction, another government agency in 1974 made plans for a computer network to link all of the government's information systems. The agency named its network FEDNET, with typical disregard for the American public's sensitivity about these schemes. President Ford vetoed the proposal. The same agency came back in 1976 with a similar scheme. This time they nicknamed it AIDS—Automated Integrated Digital Services. The benevolence of the name did not fool the White House, which again objected.

In calmer times, some information experts have proposed consolidating the federal agencies' records to *enhance privacy*. This would establish one agency responsible for the government's data about people. That agency would control entry to all computer data banks. It would be the one agency responsible for accuracy of information and for providing the individual with an opportunity to inspect and correct his or her own files. Not all the data would have to be physically removed to a central computer library; the data agency's representatives could be assigned as custodians of the data banks wherever they now exist.

Instead of leading to the consolidation of federal record

keeping, proposals for a National Data Center have led to increased concern about invasions of privacy by the federal government. As a direct result of the proposal and in the political climate created by the Watergate disclosures, Congress passed the Privacy Act of 1974, which regulates federal agencies' collection of data about individuals. The new law discourages exchanges of personal information among federal agencies.[23]

Federal records about persons may be disclosed to other federal agencies or outsiders only in the following circumstances:
–With the individual's consent.
–In response to a court order, a request by Congress, or a specific written request from the head of an agency for law enforcement purposes.
–To the Bureau of the Census, to the National Archives, or to a researcher (if the information does not name individuals or otherwise identify them).
–To another person, in "compelling circumstances affecting the health or safety of an individual" (if the information is limited to last known address).
–For a "routine use" of the record. This means that a record about you may be disclosed "for a purpose which is compatible with the purpose for which it was collected." To understand when "routine use" disclosures are appropriate, it is necessary to know just why the information was collected in the first place. This has caused federal agencies to examine why they are asking for certain data and perhaps, in a few instances, to discover that they really don't need the information. Descriptions of what each agency considers a disclosure of personal information for a "routine use" must be published at least once a year. They may be found in another volume published by the Office of the Federal Register, along with each agency's rules under the Privacy Act of 1974.
–Lastly, the Privacy Act permits the release of information about individuals if required under a separate law, the Freedom of Information Act. That law gives citizens the right to see documents and other materials that the government uses to conduct its business, except for certain materials including "personnel and medical files and similar files the disclosure of

which would constitute a clearly unwarranted invasion of personal privacy."[24] The Freedom of Information law doesn't *prohibit* the government from releasing materials that would invade someone else's privacy; it says that the government *is not required* to release such information if the agency chooses not to. But the Privacy Act would prohibit the release of that information, because the Freedom of Information Act does not require the release.

Those who seek mailing lists and similar directory-type information about individuals from government files under the Freedom of Information Act must be prepared to show that their need for the information warrants whatever threat is involved to the privacy of the individuals included in the files, according to court decisions. (Normally there is no requirement to show a need for information when you request it under either the Privacy Act or the Freedom of Information Act.)

One court denied a request by a commercial retailer for the names and addresses of all persons who have registered with the Bureau of Alcohol, Tobacco, and Firearms to make their own wine at home. The purpose of the request was mail solicitation. Another court allowed disclosure of the National Labor Relations Board's list of a company's employees eligible to vote in a certain labor election, because the requesters were law professors conducting research into union voting patterns.

"Moreover, [the privacy exemption in the Freedom of Information Act] does not protect against disclosure every incidental invasion of privacy—only such disclosures as constitute 'clearly unwarranted' invasions of personal privacy," according to the U. S. Supreme Court in 1976.[25]

Neither the Privacy Act nor the Freedom of Information Act, by the way, covers the U. S. Congress or the federal judiciary.

In spite of congressional policy against exchanges of personal information by federal agencies, there are plenty of large-scale exchanges going on. As a matter of fact, while it was passing the Privacy Act in 1974, the Congress in a separate law created a Parent Locator Service in the U. S. Department of Health, Education, and Welfare, which is authorized to query any of the government's computer systems to track down a parent who is not supporting his or her children. The system was intended to save welfare costs by finding fathers who had abandoned support of their children and left them on public assistance. Its services are available to non-welfare spouses as well. The Parent Locator Service's prime sources of last known address, of course, are the Social Security Administration and the Internal Revenue Service. Each agency can also find your last known employer easily. Each agency normally handles inquiries of that sort from other persons and agencies by forwarding a letter to the person's last known address, but not revealing the whereabouts to the inquirer. Each agency is required by law, however, to provide that information directly to the Parent Locator Service.

The Department of Health, Education, and Welfare in 1977 created variations on this parent locator scheme, but these did not have congressional sanction, nor did they square with the Privacy Act. They were called Operation Match. The computer list of welfare recipients in a certain locality was matched with a computer list of persons on the payrolls of various federal agencies. In seconds, the machine produced a list of persons receiving both welfare and federal paychecks. (Receiving two checks, in itself, may not violate regulations; but it was regarded as a strong lead to possible violators.) Only *after* it ran the matches did the department get congressional authorization, in December 1977.

The National Driver Register in the Department of Transportation is a computer data bank storing names, dates of birth, and physical descriptions of 6.2 million drivers who have had their operator's permits suspended or revoked. The information is submitted by the fifty state motor vehicle departments. When an individual applies for a license or renewal at any of those fifty motor vehicle departments, the departments will run the name through the National Driver Register in Washington to see whether the computer reports the driver as one who has a revocation or suspension in another state. If the information is timely and accurate, the system should keep bad drivers off the roads. Trouble is, it doesn't work as well as it sounds. State motor vehicle departments often issue a license before getting a report back from the National Driver Register. By the time the report of a suspended or revoked license is sent to the state, the license has been issued and it's too late to get it back without a lengthy search.

So taxpayers are spending more than $1.6 million a year for a computerized registry of more than 6 million names, and it isn't doing any good because the states use the mails to send in their inquiries or ignore the "hits" they get on the system. This is true of many computerized systems built by government and business. Big expense. Big hoopla about hardware. Big potential threat to privacy. Little evidence of an improvement in services.

There are enough exchanges of computer data between federal agencies and private agencies to blur the distinction between government and nongovernment. At least two private organizations have access to the FBI's National Crime Information Center. The National Automobile Theft Bureau, which is run by the automobile insurance companies, has direct computer access to the stolen car portion of the NCIC. Interpol, or the International Criminal Police Organization, is a private association of police officials from 120 nations that has direct computer access to the NCIC through the U. S. Department of the Treasury. This means that police in member countries—including Argentina, Chile, Iran, and Uganda—have access to Computerized Criminal Histories of United States citizens without any legal restrictions at all. Interpol's United States representative also has limited access to local criminal justice information systems in the United States, which often include details of traffic violations, names of complainants, and names of minor offenders.

Private insurance companies that process Medicare claims for the government have computer terminals on the Social Security Administration Data Acquisition and Response System (SSADARS), a nationwide computer network. The private carriers are supposed to have access only to Medicare information in the Social Security computer system. The Medicare portion includes claimants' medical condition and Medicare claims, and often the family composition, marital status, institutional commitment, income, assets, and expenditures. The over-all SSADARS network includes data on the monthly Social Security retirement or disability benefits of more than 34 million Americans and data on Supplemental Security Income (SSI) payments to up to 4.2 million eligible blind, aged, and disabled persons. State Medicaid administrators and several federal agencies have computer terminals on this same system. Social Security Administration officials see nothing wrong in the fact that profit-making insurance companies that rely totally on personal information have direct computer access to sensitive government records about citizens.

Banks feed information into the Federal Reserve System's computerized network for transferring debits and credits around the country. The Production Credit Associations that provide loans to farmers now have their 130,000 loan accounts linked to a central computer at the federally supervised Federal Intermediate Credit Bank in St. Paul, Minnesota.

How do all of these computer systems come about? The ever-confining web of government data systems that makes us feel as if every aspect of our lives were recorded somewhere in Washington did not come about because of intentional national policy. It came about because of the separate decisions of separate agencies in the government.

It would be wrong to assume that there are hundreds of government officials who deliberately set out to build a network of personal data to the detriment of American citizens. There are, however, hundreds of government officials whose first response to a perceived problem is to build a computer system for gathering information. There are hundreds of government officials who think only of efficiency, and not about threats to individual privacy and autonomy. There are hundreds of government officials who zealously pursue the information needs of their own agencies with no regard for the cumulative effect. There are hundreds of government officials who are titillated by the possibilities of computer technology and who feel naked unless they are seeking to know everything about everybody. There are hundreds of government officials who find it more exciting to

Informational Privacy

come up with a new way of collecting information than to administer creatively the programs and laws we have.

Computer sciences, in the words of retired Senator Sam J. Ervin, Jr., of North Carolina, "have accorded those who control government increased power to discover and record immutably the activities, thoughts and philosophy of an individual at any given moment of his life. That picture of the person is recorded forever, no matter how the person may change as time goes on. Every person's past thus becomes an inescapable part of his present and future. The computer never forgets."

WHAT CAN YOU DO?

By law, you have a right to examine any records kept by a federal agency that may be retrieved by your name or other identifier, such as a Social Security number (with the exception of the following: most of the Central Intelligence Agency's files, *active* investigatory files held by law enforcement agencies like the Federal Bureau of Investigation, Secret Service files used to protect the President, classified documents, and certain military promotion records). And you have a right to take an adviser with you when you see your record and a right to take a copy of your record home with you.

You have a right to dispute information in the file. The government agency, within ten days, must make the correction or notify you that you may have the information you questioned reviewed by the agency. If the reviewing official appointed by the agency refuses to make a change, then you are entitled to submit a "concise statement setting forth the reasons for [your] disagreement." Your statement will then accompany your record whenever it is disclosed after that.

All of this may be done by mail, not necessarily in person. There is no prohibition against the agency's destroying information about you. In fact, many personal records were destroyed when the Privacy Act became law. But the agency may not destroy the record after you have asked to see it. The agency may delete references to other persons in your record before you see it, but you should challenge this if you feel that inclusion of the information in your copy of the file would not be a "clearly unwarranted invasion of privacy" for the other person. A lawyer in Oakland, California, received his FBI file with the following statement: "In 1944 he married [deleted]." The bureau had deleted the name of his wife, apparently to protect her privacy. The name of an Alabama man's own mother was deleted from papers the FBI released about him, presumably to prevent a "clearly unwarranted invasion" of her privacy.

Agencies do not have centralized indexes to their data, and so you must be as specific as possible in your request. Include the date and nature of an occurrence that you feel would prompt a federal record about yourself. Here's how to make your request:

Look in the *Federal Register* catalogues for the name and address of the official responsible for individual access to the data bank that interests you. Another source of names and addresses is the *United States Government Manual*, which is available in most libraries. Here are the data systems affecting the most persons:

Social Security Administration Health Insurance Master Record, under Title XVIII of the Social Security Act.

> Director, Bureau of Health Insurance
> 6401 Security Boulevard
> Baltimore, Maryland 21235

Social Security Number Holders. All 240 million of the records include previous employers, earning records, and addresses. Send your number, or date of birth, place of birth, or parents' names.

> Assistant Bureau Director for Systems
> Bureau of Data Processing
> Social Security Administration
> 6401 Security Boulevard
> Baltimore, Maryland 21235

Medicare Enrollment Records, including records on 22 million persons enrolled in the Medicare program. Send your claim number, Social Security number, maiden name if female, date of birth.

> Assistant Commissioner for Research and Statistics
> Social Security Administration
> 1875 Connecticut Avenue, N.W., Room 1121
> Washington, D.C. 20009

Individual Master File of Taxpayers, plus intelligence, audit, and special files kept on taxpayers. Write to the Internal Revenue Service Center for the region in which you live, as listed on your tax forms. If you feel that your name is included in special files in Washington, write:

> Internal Revenue Service
> Privacy Act Officer
> Washington, D.C. 20224

National Driver Register. Check to see whether you are listed as a driver whose license has been withdrawn.

> System Manager, Room 3214
> Trans Point Building
> Second and V Streets, S.W.
> Washington, D.C. 20590

FBI National Crime Information Center, including criminal histories, stolen automobiles, and missing persons; and the *FBI Central Records System*.

> Federal Bureau of Investigation
> Privacy Act Officer
> Hoover Building
> Washington, D.C. 20535

Veterans and Dependents Identification and Locator System, including veterans or dependents who have applied for pension, compensation, education, insurance, or burial benefits. Write to the Veterans Administration Center nearest you. Include your claim number if possible, otherwise military identifying information. For Patient Medical Records, write to the Veterans Administration health care facility where you were treated.

Basic Grant Application File, U. S. Office of Education records on students applying for or receiving federal grants.

> Director of Basic and State Student Grants
> Room 5678, ROB-3
> 400 Maryland Avenue, S.W.
> Washington, D.C. 20202

Guaranteed Student Loan Program, files on applicants or recipients.

> Director, Program Systems Division
> Room 4051, ROB-3
> Seventh and D Streets, S.W.
> Washington, D.C. 20202

For records from the military services or the rest of the Defense Department, check the *Federal Register* catalogue of federal agency systems of records mentioned earlier in this chapter.

In your letter, simply say, "Under the Privacy Act and Freedom of Information Act as amended, I request a copy of any record in your files that pertains to me and a list of disclosures made of this information." Then include enough identifying information to prevent any doubt or duplication. You can usually avoid listing detailed identification if your request is signed and stamped by a notary public. Notaries, who are found at most banks, public offices, law offices, and large companies, as well as some drugstores and secretarial services, certify the identity of the individual signing a document. They charge a small fee unless you are a regular customer.

Be sure to keep a copy of all correspondence and be prepared to pay a fee for copying. (A fee for searching may be charged under the Freedom of Information Act but not the Privacy Act.) If called for, follow the necessary procedure for amending or correcting your files. If you encounter difficulty, complain to the Deputy Associate Director for Information Systems, Office of Management and Budget, Washington, D.C. 20503. This office is responsible for overseeing implementation of the act. Or write to the Chairman, Senate Committee on Government Operations, Washington, D.C. 20510, or Chairman, House Subcommittee on Government Information and Individual Rights, Washington, D.C. 20515. The latter subcommittee has published *A Citizen's Guide on How to Use the Freedom of Information Act and the Privacy Act in Requesting Government Documents*, a 59-page booklet available from the Superintendent of Documents, Government Printing Office, Washington, D.C. 20402.

From time to time, private firms advertise services to help you get your records for a fee. It's hard to see how they can save you much time or effort. Your better bet is to use the House subcommittee's guidebook, and if you're not satisfied after you have asked for correction of your records, consult an attorney or a friend who knows the workings of government.

You should also give up less information about yourself when you are asked to fill out federal forms. In each case, assume that the information you are providing will be broadcast in an extensive computer network with virtually no time limits. It's a safe assumption. Much of the information you provide will not be sensitive and you may not object to its flowing throughout the network. Other information is sensitive or *will become sensitive to you at a later time*. Again, as with private businesses, remember that not every blank on every form placed in front of you must be filled in. If the form is designed for computer use, fill in the blanks with zeros or letters denoting NOT AVAILABLE or UNKNOWN, or NOT APPLICABLE. There are criminal penalties for lying on federal forms (although there's disagreement whether you have to be notified of your rights to remain silent before you are punished for lying to a federal officer).

Find alternatives for verifying your identity, or your income, or your eligibility. If a student loan form asks for a photocopy of your tax return, find out just what information the government agency is seeking and provide that. Perhaps a letter from an accountant or lawyer verifying your taxable income will be acceptable, saving you the necessity of providing a photocopy of your total tax return with all of its personal data about deductions and miscellaneous income. If a federal program has the same eligibility requirements as a state program or another federal program, perhaps proof of your participation in that program will be acceptable, so that you do not have to provide sensitive personal information to yet another agency. A statement from a notary public or from the government clerk accepting your application verifying you are who you say you are may obviate the need for you to provide countless bits of identifying information.

Try giving a general answer instead of a specific one. List "Jones Clinic," not "Jones Psychiatric Clinic," for instance. Say "member of a civic association," without mentioning the political, religious, or other affiliation. When asked about education level say, "less than college," instead of "ninth grade."

A WORD ABOUT THE CENSUS

Inquiries by the Bureau of the Census raise special concerns. The types and number of questions have increased markedly since the United States Constitution was adopted in 1787 saying: "Enumeration shall be made within three years after the first meeting of the Congress of the United States, and within every subsequent term of ten years, in such manner as they shall by law direct." For more than one hundred years after that, the census organization would take the decennial count and then disband. In 1902 Congress set up a permanent office to collect statistics. Before 1900, individual census records were public, but since then they have been confidential by law. The bureau has a good tradition of respecting confidentiality. It even turned away the War Department when, during World War II, it demanded the names of Japanese-Americans living on the West Coast. Each employee must take an oath not to disclose any personal or business information, on penalty of up to five years in jail and/or $5,000 fine. A congressional investigation in 1970 found no violations of this oath. The Census Bureau is even exempt from the requirement that all federal agencies co-operate with the Parent Locator Service mentioned previously.

The bureau has been under considerable pressure to agree to the public release of individual census records that were gathered seventy-two or more years ago, for genealogical and other research. These old records, now held by the National Archives, could reveal long-suppressed racial ancestries or living arrangements of people who are still alive or whose recent descendants are still alive.

It is a criminal offense to fail to answer most census surveys, including the one now conducted every five years ($100 fine), or to provide false information ($500).[26] (Full census surveys used to be conducted every ten years.) There are many interim census surveys that are voluntary, including any surveys conducted more than once a year. Census takers do not tell you this, however, because they are afraid this will lessen the response rate. If you object to any of the questions asked, you should ask to see the law, if any, that requires you to answer. The law also says that a refusal to answer a question about your religion is not an offense. Copies of census reports kept by an individual or business are immune from legal process and may not be used in any judicial proceeding without the individual's consent. Before this part of the law was passed in the early 1960s, the U. S. Supreme Court had permitted an agency of government to require a business to produce census records that the agency by law could not have gotten out of the Census Bureau itself.

In 1980 the Census will again attempt to ask questions of every person in the United States on a particular day about age, sex, race, ethnic origin, marital status, employment, and relationship to the household head. There will be a dozen more questions about housing (number of rooms, rental or purchase, plumbing, and so on). In addition to these "100-percent questions," Census will mail to one out of five households a more detailed questionnaire to compile sample data on population and housing in our nation. Some census statistics are important to the individual: population figures will determine the outlines of legislative districts, the numerical "clout" of each ethnic group, and the extent of federal funding to different locales. Still, the bulk of census statistics are of value not to individuals but to businesses, which decide where to locate factories and how to market products and services from a myriad of census analyses that flow out of Washington's computers until it's time for the next survey.

Individual census data are valuable to anybody who needs evidence of age, family heritage, or citizenship. For a small fee, the Census will search its records for such information for you or your legal representative, so that you may collect an inheritance, qualify for government benefits, or know your "roots." Write Bureau of the Census, Pittsburg, Kansas 66762.

Census certificates are now accepted as valid substitutes for birth certificates by virtually all agencies. This is especially important for persons born before 1920 when birth registration was not a requirement in all states. For records pertaining to a deceased person, the application must be signed by a blood relative in the immediate family, the surviving spouse, a beneficiary, or the administrator of the estate. A death certificate must be submitted with the application (Form BC-600).

A WORD ABOUT MILITARY DISCHARGES

The armed services used to put a numerical code on each discharge certificate that indicated the reason for discharge, even if it was voluntary—homosexual tendencies, hardships, alcoholism, insubordination, slovenly habits, or physical disability. As the military now admits, "the presence of such information can be a cause of undesirable discrimination against the individual by private employers and other persons in civilian life." Many employers ask to see the discharge report, DD Form 214. Now, by law, you have a right to get a new DD Form 214, with these so-called Separation Program Numbers (SPN) deleted. Current service members should be aware of substitute codes that the military services use on current discharge papers (though not on the copy given the veteran). A member of the service is entitled to a narrative description of the code, upon discharge. To get a corrected DD Form 214, write:

Army: Commander, Reserve Components
Personnel and Administration Center
Box 12479, Olivette Branch
St. Louis, Missouri 63132

Navy: Chief, Bureau of Naval Personnel (Pers 38)
Department of the Navy
Washington, D.C. 20370

Air Force: Air Force Military Personnel Center (DPMDR)
Randolph AFB, Texas 78148

Marine Corps: Commandant
U. S. Marine Corps (MSRB010)
Headquarters, U.S.M.C.
Washington, D.C. 20380

A WORD ABOUT CANADA

In 1978 Canada enacted a law that gives Canadians the right to find out what information government institutions have compiled about them. This law, Part IV of the Human Rights Act, is similar to the Privacy Act in the United States.

The place to start is the local post office, where you will find an index of all the federal information banks in Ottawa. Then you should complete a "record access request form," available at the post office for each data bank you wish to consult, and mail it to the address listed for the data bank in the index. The government agency is supposed to send you information about yourself, unless the computer system is one of twenty-two exempted from the act's coverage. In addition, cabinet ministers have broad discretion to exempt other data systems—there are about fifteen hundred in the national government—if there is a possibility of injury to national security or defense, international relations, federal-provincial relations, or a current criminal investigation. All data banks must be listed in the index, even if they are exempted from the individual-access part of the law.

After examining your records, you have the right to request corrections. If the government does not accept your corrections, it must still include your version in your file. If an agency wants to use personal information about you for purposes other than the one for which it was collected, it must get your permission.

Canada has an ombudsman to help residents who encounter problems with federal records. The incumbent is Inger Hansen, Human Rights Commission, Ottawa, Ontario K1A 1E1.

Only one province, Nova Scotia, has a similar law covering provincial records about people.

Citizens are required to respond to census surveys by Statistics Canada, and, as in the United States, the agency has a strict legal obligation to keep personal information confidential. Tax records in Canada are confidential by law, as well. Federal law prohibits the interception of radio or telephone communications.

The law of privacy in Canada has not developed even to the limited extent that it has in American courts. Canadians rely on defamation, breach of contract, or other theories of law when they feel their privacy has been invaded. However, the provinces of British Columbia and Manitoba have declared by statute that to invade the privacy of another person is a tort for which the victim may collect damages.

There is no nationwide fair credit reporting act, as in the United States, but the Associated Credit Bureaus of Canada, a voluntary trade association, says that its members subscribe to a code of ethics that permits consumers to inspect and correct files about themselves.

British Columbia, Ontario, Quebec, and Saskatchewan have fair credit laws similar to the United States law described in Chapter 4, except that Quebec's does not limit the type of information that may be collected or used. Saskatchewan requires the licensing of credit bureaus.

Ontario, the nation's most populous province, requires that consumer investigative firms use only information stored in

Canada. Equifax Ltd., an affiliate of the leading American company in this field, is the leading company in Canada in consumer investigations. Any person knowingly supplying false information in a consumer investigation is liable to prosecution in Ontario. No information about ethnic origin or political affiliation may be kept, and criminal information more than one year old may be stored only if accompanied by the current status of the case. Arrests and bankruptcies that occurred more than seven years ago may not be included in the record. The law is enforced by the Ministry of Consumer and Commercial Relations, 555 Yonge Street, Toronto, Ontario M4Y 1Y7.

The province of Manitoba requires that private investigators inform an individual before conducting most investigations and allow the individual to challenge the accuracy of information collected.

8

Insurance Records: White-Collar Gumshoes

Although the Senate Watergate hearings in 1973 were televised nationwide, John D. Ehrlichman thought he was speaking frankly, lawyer-to-lawyer, to the seven attorneys on the Senate committee. "I imagine those of you who have been in private practice," said the former Nixon White House assistant, "well recognize there are a lot of perfectly legal ways that medical information is leaked."

Speaking of the White House burglars who sought the psychiatric records of Daniel Ellsberg, Ehrlichman said, "They might have gotten access through another doctor, through a nurse. There are all kinds of ways that one could get this information."

In an interview in Santa Fe, New Mexico, just before he went off to jail, the former White House assistant and Seattle trial attorney elaborated on his justification for assuming that his approval of a White House plumbers' operation to get Ellsberg's medical information did not mean approval of a break-in. "I'll tell you what I had in mind," he told a reporter. "I have tried personal injury cases for about twelve or fifteen years for insurance companies, and when you do that it's important for you to know what the physical condition of the plaintiff is. One of the ways you find out is to get the confidential records of the plaintiff. And the way you do that is that the adjuster goes out, sweet-talks the nurse at the hospital, or hires a doctor who talks to the plaintiff's doctor and says, 'Can I look at Tillie Jones' records?'

"There are probably fifteen ways that insurance adjusters get a look at so-called privileged records. So, if you had asked me at the time: 'Is there a way for those fellows to do this without violating somebody's civil rights or breaking into somebody's office?,' I'd have said 'sure.' In my experience there are all kinds of ways."

Ehrlichman's comments are extremely self-serving and they ignore the point that gaining access to sensitive medical information by misrepresentation violates someone's civil rights just as surely as a burglary. And the jury hearing the Ellsberg break-in case did not believe him and convicted him of a felony. Since Ehrlichman's testimony, I have been unable to find any other attorneys who will admit that they or their colleagues conduct investigations the way Ehrlichman says he did.

But private investigators hired by attorneys representing insurance companies or hired by the insurers themselves do the dirty work. Insurance representatives pleaded with the federal Privacy Protection Study Commission during its term between 1975 and 1977 not to take away their right to gather information by pretext or misrepresentation. Otherwise, they said, they could never verify claims and conduct litigation.

Insurance companies gather most of their personal information about you and me after having us sign a form authorizing them to do so. (More about that later.) With the authorization, they hire companies like Equifax, Inc., mentioned in Chapter 5 on consumer investigations, to submit a report, for a fee of ten dollars or so. However, insurers feel they also need to gather information without our knowledge or consent, as when they distrust a claim submitted. There are companies around who will do that sort of work. They are the underground gumshoes of the insurance trade.

A grand jury in Denver in 1976 indicted three investigators of a company called Factual Service Bureau, Inc., for gaining access to confidential medical information without the authorization of the patients. The Chicago-based detective agency, with offices in principal midwestern cities, is now known as Inner-Facts, Inc. An employee of the University of Colorado Medical Center was accused of co-operating in the scheme, in which Factual Service personnel allegedly posed as medical professionals to discover confidential medical data that they later sold to insurance companies. One snooper dressed as a Roman Catholic priest, others as physicians, to roam the corridors of hospitals in search of medical information about individuals who had filed insurance claims.

The Denver suspects were charged with embezzlement and criminal impersonation because Colorado, like just about all jurisdictions, has no criminal statute against stealing medical information. What was most shocking about the Factual Service case was the number of well-known insurance companies that admitted buying the services of a discredited company that advertised that it could secure personal medical information without a patient authorization. Among them were Aetna Life and Casualty Co., the Home Insurance Co., Reliance Insurance Co., Northwestern National Insurance Group, and more than fifty others.

Factual Service Bureau was found to have had access to personal data in credit bureaus (by using the code word of a Midwest bureau), National Crime Information Center, Veterans Administration hospitals, private physicians, Social Security Administration, and the New York City Police Department.

Insurance representatives will always tell you that they gather information about an individual only with prior written consent. Don't you believe it. As we have seen, the companies do not need our consent in order to have a consumer investigative company gather information from our neighbors, fellow employees, and businesses. Federal law requires only that we receive prior notification of such investigations, not that we authorize them. With regard to medical information, insurers make the same broad claim about consent, and quickly dispose of any privacy concerns in their industry. "Life insurers gain access to health care records only after obtaining prior informed

consent of the applicant or insured," said the American Life Insurance Association to a governor's commission in Indiana
studying personal information and privacy in 1976. The several
million dollars earned per year by companies like Factual Service Bureau say otherwise. Don't accuse the insurance officials of
lying; they just don't know their own industry. The president
of Aetna Life and Casualty, the nation's fifth largest insurance
company, if you can believe, said that he was totally unaware that his company bought the services of Factual Service
Bureau.

When it really matters—in checking out a large claim or preparing for a lawsuit—the insurers find a hired gun to snoop
around without the consent of the individual.

The routine information gatherings on applicants and claimants are conducted with a written authorization from the individual. It all begins with this language:

> I hereby authorize any physician, medical practitioner,
> hospital, clinic, or other medical or medically related
> facility, insurance company or other organization, in-
> stitution or person, that has any records or knowledge
> of the health, observation, diagnosis or treatment of
> either myself or any member of my family, to give to
> ____ insurance company any and all such information
> it requests with respect to such records or knowledge.
> A photocopy of this authorization shall be as valid as
> the original.

When we receive medical treatment that may be covered by
insurance, we are asked to sign language like the following:

> I hereby request and authorize any hospital, physi-
> cian, or other person who has attended or examined me
> or any member of my family, to furnish to ____ insur-
> ance company or its representative any and all infor-
> mation concerning any illness or injury we may have
> suffered, medical history, consultations, prescriptions,
> or treatments including X-ray plates and copies of all
> hospital or medical records, that same may be in-

cluded as part of the proofs of loss submitted by me to the company. A photocopy of this authorization shall be considered as effective and valid as the original.

When you strip away the verbiage, you'll see that you are requesting and authorizing "any . . . person . . . that has . . . knowledge of the . . . observation . . . of . . . myself or any member of my family, to give . . . all . . . information." We hurriedly scribble our signatures below this language when we apply for coverage or seek treatment. We are signing a blank check, with no limit of time. It's an unlimited search warrant. A dog-eared photocopy of that signed authorization in the hands of an investigator from an insurance company is the key to opening file drawers—and computer data banks—of medical and nonmedical information about us.

The authorization is no more than a contract between you and the insurance company. Like any other contract, its terms and language may be altered to your liking before you sign it.

When you sign the application authorization, you are opening the floodgates of information flow about you. A copy of the authorization is sent to the consumer investigators that we discussed in Chapter 5. An insurance agent in New York City wrote to one of his clients about this process:

> The monetary allowance permitted for the inquiry is very small. Consequently, the investigator assigned to the task is one whose normal employment possibilities are not unlimited, nor is he usually distinguished by great intelligence or zeal. Occasionally, I hear tales of these inquiries, which invariably evoke merriment, not because of any information dug up, but rather because the methods used appear to be carefully calculated to produce no information at all. The opinion appears to be general that this service is neither more nor less than useless, it is exactly useless, and I suspect, it may well be done away with. However, you are undoubtedly aware of the ways of bureaucracy, and that is the way it is.

It is probably true that the purpose of Equifax and similar reports is simply to confirm that the life insurance applicant is a warm body (how much of an "investigation" can you get for ten dollars?), but if this is true, why should the consumer put up with it? Companies that provide health coverage, unlike the life insurers, generally do without such reports. Blue Cross and Blue Shield, the health insurance plans that cover nearly half of all persons insured, even do without physical examinations for applicants.

Instead, what the "Blues" keep in their computerized membership status file includes name, address, date of birth, date of enrollment, benefit code, account number, identification number, information about dependents, marital status, and billing data. A supplementary claim history file includes details on the place and type of medical treatment for which reimbursement has been sought, a code for the attending physician's diagnosis, codes for medical procedures used, dates of service, amount of the medical bill, and amounts paid by Blue Cross or Blue Shield. When did you authorize all of this computer data collection about yourself? When you signed your application for Blue Cross coverage. Blue Cross–Blue Shield says that individuals may have access to their own files to ensure their accuracy, by telephone, mail, or in-person visit. The data bank is available to Blue Cross–Blue Shield employees at their desks by visual display computer terminals, which look like conventional television screens. Preventing unauthorized persons from taking a peek at sensitive information is difficult in such systems. The "Blues" say that each employee authorized to change elements of data in the computer is assigned his or her own access code number, like a password. These "interactive" computer terminals allow users to alter data in a system as well as to see it.

The company says that only authorized employees have access to this data bank of sensitive information. But when the applicant signs an agreement for "co-ordination of benefits" or "subrogation" when he or she has coverage by more than one insurer, the company treats this as an authorization to exchange information with the other companies.

What you're not told by health insurance companies is that they send your claims to outside data processing companies for handling. One company, Electronic Data Systems Corp. of Dallas, Texas, handles several million health insurance claims each year for health carriers, including some of the Blue Cross–Blue Shield plans. The company would probably end up processing the millions of claims to be filed under any plan for national health insurance passed by Congress. Its president, H. Ross Perot, has been a major financial contributor to congressional candidates' campaigns.

I was shocked to discover that the personnel office where I was once employed received carbon copies of the claim forms I submitted to my health insurance carrier (not Blue Cross). From the names of the hospitals, clinics, and physicians on these carbon copies, office gossips could figure out what sorts of medical treatment my family and I were receiving. And they could figure out which co-workers were using medical insurance more than others. Many employees must submit health insurance claims through their employer, with the same result. Some people have told me that they do not file claims for particularly sensitive medical treatment—cancer checkup, psychiatric consultation, treatment related to reproductive organs—even though they are entitled to reimbursement. They feel that the possibility of disclosure of this information is not worth the price. Perhaps that pleases the insurance companies, but they would be serving their customers better by coding the information on claim forms and by withholding all information—including who's submitting claims for how much—from employers.

Few consumers realize that when they apply for *life insurance* they are in fact doing business not with one company but with the whole life insurance industry. Life insurance companies—and some health insurers—have an exchange of personal information in addition to exchanges with consumer investigative companies. They exchange personal medical information with a computer data bank in Boston called the Medical Information Bureau. This relationship accounts for the additional bit of paper work you receive when you apply for insurance. It says:

> Information regarding your insurability will be treated as confidential. The insurance company may, however, make a brief report thereon to the Medical Information Bureau, a non-profit membership organization of life insurance companies, which operates an information exchange on behalf of its members. If you apply to another Bureau member company for life or health insurance coverage, or a claim for benefits is submitted to such a company, the Bureau, upon request, will supply such company with the information in its file. Upon receipt of a request from you, the Bureau will arrange disclosure of any information it may have in your file. (Medical information will be disclosed only to your attending physician.) If you question the accuracy of information in the Bureau's file, you may contact the Bureau and seek a correction in accordance with the procedures set forth in the Federal Fair Credit Reporting Act. The address of the Bureau's information office is Post Office Box 105, Essex Station, Boston, Massachusetts 02112, telephone number (617) 426-3660.

Well, not quite. I set out in April 1975 to discover what the Medical Information Bureau (MIB) has in its computer about me. It took nearly three years. The Medical Information Bureau does not regard itself as subject to the Fair Credit Reporting Act, described in Chapters 4 and 5, even though it makes consumer reports that are used in part to determine eligibility for insurance. After pressure from Congress, the MIB has said that it will comply voluntarily. As we mentioned in Chapter 5 firms regulated by the act are immune from privacy suits and so the MIB first asked me to complete "Form D-2," which relieves the bureau from just about all lawsuits for invasion of privacy based on information disclosed to me. I submitted my request without signing the release, but then agreed to sign it if MIB agreed to abide by all aspects of the Fair Credit Reporting Act. The bureau responded by instructing the medical director of my life insurance company to disclose to my physician whatever information the insurance company had submitted to the MIB. The bureau thus passed the buck to my insurance company and to my physician to fulfill its promise of disclosure. I received nothing from either. Nor from MIB did I receive any of the nonmedical information that MIB stores in its computer about me—name, date of birth, place of birth, area of residence, and last known employment.

Inexplicably, I received another letter from MIB rejecting my request.

A year later I resumed my quest, and was informed by the bureau that in July 1975 it had asked the medical director of the insurance company to disclose information to my physician. My physician said by telephone that he had received nothing. To a *Newsweek* columnist who wrote on this subject in February 1977, the Medical Information Bureau wrote that it had sent me my file a year ago. I renewed my request. My doctor wrote in May 1977 that he had received nothing from the Medical Information Bureau.

"Frankly I cannot understand your doctor's statement," said the bureau's lawyer in a letter in June 1977. "Ask the doctor to recheck his files." I did, and he found nothing.

Finally, because I had written publicly about this sad story, the bureau agreed to hand-carry the letter from my insurance company to the physician. It did so, and I asked my doctor to mail it to me. Instead, in December 1977 he sent me a letter telling me what my life insurance company wrote to him. I telephoned him and made clear that I wanted the letter itself. In January 1978 he sent it to me. There was nothing identifying the letter with the MIB and so there is no way the doctor would have known this. The letter stated my medical treatments, which had been originally reported by the doctor to the insurance company and in turn reported by the insurance company to the MIB. This did not help me to know whether or not MIB has the information accurately in its computer. Nor did MIB or the insurance company send me directly the nonmedical information it stores on me—name, date and place of birth, area of residence, and last known employment. There was no way to check the accuracy of these data, in keeping with MIB's original promise that it extends to all insurance applicants.

I pointed this out in a telephone call to the MIB, and by return mail I received a letter directly from the bureau with the nonmedical information it has on me in its computer and with confirmation that its medical code matches the data provided by the insurance company.

This whole process took nearly three years. Clearly the Medical Information Bureau has little experience in making prompt and complete disclosures to consumers under the Fair Credit Reporting Act, even though it makes "consumer reports" on millions of Americans.

You and I are relatively lucky, though. At least we know that a computer system like MIB exists, keeping codes on the health histories of 11 million Americans and Canadians for 700 member insurance companies. These companies account for more than 90 per cent of the life insurance coverage in the United States. Until 1973 the MIB was so mysterious to everyone but insurance underwriters that Senator William Proxmire of Wisconsin called it "the medical CIA." He said that a devious White House in future years won't have to hire "plumbers" to invade a doctor's office; it will merely have to hire a good computer operator who can query the Medical Information Bureau.

The bureau never even listed its telephone number in the local directory until Proxmire's prodding in 1973. To this day, learning about it is like learning about Watergate—you get bits and pieces from compelled testimony, but never the whole story. Its computer codes denote past medical diagnosis or tests (EKG readings, blood tests, X rays, and diagnoses). (MIB considers "sexual deviation" and "unhealthy appearance" as "medical codes.") Before Senator Proxmire held hearings on the bureau, one out of sixteen of its codes concerned finances, driving habits, hazardous activities, and any other gossip about sexual activities or "social maladjustment" that the insurance companies felt like reporting to MIB. The bureau says it has eliminated this nonmedical information now. It still includes codes based on medical opinions provided, not by a professional, but by a neighbor or employer. ("He seems to have high blood pressure," or "I think she once had cancer," says the neighbor to the Equifax investigator, who jots it down and reports it to an insurer. The insurer may send it on to MIB for safekeeping.)

This is how one person described the situation:

> When I was a younger man, I made an application for life insurance, and it was rejected. I could not understand why because I felt pretty healthy, and the company did not give me the reason why. Because I pressed and pressed, I finally was able to secure an off-the-record statement from the individual who had solicited the account. He said, "Well, we have information in our records that ten years ago you had cancer." I said, "Well, that is very interesting, but I am not aware of it." I asked what the nature of this cancer was. The records showed it was leukemia. I asked, "Where did you get that information?" The company indicated they had obtained it from a neighbor. The truth is I did not have cancer and, of course, I would have been dead a long time ago had I had it. Had I not pressed on that matter, I would not have known and I would not have been given an insurance policy. I brought this matter to the company's attention, and demanded that they analyze their file again, and finally they agreed that the information that had been provided them had been given maliciously.

That person was later elected mayor of New York City. Before that, as a congressman, Edward I. Koch helped pass the Privacy Act of 1974 and pushed for legislation protecting privacy in the insurance industry. (Koch made this statement in a speech printed in the *Congressional Record* of October 17, 1974.)

The notification that insurance applicants now receive about the MIB and the MIB policy permitting individual access and correction are new developments, effective in 1975. Before then, there was no way to know that the bureau even existed (violating one of the principles of fair information practices listed at the beginning of this book) and MIB officers said they liked it that way.

One of the rules of this member association is that an insurer may not reject coverage or raise rates solely on the basis of the coded report it gets by computer from Boston. But insurance executives and the bureau itself admit that there is no way of knowing whether this rule is always obeyed. If the MIB truly provides only a "red flag" to insurers to check further about an applicant and if the individual has direct access to inspect and challenge data about himself or herself, then the Medical Information Bureau concept would be acceptable. Like the National Crime Information Center, the National Driver Register, and other computerized clearinghouses, it doesn't work the way it is supposed to.

WHAT CAN YOU DO?

Medical Information Bureau policy permits you to discover information kept on you, through your physician. You should write to the MIB and ask for an application form. Either sign the waiver of your rights to sue or alter it, give the name and address of your doctor, provide your place of birth (and more identifying information if you have a common name), and do the same for your spouse. Then hope for the best. I feel that insurance companies ought to provide you with this information directly through their computer links with the MIB, and this is worth a try. Another possibility is to file suit to have the Fair Credit Reporting Act, and all of its rights and responsibilities, apply to the Medical Information Bureau. MIB clearly fits the definition of a consumer reporting agency covered by the act.

No law protects your privacy with regard to records held by insurance companies. No law permits you to inspect them or restricts their disclosure to third parties. The sole exception is a 1978 law in Virginia that entitles the customer to a written explanation of an adverse underwriting decision and an opportunity to challenge the information on which the decision was based. In other states it is still worthwhile to ask for access and to attach conditions to the information your insurance company holds on you.

No law prevents an insurance company from asking for your Social Security number or using it as your policy number. But most life and health insurance companies will agree to your request for a separate number. Auto insurers may be more reluctant to issue a policy without your Social Security number because it is used by many state motor vehicle administrations as a driver identity number. Many large insurance companies use direct computer access to motor vehicle administrations.

Laws in many states say that you may not be denied auto, health, life, or fire coverage for unfair or arbitrary reasons. If you have been denied coverage on the basis of personal information you consider irrelevant, or for any other reason, complain to your state insurance commissioner.

No law says that you have to provide any of the information requested by an insurer. Most agents want to sell insurance more than customers want to buy it. Have your agent be your advocate with the insurance company, carrying to the company the reasons why you are a good risk in spite of your desire to provide less personal information on the insurance application. Your agent probably agrees with you.

Apply for insurance with several different companies and let them compete for your business—and meet your demands for minimal collection of personal data. Shop around.

If you are insured under a group policy, the need for personal information about you is eliminated, because all members of the group are insured. Another possibility: sign up for health insurance with a high deductible amount, say $500 or $1,000. This means that you pay the first $500 or $1,000 of bills per year, and the insurer pays the rest. This type of coverage is cheaper than full coverage and is usually issued without physical examinations or intrusive demands for information. Put aside $500 or $1,000 in a savings account for medical expenses that arise and keep it in your account if you have a healthy year. Group coverage with high deductibles combines both advantages and requires little more than your name, your address, and your assurance that you have a heartbeat.

The same suggestions made in previous chapters about filling in forms apply here—especially here. Most important, edit the authorization form to your liking before you sign it. Let your agent worry about changes you make and come back to you if the home office objects. I would suggest the following alteration:

> I authorize Dr. ____, ____ Hospital, and ____ insurance company to provide evidence of my current medical condition for purposes of underwriting this coverage. This authorization applies to this application only and expires in ninety days.

You may want to include a consumer investigative firm in the authorization, or you may not. If family members are covered by the policy, indicate that the authorization covers their medical records as well. If the agent complains that you must authorize use of photocopies of this form, fill out two originals and tell the agent that should be adequate.

There is no need to authorize the Medical Information Bureau to receive information about you from your insurer, because this is not essential for the policy for which you are applying. (The Medical Information Bureau has admitted that it urges the insurance companies to report to MIB anyway, whether or not you sign an authorization.) It may be necessary, however, to authorize the insurance company to query MIB about you in this one instance. If you do, why not insist that the MIB report be sent to you beforehand or simultaneously? Don't be fooled into believing that any law *prohibits* the release of medical information directly to the individual. There is no such prohibition. The Fair Credit Reporting Act simply *permits it to be withheld from you.*

The authorization forms that you must sign when you receive medical treatment are every bit as crucial. First, do not sign any authorization if you are paying for the treatment your-self. The same applies if you are receiving treatment at a facil-ity where you are entitled to full services without charge be-cause of your status as an employee or a student or a member. Some prepaid health maintenance schemes fall into this cate-gory.

Bargain when you can. If you have just admitted a loved one to the emergency room in a crisis, you're not able to quibble over paper work. I think you have a valid right to return the next day and claim that you signed the authorization under du-ress and wish to re-evaluate it, but I can't guarantee that the admitting clerk or even the hospital director will agree.

If you or the patient for whom you are signing is already tucked into a hospital bed, then you have some leverage to bar-gain about the authorization. You may have to guarantee pay-ment of the final bill if the insurance company does not accept your edited authorization form. One possibility that may work is to alter the authorization form to your liking and casually give it back to the admitting clerk with all the other paper work. It's possible that no one will notice your changes until you're fully recovered and the insurance company is verifying your claim. My suggested language is this:

> I authorize Dr. ____, ____ Hospital, and members of its medical staff who attended me to furnish to the ____ insurance company or its representative informa-tion concerning my current treatment for purposes of verifying my claim for insurance reimbursement. I do not authorize the copying and taking of medical rec-ords from the hospital without my further consent. This authorization expires in ninety days.

An insurance company may claim that the second sentence makes its job difficult, and it may be right. It's worth a try.

9

Mailing Lists:
How Did They Get
My Name?

Usually the first thing people mention when they discover my interest in the right to privacy is "junk mail." The reason for this is not because offended persons find it difficult to remedy the situation. Clearly they can toss the unwanted mail into the nearest trash can, although the same is not true of television, radio, or telephone solicitations.

The real reason "junk mail" lists come to mind so quickly is that they are a universal experience—just about everybody gets mail advertisements. And they are the most persistent reminder that there are computer systems somewhere about which we know nothing but which know something about us. When people speak of unwanted mail as an invasion of privacy, I think, they are not so much offended by an intrusion into their private sphere as resenting having information about themselves— whether it's a name and address or a preference for a certain product—bought and sold without their knowledge or consent and without their getting compensation for it. This fits the fourth definition of the invasion of privacy "tort" listed early in Chapter 1, the use of one's name without consent for another's profit. And it fits the modern definition of an invasion of "informational privacy," loss of control over information about oneself.

The advertising industry estimates that the name of the average adult is on 80 to 150 mailing lists at any one time. "How do they get my name?" everybody wants to know. You get on a mailing list in three different ways. First, by being yourself. The fact that you are a warm body living in a particular locality places you on some mailing lists. These so-called compiled lists account for more than half of bulk mail. These lists are compiled by companies like Reuben H. Donnelley Corp. and R. L. Polk & Co. that use voter and automobile registration rolls, telephone and city directories, property ownership files, and sometimes door-to-door surveys. Some mailers' products or services appeal to such a broad audience that lists of this type—with the addresses of all people in a community—fit their needs. Through various test mailings, companies are able to refine these lists based on zip codes, census demographics, voting patterns, and other characteristics. An advertisement you receive addressed to "Occupant" or "Resident" may go not to everyone in your community or even to your next-door neighbor, only to those homes that meet the mailer's criteria. Postage and printing rates require most mailers to be even more selective in their lists.

And so you also get on mailing lists by doing something: getting your name in the paper, getting married, having a baby, buying an automobile, moving to a new home, renting an apartment, asking for utilities, owning a farm, attending school, holding a job, joining a church. These activities tell something about you and about your possible interest in a product or service. A seller of baby items will want to send advertising to new parents, not to every adult in a community. By mailing to the list of new parents, the mailer may well receive a response from 2 per cent or more of the recipients. The list of all adults in a community would bring a response rate of far less than 1 per cent.

Once a recipient responds to a mailing, that tells something else about the person. He or she not only is a new parent, but a new parent interested in buying baby products. A list of persons who have responded to a solicitation will bring an even greater response rate than the list of new parents, if used by a seller of baby magazines or toddler clothes—or life insurance.

Thus, the third way you get yourself on a mailing list is by buying products, especially through the mail. A seller of Chevrolet parts or services would be interested in reaching buyers of new Chevrolets. A company selling seeds would like to reach consumers who recently purchased garden supplies. A mail order house selling leather goods will want to use a list of persons who have bought clothing through the mail before. If the mail order house's products range in price from ten to forty dollars, it will be particularly interested in a list of persons who have made purchases in that range. And it will be even more interested in a list of persons who have purchased leather goods within that range. One of the rules of the mail business is that exchanging lists with your competitors is advantageous.

If the mail order house has a list of ten-to-forty-dollar buyers and a list of thirty-to-eighty-dollar buyers, it may send each group a catalogue tailored to their buying habits. If the list is further refined by sex, geographical area of residence, and credit rating, so much the better.

How does it work? Whenever you apply for a government benefit like a driver's license, automobile registration, birth certificate, new water service, or a license to practice a profession, your name becomes part of a list. State agencies regularly sell these names to list compilers who then rent the names to a mailer—generally at four cents a name for a one-time use. Phony addresses are included in rented lists to trap mailers who try to use them more than once without paying an additional rental. If a person responds to a mailing, either by buying a product or by asking for further information, that person's name becomes the "property" of the mailer, according to the rules of the business. The mailer adds this name to its "in-house" list, perhaps coded by the amount, type, and date of purchase. The mailer also codes each respondent according to the list on which his or her name first appeared. That allows the mailer to measure the comparative response rates of different lists (women over forty respond better to a certain mailing than men younger than thirty-five, perhaps). And it also allows the mailer to know something about you. If you responded to a list that originally included only purchasers of boating equipment for more than $400, the mailer knows you are a boater who buys products in the $400-plus range.

As the mailer compiles its in-house list, it will make this available for rental through list brokers. If your name is on the first mailer's in-house list, you will then receive a solicitation from a second mailer. If you respond to the second mailing, you will join the second mailer's in-house list. The second mailer may rent its own list to the first mailer, through a broker. This means that you will get a solicitation from the first mailer again, even though you are currently doing business with that company. Don't be offended or surprised, then, if you receive an advertisement to subscribe from a magazine publisher that already has you on its subscriber list. Some mailers have developed a computer technique for eliminating this duplication, called "merge and purge." A rented list is matched with a subscription list and purged of the names of current subscribers, or two similar lists are run together by computer to purge all duplicates. If you receive mail under slightly different names or at two different addresses, your duplicate mailing labels may well not get purged.

Just about all mass mailers use third-class postal rates, which require the mailer to presort pieces of mail by zip code. Computer lists are generally sorted in zip code sequence, but can be sorted alphabetically or by other characteristics.

Responsible retailers and mailers will rent their lists only to users whom they consider acceptable to their own customers. Users must generally submit a sample of their mail advertisement to the owner of the list. The publishers of *Psychology Today* wouldn't rent a subscriber list for the use of my newsletter, *Privacy Journal*, because my solicitation promised that the newsletter would inform readers "How to get off a mailing list."

(*Privacy Journal's* mailing list is not disclosed to others because of the sensitivities of many of its readers.)

Mail marketers call theirs a "personalized" medium of sales, and so many of them use a new computerized printer to insert your name in the salutation and body of the sales letter. A computer process called "Imaging by Jet Ink" controls tiny electrically charged droplets of ink that form characters on paper at extremely high speeds. Without a pause the computer can change the wording in any line of a document as it is printed so that it may be individualized with the addressee's name, or unpaid balance, or personal characteristics. Individually altered letters can now be printed and inserted into envelopes at the rate of 100,000 per hour.

A variation on this theme is the coding of sales letters or marketing surveys with an invisible ink that can be read only with special lighting used by the mailer. This technique has been used by magazine publishers who regularly survey the buying habits and income of a sample of their readership to impress advertisers. They promise each respondent confidentiality, and most persons think that means anonymity as well. But the publishers say they secretly code letters to know who did not respond and should get a follow-up letter and to refine the survey results later. Other mailers have been known to print a code identifying each respondent under the flap of the return envelope or under the stamp. Some have even cut and colored the paper of the questionnaire to identify the person responding.

Here are some of the sources of mailing lists on which your name may appear. Most state agencies release the name of all licensed drivers and owners of registered automobiles. The same is true of persons licensed by the state to sell real estate, practice medicine, or operate a beauty shop. One county in southern California rented its payroll list, but put an end to the practice after its employees received a solicitation to join the International Brotherhood of Teamsters. Moving companies provide names of families moving to or from a community. Hospitals often compile lists of new births. Lists of newlyweds come from the county registrar's office. The Educational Testing Service makes available to college recruiters the names of students taking college entrance examinations. A city in the

Southwest rents the names of new water customers. A California list broker will rent you the following lists, at $40 per thousand: conservative Catholic contributors, U. S. Olympic Ski Team contributors, Youth Against McGovern contributors, Korean Relief contributors, buyers of Ronald Reagan's books, or Republican contributors of $1,000 or more ($100 per thousand for that list).

If you're curious about lists where you may find your name, ask a librarian for *Direct Mail List Rates and Data*, an 800-page catalogue published semiannually by Standard Rate & Data Service, Inc., 5201 Old Orchard Road, Skokie, Illinois 60076. In it, Campbell Soup Company offers a master list of 3 million persons, child-oriented buyers, general merchandise buyers, homemaker buyers, pet owners, sports buyers, or refund respondents. *Nation's Business*, the magazine of the U. S. Chamber of Commerce, offers 7,500 names, primarily men, "who expressed their opinion on timely topics written by the editor." There's another listing for "new fathers, all of them first-timers, who have bought camera, cribs, extra decorating, insurance, food plans, etc." You can rent names of 8,500 buyers of *Encyclopedia of Love and Sex* for $30 per thousand, or 10,500 readers of *How to Avoid Probate* for $35. Or you can get a list of 52,000 "well-to-do Jewish men."

Is all of this an invasion of privacy? No, say the courts when irate consumers raise the issue. To my mind, the buying and selling of individuals' addresses and other characteristics without their consent violates the privacy principle against exploiting a person's name, face, or personal facts for another's profit. But a reason for these court decisions against unhappy recipients of unwanted mail is that communicating in this way, regardless of how annoying or wasteful it may seem to some people, is an exercise of free expression protected against government regulation by the First Amendment to the Constitution. Another reason is probably that the damage done by unwanted mail has never been shown to be serious.

Political candidates, of course, are big users of mail solicitation. The successful fund raiser for George C. Wallace's presidential campaign said once that if you contributed ten dollars to that campaign you could expect to receive about twenty-five mail solicitations in the following year from groups renting the Wallace contributor list. If you gave to Morris Udall's campaign for President in 1976, you could expect from five to ten mailings. When you contribute to a candidate or cause, you help in four ways. Part of your contribution pays for the mailing, part of it pays for future mailings, and part of it goes directly to the cause. You are also contributing your name and address, a commodity that the campaign may rent for additional proceeds. The Federal Election Campaign Act requires political candidates in federal elections to record your name and address with any contribution from you for $50 or more, and your occupation and principal place of business once your contributions to one campaign total $100 or more in a year. Federal candidates may not accept anonymous contributions of more than $50. This information about you is available for public inspection, although the law prohibits use of the information by others for political fund-raising or commercial purposes. "Commercial solicitation," however, does not include the sale of periodicals, according to the law.[27]

Charities raise 80 per cent of their funds by repeated use of mailing lists, and most of them could not survive without direct mail solicitation. Some of them are sensitive to the concerns of their contributors and therefore, instead of disclosing their in-house lists to others, send out mailings for others through their own organizations. Thus, the users of the lists never see the names and addresses. Once you respond to such a mailing, of course, your identity becomes known to the user, including your identity as a contributor to the charity that allowed use of the list originally.

There are no state or federal restrictions on the compilation or use of mailing lists, with two exceptions. New York law prohibits utility companies from renting customer lists and the telephone company from renting out the names of customers who are unlisted in telephone directories. The federal tax code prohibits tax preparers from selling or renting customer lists. I feel that mailers should seek to abide by these standards:

1. A citizen has the right to have his or her name excluded from any lists rented to other mailers.

2. A mailer should tell the recipient where it found his or her name.

3. Materials distributed by merchants, mail order houses, publishers, professions, state government agencies, and others should periodically announce their policies on disclosing names of individuals who deal with them.

4. Mailing lists that reveal political or religious affiliation or views, or reading tastes, should not be shared with others. Organizations with such lists should conduct mailings for others through their own organizations.

5. Deceased persons should be removed promptly from lists.

6. Special care should be taken in the exchange of lists with children's names.

7. Citizens should be given the opportunity to keep their names off commercial lists when registering for a government license or benefit. The costs of preparing lists by government agencies should be paid by proceeds from list rental, not tax money.

8. Mailers should periodically explain to consumers the meaning of any codes used on mail labels.

9. Questionnaires should not be coded clandestinely.

10. Controversial groups and marketers of sensitive products should send unsolicited mail in unmarked envelopes. (The National Gay Task Force, for instance, includes its return address, but not its name, on the outside of mail envelopes.)

11. Mailers should use great care in the use of residential addresses, as distinguished from professional addresses.

Whenever I propose these modest "Eleven Commandments" as voluntary goals for the industry, I am greeted with hostility or apathy by mailers. One mailer in California argued, "People with an interest in direct mail must be extremely careful to restrict any action or suggestion that might be construed to be a concession that individual privacy is indeed violated by direct mail."

WHAT CAN YOU DO?

You should be cautious when registering for a government benefit, buying a product, or seeking information. If you wish not to have your name become part of a mailing list, say so at that point. If you don't want the world to know when you become pregnant, alert your doctor before someone in the doctor's office submits your name to a mailing list. Just about all agencies and businesses say they are willing and able to respect individual requests at this point. Once your name becomes part of the list network, it's more difficult to remove your name. Write to businesses with whom you correspond asking that your name not be disclosed, or look up the addresses of mailers in the mailing list catalogue and write directly to the ones that probably have your name. But don't be surprised or outraged if you continue to receive unwanted mail. If you write to companies from whom you receive mail but with whom you have no relationship, enclose the label and ask that your request be forwarded to the owner of the list that was used. If you wish your name removed from mailing lists generally, send your name and address to the mailers' trade association, Direct Mail/Marketing Association, Mail Preference Service, 6 East Forty-third Street, New York, New York 10017. The association will respond with a name-removal form that asks for the very same information. This two-step process has caused about half the people applying to lose interest. The association will then circulate your name and address to its member companies, asking them to delete your name and address from its lists. The members are not required to do this. And, of course, nonmembers, who account for perhaps a fifth of the direct mail in the nation, are not affected by the program. The association will also *add* your name to mailing lists if that is your wish.

Some organizations provide a regular opportunity—usually by publishing a coupon—for you to request that your name not be disclosed on rented mailing lists. Among these organizations are the American Bar Association; Atlantic Richfield Co. (Arco

Oil); American Express Co.; L. L. Bean, Inc.; Columbia House record club; Diners Club; Field & Stream Club; Haines & Co., Inc. (publishers of Criss-Cross Directories); Jewelart, Inc.; McGraw-Hill, Inc.; *Ms.* Magazine; *Motor Trend*; J. C. Penney Co.; RCA Music Service; Time Inc.; and Union Oil Co.

Two federal laws are applicable. One allows an individual to get a court order forbidding a mailer to send him or her pandering advertisements that the individual defines as erotic. More than half a million persons have done this since the law was passed in 1970.[28] There is a criminal penalty for a mailer to continue to send you pandering materials after you have done this. The second statute, the so-called obscenity law, requires the Postal Service to maintain a list of individuals who do not want to receive sexually oriented material (as defined in the law). The list is circulated to publishers of that kind of material. There is a criminal penalty for any such publisher for mailing sexually oriented material to persons on this list. The publisher must also label sexually oriented mail on the envelope. Go to your local post office to fill out a form.[29]

You may want to rent a post office box. This, of course, does not stop unsolicited mail, nor does it stop mailers from buying and selling your name, address, and personal characteristics. It simply stops the flow of mail advertising to your home and may prevent a marketing company from linking your address and your telephone number. By the way, the name, address, and telephone number of *an individual* box holder may not be disclosed by the postal authorities except in response to written requests from government agencies, in response to a subpoena or court order, or for the service of legal process. (The true address of *a business* using a post office box is freely disclosed upon request.)[30]

The Privacy Act of 1974 prohibits federal agencies from selling or renting an individual's name and address, "unless such action is specifically authorized by law." Under the Freedom of Information Act, government information, even about individuals, must be disclosed to someone who requests it unless disclosure would be "a clearly unwarranted invasion of personal privacy." As we discussed in Chapter 7, a few mailing lists are not disclosed for this reason, especially if the requester does not have a compelling need for the information, beyond commercial sales.

The Veterans Administration is authorized by law to release the names and addresses of veterans and their dependents to nonprofit organizations providing services to veterans, and it does so. The list of 9 million Citizens Band (CB) radio licensees held by the Federal Communications Commission is public by law, and sold in a computer format. The departments of the Treasury and Defense and the Postal Service say they release no mailing lists without consent. The departments of Health, Education, and Welfare and Commerce usually release lists with professional or business addresses. The Federal Aviation Administration list of pilots, engineers, navigators, and control tower operators is used commercially. License applications at the Nuclear Regulatory Commission are publicly available. The General Services Administration discloses a list of persons who sought to purchase commemorative silver dollars.

The following sixteen states limit the use of motor vehicle registration information for commercial mailing purposes: Alaska, Arkansas, California, Connecticut, Hawaii, Indiana, Massachusetts, Missouri, Nevada, New Jersey, Ohio, Pennsylvania, South Dakota, Virginia, Washington, and Wyoming. Indiana, in 1977, passed one of the strictest laws; it allows mailing lists to be sold only to notify owners of motor vehicle defects or to compile statistical compilations that will not identify individuals. Individual records may be purchased for one dollar each. California's Department of Motor Vehicles requires requesters to establish their identities and state reasons for wanting individual motor vehicle information. The individual whose record is being disclosed is notified. Purchasers of mailing lists must be publicly announced by the department. But each individual on the list is not notified. California adopted this tightened policy in 1977 in response to complaints that motor vehicle lists had been used in planning crimes such as auto theft and rape. Vehicle registration, not driver's license information, is covered by these laws.

The Federal Trade Commission has issued regulations concerning the delivery of mail order *merchandise and services* (not the advertisement of them). The seller must make delivery within thirty days of your order or give you a choice of a prompt refund or an option to agree to a delay. After the thirty-day period, you reserve the right to cancel at any time, even if you agree to a delay. This thirty-day requirement, of course, applies only to the first issue of a magazine subscription. It does not cover orders for seeds or plants or collect-on-delivery (C.O.D.) orders, or book or record clubs (called "negative option" sales).[31] Commission rules also prohibit a publisher from sending you a bill that looks like an invoice if in fact you have not yet agreed to renew a subscription. If the mailer does not comply within a reasonable time to the delivery or cancellation requirement, write a letter and enclose the advertisement and your canceled check to Director, Bureau of Consumer Protection (MO-P), Federal Trade Commission, Washington, D.C. 20580.

10

Medical Records: Confidentiality Is a Myth

> Whatever, in connection with my professional practice or not in connection with it, I see or hear, in the life of men, which ought not to be spoken of abroad, I will not divulge, as reckoning that all such should be kept secret.

That is part of the ancient oath of Hippocrates, the Greek physician regarded as the father of medicine. Physicians seek to uphold the standards of the oath.

Hippocrates, of course, had not heard about "third-party payers." Neither have most other people, for that matter, except for doctors, insurance workers, and a few government bureaucrats. Medicine since Hippocrates had been a two-party affair between doctor and patient. But a "third party" now pays the bills directly, whether it's a health insurance company or a government program like Medicare or Medicaid. And whoever pays the bills wants to know what they're paying for.

It matters not that doctors are strong protectors of the privacy of their patients—and many are. The nature of third-party payments nowadays and the proliferation of computer data banks in the insurance and health industries make confidentiality beyond the control of the practicing physician.

Because of the strong tradition of the Hippocratic oath in medicine, patients—and some physicians—are shocked to discover that medical confidentiality does not exist by law. But doctors need not swear to the oath, and many don't. Nor is there any law against a doctor in private practice disclosing medical information about you without your consent. The only sanction is in the ethics of the profession.

All states but Rhode Island, South Carolina, Texas, and Vermont recognize a "doctor-patient privilege" by law. This means that the doctor may not be compelled to testify in court about medical facts received in confidence. This privilege applies generally to compelled testimony. It does not prohibit voluntary disclosures to lawyers, news reporters, investigative agencies, law enforcement, friends, or anyone else.

Where state law does recognize the doctor-patient privilege of confidentiality, the statute is often filled with so many exceptions—either drafted by legislators or interpreted by judges—that there is in fact little protection against a physician's being compelled to disclose patient information when that information matters most.

For instance, Pennsylvania will protect a doctor from testifying only if the medical information is "derogatory." California and Michigan require the patient to waive the privilege when he or she is the plaintiff in a civil suit. Imagine a doctor being compelled to reveal a 1960 hemorrhoids operation or a 1969 mastectomy because a patient happens to have to sue to recover for back injuries in an automobile accident. In Idaho, the privilege is of no use in personal injury actions. In Maine, a judge may ignore the privilege.

Alabama, Connecticut, Georgia, Maryland, Massachusetts, and Tennessee recognize a privilege only for psychotherapists, not physicians. So medical privacy is a myth—in spite of the patient's strong expectations and the tradition of Hippocrates.

The most damaging invasions of privacy are caused by doctors, nurses, and other medical staff who simply gossip too much. They are often anxious to talk to the press or anyone else about a well-known patient's condition without checking first with the patient or the family. Or they carelessly discuss patients' conditions at parties or when treating other patients. It's not at all uncommon for a doctor to tell you that so-and-so was in last week with such-and-such a problem. It may be that the second person's condition was quite routine, but it's no one else's business. It's the individual's right to decide whether medical information, even routine information, is disclosed in such a fashion. These same practitioners will earnestly tell you why the patient himself or herself ought not to know the same medical information.

This disparity in respecting confidentiality is illustrated by a tale of two doctors. One, George R. Caesar, M.D., of Marin County, north of San Francisco, California, went to jail for three days and spent loads of money in legal expenses to protect his patient's privacy. A psychiatrist, he refused to answer questions about the psychotherapy of one of his patients in civil litigation she initiated to recover damages for two auto accidents. Dr. Caesar told the trial judge that to describe his patient's therapy would result in harm to her. After the United States Supreme Court chose not to accept his appeal in 1977, the psychiatrist was locked up.

In New York City, one of Dr. Caesar's colleagues decided to write a book that reported verbatim and extensively her patients' thoughts, feelings, and emotions, their sexual and nonsexual fantasies, their life histories, their most intimate personal relationships, and the disintegration of their marriages. She published the book eight years after their treatment. The names of the patients were not used, but the patients claimed that it was not hard to figure out their identities. Whether or not their identities could be determined, the trauma of reading in a book a blow-by-blow account of one's revelations to a psychiatrist is damaging enough.

All of this was done in the name of scientific research. The patients were unable to prevent publication of the book because the courts did not want to restrain the doctor's right of free expression, prior to publication. But the patients may be able to recoup a money award for invasion of privacy now that the book has been published.

Those are the most aggravating invasions of privacy, but the most *frequent* disclosures of medical information result from each patient's signing language authorizing "any licensed physician, medical practitioner, or other person" to disclose information. This is necessary, as we have seen, whenever we apply for insurance coverage or seek payment by a third-party payer. Practitioners seem to think that whenever a patient hurriedly signs this language he or she is knowingly granting access to any and all medical information in the file.

According to the employee newspaper of Equifax, Inc., one of its field investigators may present a photocopy of this signed authorization at the prestigious Mayo Clinic in Rochester, Minnesota, and be able to review personally a patient's *whole medical file*.

The patient clearly signed the form to qualify for insurance coverage or to file a claim. That means to me that the patient is authorizing hospital personnel only to answer inquiries about an insurance applicant's medical history or about a claimant's recent treatment. I don't regard that signed authorization as a license for a stranger to have visual access to the whole medical file. But most hospital staffs do. Some hospital records administrators even allow consumer investigators to take away photocopies from the individual's file. Question them on this and you'll get the reply, "Well, we release information only with the consent of the individual. And when the individual requests us to disclose, we have to comply."

Mayo Clinic now allows anyone with a photocopy of a signed authorization to sit down and peruse the patient's file. "Only limited information has been available from this clinic in the past. With a personal review of the patient's clinical record now permitted," reported the Equifax management to its seven thousand information gatherers in the United States, "we can make a comprehensive report of the patient's history and current status. The report would contain more information than can normally be found in a combination of doctor and hospital records. . . . Our Rochester branch office's breakthrough, that allows us to *personally review* clinical records, can be a 'shot in the arm' toward new volume—especially [Equifax's Underwriting Medical History Service] volume."

I asked Mayo's lawyer about all of this and his response was simply, "Information from a patient's medical records is disclosed only when [we are] required to do so by law or when specifically directed to do so by a patient or his legally authorized representative."

Once the patient's signed authorization opens the floodgates of medical information, that flow continues to the insurance investigator, to the insurance company, to the Medical Information Bureau, and often to an employer. If the government is paying the bills (as it does for 50 per cent of the medical bills in the nation), the flow goes in another direction, to the government agency that administers the CHAMPUS (military), Medicare (federal), or Medicaid (state) programs. Often, however, even if the government is paying, the information flows by way of a private insurance company. Insurers like Aetna, Mutual of Omaha, and Blue Cross–Blue Shield act as Medicare "intermediaries" to process payments for the government. They use computers to do the job; they probably couldn't handle the volume of claims without computers.

Some government bureaucrats get the idea that this information is their personal property. Just before he left office, the secretary of health and welfare for California under Governor Ronald Reagan walked off with 1,500 reels of computer tapes containing the medical records of millions of persons in California's medical insurance program, Medi-Cal. The man wanted to use them for academic research, but the state got them back.

Like insurance, computers have changed the face of medical information flow. Many hospitals and clinics use computers, of course, to diagnose and treat illnesses. Many use them to administer their programs. Many more use them to process medical information about patients.

The following is the minimum amount of information gathered by the typical hospital on each patient: a unique numerical identifier, date of birth, sex, race, address, admission date,

discharge date, attending physician's identifying number, operating physician's identifier, primary and secondary diagnoses,
the dates and natures of all procedures performed, the disposition of the patient (sent home, transferred elsewhere, or died),
and expected source of payment. This is the U.S. recom-
mended daily allowance of information about hospital patients.
Private or public hospitals, even if the patients are among the
13 per cent in the nation who pay their own medical bills
directly, disclose this information to the National Center for
Health Statistics in the U. S. Department of Health, Education, and Welfare, to hospital associations that monitor health
care, and to hospital accrediting bodies. I don't recall authorizing these disclosures of my hospital record, do you?

In some cases, welfare departments and various community
service organizations get the same data.

If you are hospitalized in some states—Missouri, for instance
—these data on you are shipped out of state to a computer system in Des Moines, Iowa. Your name is not included, but your
census tract number is: that's the designation for your immediate neighborhood of five thousand or so persons. If you saw a
computer printout of the hospital data on your five thousand
closest neighbors, without their names, could you figure out
who's had what? Perhaps.

The Iowa Hospital Association runs all of this "input" from
each hospital through its computer in Des Moines and returns
to the hospital a pile of monthly printouts that tell more than
anyone ever wants to know about what's going on in that hospital: a list of all patients discharged that month, a list of all
deaths, a list of patients with similar diagnoses, a list of patients with similar operations, a list of each physician's work-
load, a list of patients in each department, pages and pages of
cumulative data on the number of patients treated, average
length of stay, and even the numbers admitted on each day of
the week. Hospitals pay good money for all of this, on the
theory that it helps them manage their places better. One of
the compilations may prove a point at a staff meeting, but as
often as not the computer analyses get stuffed away somewhere.
There is, then, little hope that when your name appears on the

monthly computer list of dead patients, this will mean that a member of the staff will be sent by to do something about you. Patients would be willing to bear the risk of disclosure of this sort of sensitive information if they were confident that the information was being put to good use in administering health care.

There is a similar "quality-control" program sponsored by the federal government. These are the so-called Professional Standards Review Organizations (PSROs) located in each county to assess the quality of medical treatment. Funded and monitored by the federal government, these PSROs have revolving groups of private practitioners who review the services of their professional peers. They do this by evaluating patient profiles that are shipped in bulk—usually in computer form—from doctors, clinics, hospitals, and nursing homes to the PSRO. By law, the patient information is supposed to be coded "to the greatest extent practical" to conceal patient identity. If that code is the Social Security number, there is not much security for the individual's privacy. If a PSRO finds it impractical to code the information, there is even less security. A patient seeking private or public medical treatment is not agreeing to have his or her case scrutinized by a random selection of doctors in the community, but that in fact is what is occurring.

This automated transfer of patient data to an outside evaluation group has established the prototype for the massive amounts of patient data that will be required to administer the proposed national health insurance plan. It is a network of extremely sensitive personal information that has been established bit by bit without any realization by the American people of what was happening.

State governments also maintain similar computer data banks with medical information in them, even on patients getting private medical treatment. In Maryland the following information must be submitted to the state on each woman who has an abortion: age, race, marital status, reason for the operation, method used, complications, source of referral, source of payment, whether sterilization was performed, address, previous abortions, and term of fetus. All of this information on 20,000 abortions is stored in a computer at the Department of Health in Baltimore, which reports cumulative data to interested organizations. Women are listed not by name but by a hospital or clinic identifying number. If that number happens to be the same as the woman's Social Security number it is not difficult to identify her. With typical disregard for individuals' concerns about medical privacy, Maryland bureaucrats named their system the Maryland Abortion Surveillance Unit. New York City has a similar data bank on abortions. Health planners, researchers, lawmakers, and lobbyists want the data to determine the frequency of abortions in different segments of our society, as well as the social and physical consequences. They need the identity of the women, they say, in order to follow trends and locate problem cases that are discovered only long after the operations. But few facts about a person are more sensitive and less suitable for an impersonal data bank. A young woman who has still not recovered from her shock related this experience in *The New Yorker:*

> I went into the hospital early in the morning, and was home in bed early that evening. At seven the next morning, the telephone rang. A woman [said,] "We know that yesterday morning you murdered a six-week-old baby girl, and we'd like to offer you some guidance." [The caller left an inaccurate telephone number and only her first name.] Then I called my doctor, and he told me that anti-abortion groups pay nurses for lists of women who have had abortions, the same way diaper companies used to pay nurses for lists of women who had given birth.

The state of Maryland also maintains a Psychiatry Case Registry that includes the following on private and public patients: age, sex, race, socioeconomic status, residence, marital status, diagnosis on admission and discharge, type of therapy, number of interviews, suicide attempts, improvement in condition (if any).

When a government agency gathers all of this information, does it raise possibilities of a constitutional invasion of privacy?

You would think so, but the U. S. Supreme Court has ruled that it does not. "Disclosures of private medical information to doctors, to hospital personnel, to insurance companies, and to public health agencies are often an essential part of modern medical practice even when the disclosure may reflect unfavorably on the character of the patient. Requiring such disclosures to representatives of the State having responsibility for the health of the community, does not automatically amount to an impermissible invasion of privacy," the Court said in 1977.[32] The Court upheld New York State's requirement that druggists send a carbon copy of prescriptions (identified with the name of the patient) for certain dangerous drugs to a computerized file in the state capital. It argued that collection of information that has always been regarded as legitimate is not rendered unconstitutional simply because new technology makes its operations more efficient. Justice William J. Brennan, Jr., in concurring with the Court's opinion, noted, however, that there may come a time when there is "the necessity of some curb on such technology." The Fourth Amendment, he noted, "puts limits not only on the type of information the State may gather, but also on the means it may use to gather it."

When psychiatric information is released to third parties, the problems for the patient are particularly acute. Psychiatrists say they release information only: when knowingly authorized by the patient; when other professionals assist in treatment; when required by a court order; when the doctor honestly believes that the patient will do serious injury to himself or herself, to another, or to the community; or when the survivors of a deceased patient authorize disclosure.

Because of this code, few patients would expect that when they seek treatment for mental illness, their names and case histories would end up in a computer in Rockland County, New York. But that is exactly what happens to mental health patient records in Connecticut, the District of Columbia, Hawaii, parts of New Jersey, New York, Rhode Island, and Vermont. Only the state of Connecticut has a law authorizing mental health records to go to an out-of-state computer. New York law requires that the records in this computer system be kept confidential and immune from judicial process This Multi-State Information System provides participating facilities with countless analyses of their patient data and up-to-date reports on individuals. Mental health treatment is thus supposed to be made more efficient.

Public mental health facilities, alcohol and drug clinics, state hospitals and their clinics, general hospitals, child guidance clinics, private hospitals, mental health centers, children's residential treatment centers, outpatient centers drug addiction centers, halfway houses—all of these are hooked into the Multi-State System, by either direct computer terminals, telephone lines, or mail. It would be hard to find a patient at any of these facilities who is aware of this. "The system," says its director, "is designed to keep exact records of the location and status of each patient."

Psychiatrists and psychologists are particularly uncomfortable about providing detailed diagnoses to insurance companies, but this has become necessary so that patients may collect reimbursement for therapists' bills. Some practitioners and insurers have co-operated on a system of spot-checking or coding of mental conditions to cut down on the information submitted to the insurance companies. An insurance agent in Boston decided to query psychiatrists about this and discovered that three fourths of the 900 in his survey said that they fear a breach of confidentiality by insurance companies. Consequently, as one respondent put it, "I distort my diagnosis for health insurance purposes. Others do the same—meaning that insurance companies do not have reliable statistics." (Virtually all of the psychiatrists felt that mental patients are better risks than others, even though employers and insurers seem not to agree.)

The survey reminds me of a cartoon in an old issue of *The New Yorker* magazine, in which the patient settles down on the psychiatrist's couch and exclaims, "Today I'm not going to talk about my goddamn mother. I'm going to talk about my goddamn insurance company."

WHAT CAN YOU DO?

When you receive medical treatment, you are entitled to receive a clearly written account of how your personal information will be disclosed and how it will be used. And you should know what safeguards the recipients of your information use to protect it, to update it, and to prevent its use for purposes different than the one originally specified. You are entitled to full information about your health conditions. When health data is used to determine payments and claims or for any nonmedical social or governmental programs, you are entitled to inspect whatever is released in your record. You should have a right to see any part of your medical files, including your doctor's working notes. Your doctor should be given the opportunity to advise against this, if the doctor feels that it would be harmful to your medical interests. If you still insist on seeing the records, you should be able to do so, or, if your doctor advises, have another professional of your choice inspect the records for you.

This, anyway, is the recommendation of a 1976 federal study on health records. It is not your right by law. In some rare instances, as in Massachusetts and Florida, state law permits you access to your own hospital file. The Privacy Act of 1974 permits you access to medical files about you held by a federal agency. Regulations under the law, issued by the Veterans Administration, Indian Health Service, or other health care agencies, say that a federal physician may choose to have the disclosure made not directly to you but to a physician of your selection. Some hospitals allow individual access as a matter of policy.

I have never known a person to roll over and die upon learning of his or her true medical status, but many practitioners claim that full disclosure, especially of mental health information, can be detrimental to the patient. (Try to tell that to a person like the late Hubert Humphrey.) I am not qualified to debate that point, but two things I know. First, there can be no legitimate objection to a "medical advocate," if necessary, representing the patient to secure full and prompt disclosure of an individual file held by a hospital, clinic, or doctor. A family member could play this role. And second, any medical information that is available to nonmedical professionals ought to be available directly to the patient. This includes information known to nonprofessionals in a hospital, insurance company, government agency, or other organization. The purpose, of course, is to assure the individual that information in his or her file is accurate and up to date before it is disseminated and before crucial decisions are based on it.

The American Medical Association is wary of providing the patient, or a nonprofessional proxy, with direct access to his or her own medical records. The American Hospital Association endorses the idea of direct patient access. So does the Secretary of Health, Education, and Welfare's Commission on Medical Malpractice (1973). "Lying to patients for their own good has often seemed excusable to philosophers and physicians alike," according to Sissela Bok, author of *Lying: Moral Choice in Public and Private Life*. After reviewing practices in the medical profession in 1976, she discovered that telling the truth is not a requirement in the various codes of ethics developed by the profession through the years.

Where there is no legal right to see your own medical records, you are still entitled, often by law, to have them transferred to a hospital or clinic of your choice. You are entitled, as a matter of law, to have access once you sue the practitioner or institution for malpractice or other wrongdoing.

It is always important to discuss with your doctor in advance your concern about the disclosure of your medical information to outsiders so that the practitioner will act accordingly. Make clear that you are not authorizing informal disclosure to the doctor's friends, colleagues, or golfing partners. And if you have any doubts about what you are agreeing to when you sign a form authorizing disclosure of your medical records, speak up. Make those doubts known. In the course of all of this, you will discover just what information is disclosed about you.

Laws in the various states require doctors to report to state agencies instances of the following, usually without the consent of the patient: cancer, child abuse, contagious diseases, narcotics use, venereal disease, violent injuries, and, of course, births and deaths. A few states require reports on abortions, alcohol abuse, driving impairments, handicaps, occupational diseases, rabid dog bites, or tuberculosis.

Some companies now sell a so-called medical identity card that you may carry with you at all times. One variety has a brief summary of a condition you have (like an allergy or chronic disease) that may require emergency treatment; others summarize your medical conditions; and a third kind includes your whole medical file reduced to microfilm. The possibilities for abuse are endless. The information could be sold to insurance investigators snooping for pre-existing conditions. It could be rented to marketers who want to advertise equipment and services for persons with particular medical conditions, such as diabetes or hay fever. I have not heard of abuses like this occurring, but it's smart to write on any form that you fill out for one of these ID cards: "This information is submitted only for purposes of recording it on my own medical identity card and may not be preserved by [the card-issuing company] or disclosed to anyone." If your application for a medical ID card is rejected, you'll be alerted to try another company that provides the same services.

Better still, why not get your own medical ID card or bracelet made locally at a place where you do not need to leave a trail of medical information about yourself?

11

Privileges:
Your Right to Have
Confidants

What you tell your lawyer, priest, spouse, or physician in confidence usually cannot be disclosed in a court of law without your permission. This legal principle is called a "privilege." Most professionals zealously resist if they are compelled to testify about information they received in a privileged communication. This was the case with the therapist mentioned in the preceding chapter who spent time in jail rather than disclose a patient's comments. Because of this, many people think that professionals are prevented from voluntarily revealing the same information outside of a court. They are not. They are limited usually by professional ethics, but not by law.

At a cocktail party or on the golf course, an attorney or a doctor is often lax about protecting the confidentiality of a client or patient. Doctors often talk to the press about the medical condition of a famous patient, without consent. A Protestant minister based a sermon on the final words he heard from a public official who died in 1978. Journalists in Washington who devotedly protect their right not to be compelled to reveal the names of informers freely disclose them voluntarily to friends and other reporters after leading the news source to believe that he or she was speaking in confidence.

In *Couch* v. *U.S.*, Supreme Court Justice William O. Douglas explained succinctly, as he so often did, what the privilege represents: "One's privacy embraces what the person has in his home, his desk, his files, and his safe as well as what he carries on his person. It also has a very meaningful relationship to what he tells any confidant—his wife, his minister, his lawyer, or his tax accountant. The constitutional fences of law are broken down by an ever-increasingly powerful Government that seeks to reduce every person to a digit." Douglas was disagreeing with a 1973 Supreme Court decision that refused to recognize a privilege for conversations between accountant and client, except where a state legislature has created such a privilege.

Privileges are recognized by court rules, by state law, by federal laws that restrict the use of federal information, and by principles developed through the years by the courts. Except in the case of a journalist-source privilege, the privilege belongs to the client, patient, or penitent, not to the professional. It is the individual's to assert and to waive, not the professional's. The following privileges are recognized in various court jurisdictions:

Attorney-client. This is the longest-recognized, and its rationale is that a person must be able to talk candidly about embarrassing and incriminating information in order to get complete legal help. Whatever you tell *your* attorney (not any attorney) in a relationship as a client—and whatever may be overheard by or disclosed to the attorney's staff—is immune from compulsory process by a civil or criminal court. This privilege does not include the fact that you are the attorney's client or, usually, the fees involved. It covers your comments about consummated acts, including crimes, but not contemplated or continuing acts or tangible evidence given to a lawyer. It does not cover routine business conducted by someone who is an attorney, like tax returns or real estate sales.

In addition to the privilege, each attorney must abide by the Canons of Professional Ethics of the American Bar Association, which state:

It is the duty of a lawyer to preserve his client's confidences. This duty outlasts the lawyer's employment, and extends as well to his employees.

Doctor-patient. This applies to communications from the patient (as to his or her medical condition usually) and also extends to the physician's advice, hospital records, and X rays. The rationale is that a person might be deterred from disclosing embarrassing and personal facts necessary for adequate medical treatment if he or she fears later disclosure. State laws recognizing this privilege include psychiatrists where they are licensed medical practitioners. Some states have separate statutes to cover psychologists, "psychological associates," nurses, marriage counselors, psychiatric social workers, or dentists. Maryland protects communications to a fellow patient in group psychotherapy. Utah and Montana protect communications to speech pathologists.

Some state laws recognize the privilege in criminal cases, not in civil cases; other states, the reverse. Most states recognize it in both instances.

In spite of the recognized medical privilege, doctors in most areas are required to report to the state cases of certain diseases, child abuse, violent wounds, or narcotics abuse. Reports of venereal disease, where required, may often be made anonymously. Until 1976 Maryland required all physicians to report to the motor vehicle department any data on patients whose driving might be impaired for medical reasons. The reporting is now voluntary, not mandatory.

In addition to the privilege, doctors are bound by a medical code of ethics that requires them to keep patient information confidential, unless there is consent to reveal it.

Husband-wife. Courts have recognized that the testimony of one spouse against another may not be very reliable and would diminish trust in that relationship. Neither spouse can be very comfortable around the home if there's the possibility that what is said there may be revealed involuntarily at a later time. Once that relationship has broken down, the rationale disappears, and so one spouse may testify about the other in a divorce proceeding. But the termination of the marriage by divorce or death will not mean that a person can later be compelled to testify about communications made by the ex-spouse during the marriage. On the other hand, what is spoken before the marriage is not covered by the privilege, even after the couple is married. A defendant in Georgia a few years ago married the witness to his alleged crime and sought to prevent her from testifying. Sorry, said the judge, her testimony is not barred by the marital privilege.

You cannot have it both ways if the marriage is nullified. That means that the marriage never happened and so the husband-wife privilege does not protect whatever was said during that relationship. As would be expected, judges will not recognize the privilege when a crime by one spouse against the other is at issue or, in recent years, when abuse of a child is at issue. If you are "living together" in a state that recognizes the arrangement as a marriage, you may well be able to claim the privilege.

A municipal judge in Thornton, Colorado, was not successful in penetrating the confidentiality of the marital relationship. After a man was arraigned on a traffic violation before the judge, he muttered something to his wife as he was leaving the courtroom. The judge recalled the man and ordered him to reveal what he had said. The man refused and was cited for contempt of court. The Colorado Supreme Court, though, ruled in 1977 that marital privilege protects the conversation from forced disclosure.

Priest-penitent. The First Amendment of the Constitution recognizes the strict separation of Church and state that has been a part of American democracy. For an arm of the state, a court of law, to compel a member of the clergy to testify about conversations with a member of a church or synagogue would violate this principle. Further, where the conversations involve confessions, as in the Roman Catholic Church, the state would be diminishing the opportunity for candor and unfettered practice of religious worship. Priests, ministers, and rabbis are not supposed to disclose such communications even outside of court, according to standards of most religious associations.

Accountant-client. About fifteen states recognize this privilege, although purists say that such state laws are simply the product of lobbying by special-interest groups.

Journalist-informer. This privilege does not cover the content of communications by an informer to a news reporter, only the informer's identity. This is intended to prevent a chilling effect on a news organ's freedom of expression (as would be the case if a news reporter could never promise confidentiality to an informer). About a dozen states recognize the confidentiality of news sources, but elsewhere many courts find reporters in contempt of court for not revealing the source of information. A news source has no recognized right to conceal his or her identity as a source if compelled by a court. The privilege, where it exists, may be raised only by the reporter.

The general rule that confidential communications between persons in particular confidential relationships may not be compelled by a court has brought about traditions in each of the recognized professions to protect the confidentiality of personal information out of court. But remember that only a tradition and sometimes a code of ethics prevents voluntary disclosure, not a law.

There are other relationships that have been regarded as confidential and sometimes are recognized as such by law. The counselor-student relationship is one. The confidentiality of academic research is another. "Compelled disclosure of confidential information would without question severely stifle research into questions of public policy, the very subjects in which the public interest is greatest," said a federal judge in San Francisco in 1976, in refusing to allow an industrial supply company probe into a Harvard professor's reports on interviews with employees of an electric power company being sued by the supplier. Chances are, if the need for the information were greater, as in a criminal case, the court will order disclosure of the academic research.

A few states, New York and California among them, recognize the right of a victim of a rape to withhold testimony, in certain circumstances, about her prior sexual activities. This is intended to protect her privacy, in spite of the constitutional right of a defendant to confront fully any witnesses against him.

There are important bits and pieces of information that may be withheld from legal process in addition to privileges covering persons. A prosecutor may protect the identity of sources generally. A witness usually may protect the identity of political or religious affiliations and beliefs. How you voted is a secret, but if there is proof that you voted illegally your right to a secret ballot may not be recognized by a court. State and federal laws say that certain information submitted to government agencies—like the census information mentioned in Chapter 7—may not be compelled by a court.

If you are involved in a lawsuit and offer to settle with your adversary, this may not be admitted into evidence in a trial. There would be an implication of fault, perhaps, in any offer to settle. But it's the job of the judicial system to encourage offers of settlement, not discourage them. So such offers are not mentioned in court.

Materials seized illegally may not be admitted into trial, either, such as documents stolen from your home by police without a warrant or tape recordings of wiretaps installed without a warrant or without consent.

The most important privilege recognized in American law is one that you share with yourself, and no one else. Your thoughts, your secret expressions, your words spoken to yourself may not be admitted into evidence if they tend to incriminate you. This principle of the Fifth Amendment to the Constitution has been significantly modified in the past decade with court decisions concerning what is "incriminating" and which testimony is compelled and which is voluntary. Also, federal law allows courts to compel testimony that is self-incriminating if you are granted immunity from prosecution on the basis of what you say in court. The Fifth Amendment protection extends only to testimony that would tend to be incriminating, not merely embarrassing or damaging.

Once again, in Justice Douglas' words (*Couch* v. *U.S.*), "When it comes to the 'forcible and compulsory extortion of a man's own testimony or of his private papers to be used as evidence to convict him of crime or to forfeit his goods,' that is an illustration of the manner in which 'the Fourth and Fifth Amendments run almost into each other.'"

12

School Records:
Where It All Begins

What is the starting point for the invisible threads of information that Solzhenitsyn wrote about in *Cancer Ward*? It is in the school system, of course, the first place where each of us is required to relinquish personal information about ourselves for the record. And we soon learn that the information is used to make decisions about us without our knowledge. We soon learn to respect "the people who manipulate the threads."

A Providence, Rhode Island, mother was so outraged at what she discovered in her eleven-year-old son's school file that she scooped up the whole mass of materials and walked out of the principal's office. The woman, Carol Rodi, was taking advantage of a federal law that permits parents—and students over the age of eighteen—to inspect files about the student. The law does not permit you to carry the records away, however, and Mrs. Rodi was threatened with arrest.

The mother discovered obscene notes written by her boy's classmates and references to private family matters. "I am the mother. These records are about my child and they are not staying in this building any longer," she said.

The woman had come to see her son's records because she feared they might include material that would adversely affect his chances of transferring to another school. The federal law was passed in 1974 for purposes exactly like that. Until then the Providence school system, like many others not covered by a state law on the subject, refused to let parents or pupils see individual files affecting the pupils.

The school officials in Providence agreed with Mrs. Rodi that nearly half of the 111 pieces of paper in her son's file were irrelevant and did not belong there. Mrs. Rodi, when promised that the irrelevant items would be destroyed, returned the file to the school, but not before photocopying the contents.

The Providence parent was right to nip this in the bud (even if she was wrong to remove the pupil folder from the school). Cumulative records like her son's follow a child throughout his school career, and beyond. It is not at all surprising for an eleventh-grade teacher to read in a pupil's file that the kid was disruptive—or "immature"—in the second grade. And not surprisingly, the eleventh-grade teacher treats the pupil as if he or she were potentially disruptive in the eleventh grade.

For example, a fifth grader in the San Francisco area had this entry in his records: "Kindergarten: Follower—sometimes cannot find 'anything to do.' Must always be outer directed. Inclined to be naughty. Mother is casual. Young—often loses control. Easily frustrated. 'Babyish.'" That was five years before! And it's hard to know whether some of the remarks refer to the child or the mother.

One seven-year-old has effectively been barred from public schools because of such gibberish in her files. After she had trouble in kindergarten, her parents sent her to private school. Her new teacher was shocked at how vitriolic were the comments in the public school record. The parents then wanted to return her to the public school system, but teachers there had read the earlier reports and wanted nothing to do with her.

Many people, of course, manage to overcome what's said about them.

Some years ago, a pupil's file included the evaluation that he was "retarded." He was expelled from school.

Many more years before that, a teacher said about another student that he was hopeless as a composer of music.

And years before that, a third little boy was rated a poor elementary student by one of his teachers.

The records were those of, respectively, Thomas A. Edison, Ludwig van Beethoven, and Isaac Newton. It's said that Winston Churchill flunked the sixth grade and that Albert Einstein lagged seriously behind his peers in learning to read.

Student counselors keep assessments of this kind in their files along with notes about their conversations with students on very sensitive subjects: their views of their parents, their home life, possible pregnancies or venereal disease, drug and alcohol use, sexual activities and fantasies. The Philadelphia school system was split down the middle a few years back on whether that information ought to be shared with the parents of the student who discloses it. Half of the administrators and parents insisted that a counselor has an obligation to inform the parent when a student discloses drug use, pregnancy, or other sensitive information. These parents felt they especially had a right to know if their own son or daughter had told a counselor about behavior that might involve law violations, health care, or the welfare of another person. The other half agreed with a representative of the school counselors, who argued, "Perhaps they have forgotten what it is like to be a teen-ager, to live in a nowhere world, not yet an adult but certainly no longer a child, trying out your own independence and questioning the wisdom of your parents. The teen years are not a rational time and if a student, despite our efforts and encouragement, cannot be convinced to tell his parents that he has VD, would you have us refuse to give him information on the agencies that can, under the law, diagnose and treat him without his parents' consent? Or would you have us violate his confidence and risk his running away—or guarantee that his friends do not get helped at all?"

Within a year, both sides seemed to have agreed to a compromise under which a parent would be informed whenever a counselor referred a student to an outside agency for help. The states of Connecticut, Idaho, Kentucky, Maine, Michigan, Montana, Nevada, North Carolina, North Dakota, South Dakota, and Washington recognize student-counselor communications as privileged—immune from compelled disclosure. Michigan, Nevada, Oklahoma, and Oregon protect communications between students and teachers.

If there is no guarantee of secrecy, the result is obvious. Students who most need help will not seek it, for fear of punishment by their parents, ridicule by schoolmates, or creation of a "paper prison" of records that will haunt them for the rest of their lives, shattering a career choice or college admission.

To prevent this, the federal law that granted individuals access to their own school records also limited the disclosure of those records to outsiders. The law, the Family Educational Rights and Privacy Act of 1974, is often called the Buckley Amendment, after its sponsor, former Senator James L. Buckley of New York. The Congress passed the law at a time when it seemed that everybody *but* parents and students themselves had access to student files. Employers, law enforcement, news reporters, military and graduate school recruiters, accrediting agencies, researchers, and even an auto insurance company offering a "good student discount" were able to get access to records about individual students.

Stewart Schwartz told his landlord that he was able to pay only half of his semester's rent at one time, and so his landlord called the financial aid office at Cortland College in upstate New York where Schwartz was a student. The landlord asked for information about Schwartz and was told about a forthcoming loan due to Schwartz. The landlord then confronted Schwartz with the exact amount of the loan and the name of the bank that was handling it. He demanded the full amount of the rent. Under the Buckley Amendment, a college is no longer able to disclose that sort of information about a student.

Several years before passage of the law, a survey of college registrars showed that fully nine out of ten answered yes to the question "Do you make available to local, state, or federal government agencies, such as the FBI, police, civil service, or military intelligence, the academic and personal information deemed pertinent to the query without the student's permission?" Under the Buckley Amendment, a college is no longer able to disclose that information.

As soon as you apply to college, you find yourself providing lots of personal information for a thick dossier about yourself: test scores, medical history, family finances, summer employment, letters of recommendation, after-school activities. Upon registration, you are most likely asked for your Social Security number so that the college's computers can keep all of the information straight.

Many colleges have joined together to consolidate the admissions procedure. Nearly one hundred of the nation's leading colleges now use an identical admissions form so that the applicant need fill out only one form and send photocopies to each of the colleges that interest him or her.

Law school admissions have been consolidated in the Law School Data Assembly Service, run by the Educational Testing Service in Princeton, New Jersey. It compiles the usual admission and scholarship information submitted by applicants for use by the various law schools. ETS has linked several of the law schools into this computer system with their own terminals. The system is "interactive," which means that each law school using a computer terminal may alter the data in the system. Each law school is supposed to have access only to information on applicants who have designated that law school as a recipient of an application.

The Educational Testing Service, which is generally known as the administrator of nearly four million college, graduate, and employment tests each year, also administers the College Scholarship Service. This service processes student financial aid information on more than a million families a year to help 1,200 member organizations—including state and federal agencies—make decisions on scholarships and other financial aid. The core of the program is the multi-paged Financial Aid Form, formerly called the Parents' Confidential Statement. The College Scholarship Service evaluates each of the forms that it receives to determine a family's ability to pay college costs. It sends its analysis and a copy of the form to each institution designated by the applicant. Parents are usually astounded by the amount of family financial data that is required —far more than on the average person's income tax return.

The kicker comes at the end of the form, where each parent or applicant is required to sign this statement:

> I agree that to verify information reported in this form I will on request provide to the CSS or any of the authorized recipients, including the BEOG program, an official photostatic copy of my state or U.S. income tax return.

BEOG is a program of basic education opportunity grants administered by the U. S. Office of Education. This statement is required even though not all colleges or scholarship programs require inspection of your federal tax returns. As more and more colleges feel that financial aid is going to families that underestimate their financial worth, some are asking to see the income tax returns. To the extent that the form is used to determine eligibility for federal financial aid, there are federal penalties for false statements.

The College Scholarship Service agrees to keep this information confidential except from organizations you wish to receive it, but no law requires the service to do so. The Buckley Amendment regulates only federally supported colleges and public school systems. State laws protecting the confidentiality of school records cover only public institutions. Nor is there any law that gives you a right to review the sensitive personal information the Educational Testing Service has on you to make sure that it's accurate. The service provides this access as a matter of policy, sometimes charging a small fee. The address is Educational Testing Service, Princeton, New Jersey 08540.

There is a comparable scholarship processing service run by American College Testing (ACT), Student Assistance Programs Division, P.O. Box 767, Iowa City, Iowa 52240.

Once admitted, the college student becomes the most surveyed, researched, and probed individual on the face of the globe. At more than 250 colleges, intimidated freshmen are confronted with an American Council on Education computerized questionnaire even before they can unpack their bags. Where do you plan to live? Where would you prefer to live? What influenced you to come to this college? Your parents' income? Their educational level? Your race? Religion? Do you identify with your neighbors, your religious peers, persons of your own sex, persons of your own ethnic group, or persons of your same age? Rate yourself in the highest 10 per cent, average, or below average in academic ability, athletics, the arts, cheerfulness, defensiveness, drive to achieve, leadership, mathematics, mechanics, originality, physical attractiveness, popularity, popularity with the opposite sex, public speaking, self-confidence (intellectual), self-confidence (social), sensitivity to criticism, stubbornness, understanding of others, writing ability. Are you interested in making money, raising a family, or helping others? Where do you stand on various political issues?

> Use only black lead pencil. Make no stray markings of any kind. Your response will be read by an optical mark reader.

The questionnaire is voluntary, but most of the thousands of freshmen who receive it adjust quickly to filling out and signing whatever is put in front of them. Much of what they fill out just before or after this form *is* mandatory. For all the harried freshman realizes, these sensitive data are being collected to devise his or her curriculum, to report home to parents, to determine eligibility for college programs, or to help the campus police keep order. The end result of the intrusion is an annual press release that purports to tell just what the current generation of college students thinks—STUDENTS MORE CONSERVATIVE, STUDY SHOWS or COLLEGE STUDENTS MORE LIBERAL ON SEX THAN PARENTS.

One trend is certain. College students today live and study on a campus where physical safety is a prime concern and trust in one's fellow students is the height of naïveté. When I attended college in the early 1960s, I rarely worried about locking my dormitory door or carrying student identification. Cafeteria workers recognized each student who showed up for meals. By 1964 the rallying cry of the student revolt at the University of California at Berkeley was, "I am a student. Do not bend, fold, spindle, or mutilate."

By the end of the seventies, American college students had

been taught to accept the need for tight security and a computerized identity.

Georgetown University in Washington, D.C., has its own way of keeping tabs on students who live in the dormitories located on its urban campus. Faced with increased criminal activity in dormitories—and undoubtedly faced with a zealous computer salesman—the security force at the university has installed a computerized lock system that requires each enrolled student to insert his or her numbered plastic card into the dorm door. The lock is connected to a computer that knows whether the holder of the card is authorized to enter the building. If a student has been expelled or hasn't paid a bill, the computer can be told overnight to reject that student's card. The computer doesn't keep a log of which student ID numbers are entering which dormitories at which hours—and with what other numbers—but it could do so very easily. And it could provide this daily log to parents, too, very easily.

Human nature defeats the machines in the end, of course. Students insert their cards into the computerized lock and gain entry to their dormitories. Then, naturally, they hold the door for whoever else might be following, thus defeating the security system.

Students at the University of Tennessee must place their hands on a computerized sensor to get into the cafeteria line each day. The device compares the length of each finger on the hand with a computer-stored hand profile of each student authorized to use the cafeteria. Experts said that the geometry of each person's hand is unique—shared with no one else, like a fingerprint. And, of course, students' hands are not transferable like plastic ID cards.

What all this means is that the spontaneity of college life has disappeared in an age of fancy security devices and computer data banks. Instead of taking risks and raising a little hell, students now know that they are catalogued and identified at every turn. By graduation time, the young person has left behind countless bits and pieces of personal information, most of it computerized so that it can be retrieved instantly, stored at minimal cost, manipulated without the individual's knowledge. There is the possibility that it can be linked with other data about the person stored in other systems—the Educational Testing Service, the military, employers, research centers.

With this in mind, Congress passed the Family Educational Rights and Privacy Act of 1974.[33] It says that federal funds shall be denied an educational institution that has a policy or practice of releasing educational records about students without written consent of the parents. There are exceptions to this federal policy of nondisclosure. Records may be disclosed without consent to other school officials who have an educational interest, including officials elsewhere in the school system; to officials of other schools in which the student seeks to enroll (if parents are notified of the transfer of records); to federal and state regulatory agencies; to organizations processing financial aid; to educational researchers who certify that individual information will not be disclosed further; in compliance with a court order, if the school attempts to notify the parents; in an emergency, especially if time is of the essence. These disclosures may be made only if the recipients promise not to disclose the information further and if a record of all these disclosures is made a part of the student's record.

Obviously, the law would be a nightmare if it prevented a school from publishing a list of student addresses or from releasing the height of a basketball player or the name of the valedictorian without consent, and so it makes allowances for these sorts of disclosure. Under the law, the school must publish each year the categories of such routine information it plans to release—called "directory information" in the law. This includes student's name, address, telephone number, date and place of birth, major field of study, participation in officially recognized activities and sports, weight and height of athletes, dates of attendance, degrees and awards received, the most recent institution previously attended, "and other similar information." If you object to any of this information being released about you, you must speak up. Otherwise the school is able to release it routinely upon request.

WHAT CAN YOU DO?

The same federal law gives you as a parent the right to inspect your child's school record. If the student is eighteen years or older, he or she has that right in place of the parents. Schools and colleges must notify you of your rights each year.

You are entitled to see only what are "educational records," and the law says that excludes personal notes kept by an individual teacher or records that are used for law enforcement and kept separate from educational records. Rejected applicants have no rights of access. As a former student, you have a right of individual access to your student records, but this does not include alumni records. Medical records may be disclosed to a medical professional of your choice. Students, not employees, have rights under the act.

The school has forty-five days in which to meet your request, and it may not destroy records in the meantime. You have a right to make notes or to take photocopies if this is, in effect, the only way you can inspect the record. As a parent, you are presumed to have authority to inspect your child's records unless the school has been given evidence of a court order or state law to the contrary (usually because you no longer have child custody). The school may block out information about another individual in the records you inspect. A student is not entitled to see parents' financial statements without their consent.

If you believe that any part of the record is inaccurate or misleading, you should ask school officials to change it. If the school refuses, it must promptly inform you that you are entitled to a hearing on the validity of the record. If your complaint is upheld at the hearing, the school must place your side of the story in the record and make sure that it always accompanies the file. The hearing officer will be an employee of the school system or college—or may be an outsider—but that person may not have a direct interest in the outcome. You are entitled to a written decision after the hearing.

If you are still dissatisfied, you may complain to the Department of Health, Education, and Welfare, which enforces the law. Its address is Privacy Office, Department of Health, Education, and Welfare, Washington, D.C. 20201. You should label your envelope "FERPA complaint," because federal officials seem to respond better to initials.

Remember that the law calls for the termination of federal funds for a school system or college that does not comply. This is an extreme remedy, and so don't hold your breath expecting that your single complaint will make the difference. HEW will attempt to resolve the complaint and, even if this is unsuccessful, your complaint may still contribute to reform at the institution.

At least one judge has ruled that the law implies a right for you to sue directly to enforce your rights under it, but this is not a part of the language of the law. There is no doubt that the records compiled by school systems are private facts, entitled to the full protection of the constitutional right to privacy. In 1973 the United States Supreme Court took the extraordinary step of permitting parents to challenge a congressional committee's circulation of a report because it contained unnecessary personal information about individual students. Generally, whatever is said in the course of Congress' business is immune from any limitations by either the executive branch or the judiciary because of Article 1, Section 6, of the United States Constitution. But a 450-page report on the difficulties of the District of Columbia school system included 45 pages displaying absentee sheets, lists of absentees, test papers, and disciplinary papers concerning specifically named pupils. There were the failing grades of twenty-one youngsters, and letters and memos discussing specific students' disciplinary problems. The Supreme Court agreed with the parents of the students that the invasions of privacy were so gross as to warrant the unusual remedy of a trial challenging circulation of the 1,000 printed reports.[34] This decision implies that students have a constitutional right to privacy in the personal information collected about them and can enforce that right by themselves in the courts, whether or not the Buckley Amendment applies.

A national organization of parents and educators was instrumental in pushing the law through Congress and continues to monitor its effectiveness. The group is National Committee for Citizens in Education, Suite 410, Wilde Lake Village Green, Columbia, Maryland 21044. It provides a toll-free "hot line" for you to call for more information about the law on student records. Dial 800-NETWORK.

A school or university may *request* you to waive your rights to see particular records, but it may not have you waive your rights generally. It may not *require* a waiver. Students who apply for admission to institutions of higher education are commonly asked to waive their right to see letters of recommendation once they become a part of their file. The law permits waivers of this type, but only if you are notified who has provided such letters about you. Institutions may not force you to sign a waiver as a condition of admission or of any other benefit, but most institutions come pretty close to violating this requirement. Many teachers simply will not write letters of recommendation unless you waive your rights under the law. Universities yelled and screamed when the law was passed in the summer of 1974. They said that professors could no longer be candid and truthful if the subject could eventually see what was written. A Wisconsin teacher wrote to the Department of Health, Education, and Welfare that he would be shot if one of his former students saw what the teacher had written about him. By November 1974 the universities had convinced Congress to amend the law and allow for waivers.

If you do not wish to waive your rights to see letters of recommendation at a later time—and there is no reason why you should—you should include your reasons why. Here are some good reasons: (1) You want to make sure that the information is correct. (2) You want to know your weaknesses and strengths. (3) You want to gauge your progress. (4) You want to know whether the person who wrote on your behalf would write an appropriate letter on another occasion. (5) You believe in the principle of individual access intended by Congress. (If your reasons are not benign, you should perhaps not list them.)

You should include your reasons because recipients of letters of recommendation for which there is no waiver tend to think that the subject of such letters is a troublemaker or that the letters are not accurate. Two University of Georgia psychologists reported in a 1977 experiment that evaluators tend to favor the applicant who chooses not to see his or her own file, regardless of the content of the letters of recommendation. Can there be any doubt why many students are *insisting* upon waiving their rights of access even when not asked to do so?

Most states have laws that are similar to federal law. In a few instances, they provide additional protections for students and parents. In California, for instance, pupils over the age of sixteen, not eighteen, may see their own files. Nebraska and Wisconsin state laws require the destruction of disciplinary records after graduation. And Rhode Island has a state law that parents will appreciate. In that state it is a misdemeanor to circulate a questionnaire, without the approval of state and local authorities, that is "so framed as to ask the pupils of any school intimate questions about themselves and/or their families, thus trespassing upon the pupils' constitutional rights and invading the privacy of the home."

There is no protection, anywhere, against young children blurting out family secrets at "show and tell" time or at any other period in the school day. The primary threat to family privacy is, of course, elementary school pupils telling stories in class. Humorist Erma Bombeck wrote in her syndicated column of December 15, 1975, that parents should fear the CWT more than the CIA, FBI, or IRS. "There isn't a parent who doesn't dread a meeting with the Creative Writing Teacher," she wrote. "The CWT knows everything . . . from what your kid did last summer to family relationships, ancestry and intimate details of heretofore unpublished home life. Unless we administer an oath to the CWT to hold privileged information in the strictest confidence we are in for some serious problems."

13

Social Security Numbers:
Everybody Wants Them

"It wouldn't bother me in the slightest to be numbered in every file that was kept on me by the same number. It's something that can bring greater efficiency in the business. I can see no negatives." That's the opinion of Thomas J. Watson, Jr., retired chairman of the board of International Business Machines Corporation (IBM).

Griffin Bell, just after he was appointed Attorney General of the United States, told a congressman, "Many people today, particularly old people, refuse to give you their Social Security number because they think you are getting ready to invade their privacy in some way, and if you get that number, you will find out everything about them."

The world seems to be split into two groups: those who feel that increased use of the Social Security number is no threat to their privacy, and those who feel that there is a threat. I'm among the second group. The number, among other things, has become a symbol of individuals' resistance to being mass-processed in a machine age. It is legitimate for people to expect to be known by a name, not a number. People feel that they need not be enumerated just because of a single encounter with a clerk. Many Americans came to this country to escape just that sort of enumeration. They pride themselves on the fact that there is no requirement here that "your papers be in order" when you walk the streets—or do anything else. And they resent being regarded as non-persons unless they present a number that somehow vouches for their validity.

There is also a technological reason why an individual should not provide his or her Social Security number to anyone who asks. One great fear we have is that each of the computer systems we have thus far discussed can somehow pool their resources and bring to bear on us a whole lifetime of data about us for decisions about us, about which we have no knowledge. Right now, there are limited exchanges of personal data among these automated systems. Each of them has our name and our facts. And most of them have our number—our Social Security number. The number is the one means that makes it easier for *all* of these disparate computer systems to link information about a particular individual. If we deny our Social Security number to a particular data gatherer, this will make it a little more difficult for that data gatherer to share our information with another system that has information about us.

And there is a practical reason why a person should not provide the Social Security number to anyone who asks. In spite of the clear legend that used to appear on the card, NOT FOR IDENTIFICATION, the Social Security card, and its number, *are* used for identity by private and public agencies. It is an absurdly unreliable identifier, but most of the identity checkers in our society don't know that. This means that with your Social Security number I can impersonate you in several contexts. I can probably get bank information and tax information and Social Security information over the telephone. I can probably get your grades in college. I can get military information and veterans information. I can get credit information. An amazing number of clerks in this nation will simply assume you are who you say you are when you just produce a Social Security number that matches the number of the person you are claiming to be.

For that reason, I don't want my Social Security number floating around. I don't want to put it on a check at my grocery store so that a clerk passing through the office can copy it down and pose as me. I don't want to give it to the gas company so that somebody there can discover my bank balance. Before I was wise about some of these matters, I provided my Social Security number to my law school upon registration. Five years later it began appearing on the outside of mailing envelopes from the school alumni office. I would object if my American Express number appeared on the outside of mail, and I object when my Social Security number is publicly known as well. Still, many employers design payroll forms so that the individual's Social Security number appears through window envelopes. And anybody can get your Social Security number at the motor vehicle department, for one dollar or less, in those states that ask for the number when you apply for a driver's license or renewal. These include Arkansas, Florida, Georgia, Idaho, Indiana, Iowa, Louisiana, Maine, Maryland, Nebraska, North Dakota, Oklahoma, Rhode Island, South Dakota, Vermont, and Wyoming. (In some of these states you are given a license if you choose not to provide your Social Security number, but in most the number is mandatory and you may not drive without it.)

Further, the following states display the number on the driver's license so that it is readily available to anyone who asks to see your permit for identification: Alaska, Arizona, Colorado, Hawaii, Illinois, Kansas, Kentucky, Massachusetts, Mississippi, Missouri, Nevada, New Mexico, Ohio, and West Virginia. The District of Columbia has the same policy.

Confronting the nation's mania for collecting the Social Security number seems a losing battle. In many states the three agencies with nearly universal registration of citizens—motor vehicles, voting, and taxation—want the number. Banks want it (and by federal regulation are probably entitled to it). The bar associations in many states want it before you can practice law, although on objection some have been known to drop the request. The United States Supreme Court requires it of every attorney who argues a case there. Why? To eliminate duplication in its computer record of lawyers, the Court says lamely. You need it to attend a meeting or party at the White House.

Why? Because the Secret Service keeps a computer list of names and numbers of potential troublemakers. Most visitors figure they'll get turned away at the door of the mansion if they don't meekly provide the number, but the Secret Service has been known to drop the request if you object.

You need the number to enroll at just about every college and university. Some school systems, like Baltimore's, enumerate their students en masse in the ninth grade.

You need to supply a Social Security number to vote in the Commonwealth of Virginia. This is part of the state's constitution and has been held valid by courts. Other states ask for your Social Security number when you register to vote, but this is a matter of administrative policy, not law. In those states the request is dropped if you object. In spite of the court decisions there is no doubt in my mind that demanding a Social Security number for voter registration unduly burdens the right to vote, in violation of the United States Constitution. Providing a Social Security number involves giving up a bit of your privacy. Privacy is regarded as a constitutional right. The state may not force you to give up a constitutional right unless it has a compelling reason for doing so. Virginia's compelling reason is weak: "The computer needs the Social Security number." Shouldn't there be a place in the United States for a citizen, especially one in the late teens, to choose not to be enumerated by the federal government without sacrificing his or her right to vote?

There is no escape. You need a Social Security number in order to get a fishing or hunting license in West Virginia.

Farsighted persons knew where all of this was leading when the Social Security system was begun in 1935. An Italian immigrant told his children, "They are going to require a number for all of us. There goes our family name, it will no longer be important." The United Mine Workers and the United Steelworkers immediately worried that Social Security numbers could be used by employers to blacklist pro-union men involved in the labor strife of that period. They persuaded their friends in the New Deal administration to allow individuals to receive a new Social Security number when "showing good reasons for a change."

A request for your Social Security number that is related to its original purpose—namely, to account for retirement and survivor benefits—is legitimate. In 1943 President Franklin D. Roosevelt authorized other uses with Executive Order 9397, which ordered any federal agency that uses account numbers on individuals to use the Social Security number. That included the Internal Revenue Service, which now uses the number as an individual taxpayer number. The state tax authorities do the same. Not surprisingly, the number is needed whenever a transaction with a private or public agency will produce taxable income for the individual. Recipients of public assistance must provide their Social Security numbers. Under the Aid to Dependent Children program, that means children, even newborn infants. The father of a newborn baby in New Hampshire was asked for the child's Social Security number on his first visit to the hospital. "Number?" said the father. "We don't even have a name yet!"

The nurse responded, "Oh, that's okay, we don't care about a name. We just need the number."

There are many people in this country with responsibility for personal information data banks who think that a compulsory program of enumeration from birth would make things a lot more efficient. We have drifted in that direction, to be sure.

We have not reached the Swedish system yet. In Sweden each citizen is issued a unique personal identity number that incorporates the date of birth explicitly. A Swedish child born on April 22, 1979, for example, would have an identifier like 79 04 22 007 9. The first two digits denote the year, the second two the month, the next two the day; and the next three form a serial number showing the order in which the child was registered that particular day—odd numbers for males, even numbers for females. The final digit is a check on the accuracy of the first nine. If, in this example, that digit were anything but a 9, an expert would know that the number is erroneous. This check was selected by multiplying 1 times the first digit (7), 2 times the second digit (9), 3 times the third (0), and so on, adding the total (126), and then adding that total (1 plus 2 plus 6), to get a "fail-safe" digit of 9.

The properties of the U.S. Social Security number are far different from those of the Swedish serial number. The first three digits of your Social Security number tell the state in which you received it. New Hampshire, as in presidential primaries, leads the way, with 001 to 003; New York has 050 to 134; Pennsylvania, 159 to 211; Illinois, 318 to 361; Texas, 449 to 467; and California, 545 to 573. The middle two digits tell approximately the year of issue. An odd number less than eleven (05 or 09) was probably issued before the late 1930s, and an even number from 10 to 98 was issued after that. About ten years ago, previously unused even numbers (02 or 08) began to be issued. The final set of digits is a serial number with no special meaning; your digits are determined not by when you were born but by when you go to your local Social Security office to apply for a card.

The number, then, is not totally anonymous. You can tell from it the owner's approximate age and the state of residence where he or she first received the number. For example, in a college class of one hundred or so in which grades are posted by Social Security number, it's not hard to pick out the out-of-staters, or to identify the lone person in the class with a distinctive accent (a New Yorker at the University of New Mexico or a Southerner at the University of Maine), or to identify the lone person who is much older than the average student. In this instance, and others, the Social Security number is not totally anonymous.

The Social Security number has no fail-safe device to check the accuracy of each number internally. The middle set of digits or possibly the first three may give you away if you use a fictitious number, but that is all.

Nor is the number issued in sequence to each applicant.

Nor is it universal; a few law-abiding Americans do not have one.

Most important to those who resist a mandatory enumeration in this country, the Social Security number is not unique for each individual. Thousands of Americans have identical numbers. More than 4 million persons have more than one each.

Account number 078-05-1120 was the first of many numbers referred to by Social Security insiders as "pocketbook numbers." It first appeared on a sample card inserted into wallets sold nationwide in 1938. Many people who bought the wallets assumed the number to be their own. And so they used it. That same Social Security number began to appear on hundreds of employers' quarterly reports on income and tax withholding—5,700 times in 1943 alone. Even now, that number appears on a half dozen reports each year. There are about twenty other "pocketbook" numbers being used by oblivious citizens around the country!

A 1973 study by the Department of Health, Education, and Welfare, of which the Social Security Administration is a part, noted that the Social Security number had become very nearly a universal identifier for all Americans in fact, if not in law. It said, "We recommend against the adoption of any nationwide, standard, personal identification format, with or without the SSN, that would enhance the likelihood of arbitrary or uncontrolled linkage of records about people, particularly between government or government-supported automated personal data systems." Still, the trend has continued unabated. Wherever you apply for a government or business service, folks seem to want your Social Security number as much as your money.

This is true even though computer technology now makes it feasible to manage data banks on millions of persons without the Social Security number. One methodology reduces names to a numerical code so that variants of the same name would turn up near each other in a computer search. One's date of birth, or mother's name, or address could be added to the code to further reduce possibilities of duplication. There have been refinements that now allow companies that process large numbers of names—insurance companies, for instance—to do without customer account numbers altogether. When a customer makes an inquiry, the clerk may retrieve the record in question, via a computer terminal, without ever having to ask for a number. How sweet it is. The Medical Information Bureau discussed in Chapter 8 processes its 11 million records without using Social Security numbers at all.

When you are told that you must provide your Social Security number to avoid duplication with the records of someone else with a similar name, don't believe it. The main purposes for asking for Social Security numbers nowadays are: first, to preserve the option of linking separate data banks or to query other data banks about you; and second, to lead you to believe that this is being done now.

Next time you're invited to visit the White House, or to go fishing in the mountains of West Virginia, see if you can't get the bureaucrats to do without your Social Security number.

WHAT CAN YOU DO?

If you are receiving any taxable income in the transaction, demands for your Social Security number are legitimate.

There is no law that requires you to provide a Social Security number to any nongovernmental organization, such as a bank, insurance company, utility, hotel, or private college. Nor is there any law that requires that organization to provide you services if you choose not to provide your number. You simply must negotiate, without the benefit of law on either side. Some organizations ask for the number, but respect a customer's request for an alternative account number. You should definitely resist any company that wants to display your number openly, as on the face of your checks, on student ID cards, or on mailing labels.

The Privacy Act of 1974, discussed in Chapter 7, restricted somewhat the demands for your number from government agencies, local, state, and federal. But the Tax Reform Act of 1976 (to be discussed in Chapter 15) added to the loopholes. Here's the current picture:[35]

No federal, state, or local government agency may deny you any right, benefit, or privilege for refusing to provide your Social Security number, unless there is a law or regulation on the books (adopted prior to 1975) that specifically authorizes the demand for the number. A written or oral policy of an agency won't comply with the law; it must have a law or regulation on the books.

This law covers publicly supported institutions of higher education and public school districts.

There is an exception to this law: state agencies may demand and use the number in administering tax laws, motor vehicle and driver registration, or public assistance programs. Or they may use the number to track down a parent not supporting his or her family.

Even if the agency has the required authorization in law or regulation, the Privacy Act of 1974 requires the government agency to name the authorization when it asks for your number, tell you whether a response from you is voluntary or mandatory, and tell you how it plans to use your number. Failure to do this violates federal law. There is a misdemeanor penalty for deceptive use of the Social Security number by you and for unlawful disclosure of it by a government employee. This law, remember, applies only to federal, state, and local government, not private organizations.

Courts thus far have turned a deaf ear on complaints that demands for the Social Security number are either an invasion of privacy or a denial of equal protection under the laws. One reason for this is that judges who have heard these cases have not shared the sensitivity that many citizens have concerning the increased use of the Social Security number as a universal identifier. This may change in time.

You have a right to get a new Social Security number, but your reasons for wanting one and your proof of identity will be increasingly scrutinized. This is because of concern that aliens who have entered the United States illegally have received Social Security cards so that they may get jobs.

A WORD ABOUT SOCIAL SECURITY ITSELF

In most instances, there is no penalty for refusing to provide information to the Social Security Administration. However, the following reports are mandatory once you are declared eligible for Social Security benefits or supplemental security income payments:

> –Yearly earnings that exceed the exempt amount.
> –Certain work performed outside of the United States.
> –The departure of a child entitled to benefits.
> –A change in income, resources, household composition, living arrangements, or other circumstances affecting eligibility for supplemental security payments.

There are penalties for withholding these kinds of information. The Social Security Administration publishes a list (Form SSA 5000) of thirty-five instances in which information about you may be disclosed—mostly to other federal agencies administering payment programs and to private companies that help administer Social Security's programs.

14

State Government Files: Another Library of Personal Information

A group appointed by Governor Otis R. Bowen of Indiana took the time in 1976 to count the state's files on individuals. It found 200 different systems of records with information about people scattered throughout the state government. There were 82 million names in all, in a state with a population of a little more than 5 million (ranking eleventh in the nation). The Bureau of Motor Vehicles, the Department of Revenue (taxation), the Board of Health, the State Police, and the Employment Security Division (unemployment compensation) account for nearly half of the 82 million files. About 60 of the 200 systems are automated.

The state stores about sixteen files for every one of its citizens. By contrast, the data kept on individuals by federal agencies amount to about eighteen files per man, woman, and child in the United States.

Here is an inventory of the personal information that a typical state collects on its citizens, and, in Indiana's case, the number of records systems where the information is stored:

Name	194
Social Security number	95

Driver's license number	17
Other unique identifier	52
Age	137
Birthplace	55
Parents' birthplace	9*
Family history	18
Marital status	63
Next of kin	24
Number of children	41
Brothers and sisters	18
Race	46
Ethnic group	22
Religious preference	12
National origin	13
Appearance	19
Physical characteristics	37
Physical disabilities	43
Current and past addresses	157
Military service	36
Membership in groups	3†
Political affiliations	1‡
Tax information	11
Income	22
Property ownership	22
Assets and debts	16
Expenditures/credit rating	8
Checking and savings accounts	16
Home ownership	15
Public housing occupancy	5
Mortgage information	12
Condition of living quarters	8
Educational level	65
Grade average or class standing	15
Occupation	72

* Included in vital statistics and adoption records.
† Required of some state officials, mental health patients, and law enforcement academy employees.
‡ Law enforcement academy employees.

Occupational preferences   10
Employment history   58
Employer   68
Occupational licenses   51
References   34
Police records   20
Security and other investigations   45
Civil/criminal court involvement   47
Medical information   50
Dental history   12
Psychiatric information   28
Personality inventory   11
Alcohol or drug addiction   24
Motor vehicle ownership   13
Food purchases and consumption   8

William R. Bryant, Jr., a state representative in Michigan,
took a different approach. He figured out the kinds of information his state had compiled on Jane Doe, a make-believe citizen
who had a nervous breakdown after she lost her job and accepted Aid to Dependent Children payments. She had been
convicted for passing a bad check after her husband deserted
her, but is now remarried and steadily employed. "It is evident
we know her better than her mother does," says Bryant.

The state has a juvenile record on Jane Doe as a result of a
beer party she attended when she was fifteen. Her pre-sentence
report and her files from the state mental hospital contain subjective and intimate details about her.

The Corrections Department has Jane's personal history, her
education, psychiatric evaluation, judgments as to her social ad-
justment, and interview reports. It has her criminal record, the
rap sheet, the pre-sentence report, the judge's statement, fingerprints, medical test, and counselor's report. It has her physical
characteristics, birth date, ethnic origin, marital status, Social
Security number, religion, education, occupation, dependents,
use of drugs or alcohol, mother's influence, father's influence,
family history, psychosexual indications, IQ, reading level, and
handicaps.

The Department of Mental Health has her birth date, sex, income, number of dependents, marital status, ethnic group, retardation or education, insurance coverage, referral source, job, diagnosis, previous mental health services, degree of impairment, name of parent or guardian, evaluation at discharge, final diagnosis, and additional staff comments.

Social Services has a file on her—with age, sex, address, education, truancy or other school problems, income, mental and physical condition, employment, dependents, marital information, intellectual potential, religion, criminal record, source of support, vocational experience, family background, and reports from caseworkers.

The state agency processing unemployment compensation has still more data on her. The motor vehicle administration knows her address, birth date, sex, license restrictions, convictions, arrests, traffic violations, and accidents, including injuries and fault, if any. The taxation department has on its computer her address, Social Security number, occupation, marital status, dependents, income, property tax paid, income tax paid to other states, contributions, and alimony or child support.

Hanna Weston, a college teacher who campaigns for strong privacy laws in Iowa, took still a third approach. She tried to find out as much as she possibly could about a friend from state files. The friend happened to be a state senator, who agreed to the search so that she could determine the need for legislative safeguards on all of this personal information. In three hours in the state capital of Des Moines, Ms. Weston found out her friend's birth date and age, full name and maiden name, current address and phone numbers, address and occupation in 1948 and 1951 (from her children's birth certificates, which are public records), parents' full names and her marital details (from her marriage license on file), doctors who delivered her children, Social Security number and political party affiliation (from voter rolls), state government salary and travel expenses, valuation and taxes on her residence, driving record, liens and small claims pending (there were none), the fact that she and her family were covered by Blue Cross–Blue Shield and the claims, if any, filed in the prior eighteen months, and, from her driver's record, her height, weight, hair color, and eye color. Ms. Weston found out comparable information about her friend's immediate family, all without deception and all within half a day. "And I am an amateur," said Ms. Weston. Imagine what professional investigators can discover about you, all from public records.

Much of this information is available not simply to the curious person who shows up to request it, but to private firms who get it wholesale by way of computer networks. Major auto insurance companies, for instance, have direct computer links to the driving records stored by the states. Compilers of mailing lists and city directories have comparable computer access to government files. In fact, many state agencies go to these private companies to get the computer information they need in their own files because it is available in quick and orderly formats.

These information systems are often built simply because a state has federal money earmarked for that purpose. This is true of federal funds for law enforcement, for welfare, and notably for the prevention of child abuse. The Federal Child Abuse Prevention Act of 1974, drafted by then Senator Walter F. Mondale, made $90 million in federal money available to the states, not so much to attack the problem directly but to gather information about it. The presumption of these programs is that the more information we record about the occurrences, or possible occurrences, of a social problem, then the more able—and willing—we will be to solve the problem. To qualify for this sudden flow of dollars from the Department of Health, Education, and Welfare, states had to agree to build computer systems to store reports on possible instances of child abuse. In their rush to get the money, state officials rarely stopped to consider whether the information they would be gathering would be reliable, whether it would invade the privacy of its citizens, or whether it would help at all to prevent the battering of children.

In the process, many persons have suffered. When a young couple in Milwaukee took their newborn infant to a hospital with eleven fractured bones, they were accused of child abuse.

The parents were duly reported to a county child abuse information system and eventually to a statewide system. The county welfare department sought to remove the child from the parents' custody. The two insisted on their innocence. "I could tell something was wrong," said the mother. A doctor suggested they get psychiatric help. A social worker predicted that they would be divorced before long.

One nightmare ended and another began when a specialist finally determined that the baby was actually suffering from a rare metabolic birth defect—terminal in nature—that makes the bones extremely weak and brittle. There had been no beatings. "We have a switch from child abuse to parent abuse," said a family counselor, who was trying to help the family get its name out of the federally funded child abuse information systems to which it was reported.

A woman in Maryland ended up in one of those systems when a neighbor reported that the woman's child was being abused—because the neighbor *didn't* hear the baby crying. The allegation proved unfounded but remained in the computer.

Neighbors in a small town in Oregon suspected that a seven-year-old girl was being beaten and called the sheriff. Three times the sheriff reported the complaints to the state Children's Services Division, where it was duly recorded. But nothing was done in response to the reports. The child was found beaten to death less than three weeks later. The reporting system may result in sophisticated data about child abuse but it did not prevent the death of a child.

There are 1,001 objections to legislative attempts to build safeguards into these computer systems—to ensure accuracy, to prevent inappropriate uses of the information, to limit needless information gathering. When a member of the State Assembly in California introduced such a bill in 1976, this is what he heard:

> –The State Department of Finance objected to "excessive costs" in the range of $10 to $34 million.
> –The Department of Motor Vehicles said that it

would have to send notices, perhaps annually, to 14 million licensed drivers in California.

–The County of San Bernardino told the legislator, "Your bill would mandate a nightmare of added paperwork to current county procedures."

–The Department of Justice: "As a matter of public policy criminal justice agencies should not be subject to its provisions."

–Computer Services, Rockwell International: "This would be an impossible restriction comparable to crippling the interstate use of telephones, radio transmission and aviation."

–Forest Lawn Memorial Parks and Mortuaries: "This legislation would interfere with related business activities for which the company-owned computer is being used."

–The California State University and College System: "The bill fails to take into account the unique educational function of our University system."

–East Bay Municipal Utility District (EBMUD): "Customer billing should be excluded."

–Creative Socio-Medics Corporation: "Medical records, especially mental health records, must be treated as a separate issue from other computerized records."

–State Teachers Retirement System: "We comply with the spirit and intent of the bill, and to impose additional reporting requirements would be unnecessary and result in higher administrative costs."

–TRW/Credit Data: "The all-encompassing regulations . . . if enacted verbatim would prove detrimental if not destructive to the credit industry without meaningful benefit to individuals in search of credit."

–California Highway Patrol: "The ability of this department in providing effective programs in crime prevention will be deterred by passage of this bill."

Members of a federal Privacy Protection Study Commission, including an accountant, an insurance company president, and a computer scientist, determined in 1977 that the cost to implement privacy safeguards is modest, and that when these protections are designed in a system from the start the cost is negligible. As we have seen, credit bureaus, educational institutions, and federal government agencies have had to comply with these restrictions for a few years now, and they have done so without excessive expense or paper work. One consequence of privacy legislation, in fact, is that record keepers *save money* by gathering less data.

WHAT CAN YOU DO?

Some states have passed laws, similar to the federal Privacy Act of 1974, giving citizens the right to inspect and correct records about themselves in state files. Between 1974 and 1978 Minnesota, Utah, Arkansas, Massachusetts, Virginia, Ohio, Connecticut, Indiana, and California passed so-called fair information practices acts. These laws cover only state government records and generally exempt law enforcement records. They provide penalties and fines for state employees who refuse to allow a citizen to inspect and correct individual files. Medical information is usually disclosed to a professional chosen by the individual. Most of the nine states allow the individual to include his or her side of the story if a dispute remains over the accuracy of the information.

If you live in these states you should write or call the state agency that has information on you to arrange to inspect it and check its accuracy and relevance. The state of California has a toll-free number for residents anywhere in the state to get information about seeing their own records: 1 (800) 952-5562.

If you live in a state without a fair information practices act, you may be able to gain access to your files by arguing fundamental fairness. Many states have so-called freedom of information acts, or sunshine laws, that permit citizens access to governmental materials. One of these laws may be used if you wish to have access to information about yourself.

Kentucky state law allows you access to state files, but does not allow you to correct the information. The cities of Dayton, Ohio; Wichita Falls, Texas; and Charlotte, North Carolina, have passed ordinances with similar rights and protections. These state and city statutes limit the disclosure of personal information about individuals to other agencies and outsiders; require agencies to eliminate outdated, irrelevant, or inaccurate data from their files; require safeguards for protecting the security of the information; and usually require new computer systems or substantial changes to existing systems to be approved by a central agency in the government.

There are hundreds of laws and regulations that provide for the confidentiality of particular records held by state agencies. If you feel that information about you has been disclosed unfairly, check to see whether one of these laws or regulations was violated.

State government agencies often use the services of credit bureaus (discussed in Chapter 4) or consumer investigative firms (discussed in Chapter 5). The Fair Credit Reporting Act permits this if the reports are for a credit or business transaction, for employment, or for determining eligibility for a license "or other benefit." The law appears to allow reports in the latter instance only if the government agency has a legal obligation to consider an applicant's financial responsibility. If a government agency requests such a report on you, then you are entitled to the notices described in Chapter 4 (under "What Can You Do?").

There are times when a government agency becomes a consumer reporting agency itself, as when the department of motor vehicles sells a report to an insurance company concerning your entire driving record, including arrests for speeding, drunken driving, and involuntary manslaughter. The Federal Trade Commission has ruled that state motor vehicle agencies become subject to the Fair Credit Reporting Act when such reports are used as a factor in establishing eligibility for insurance. If this is the case, a motor vehicles department, regardless of state law, must provide you with the "nature and substance" of the information it sent to the insurance company, reinvestigate the information upon your request, and include your amendment to the file if you dispute the reinvestigation. And the insurance company must identify the state motor vehicle department as the source of information on which your insurance was denied or your rates raised.

A WORD ABOUT ADOPTION RECORDS

Until recently, adopted persons rarely searched for their biological parents even if they were curious about who they were. Thinking about a search was considered to be a sign of ingratitude toward one's adoptive parents. Now many adopted children want to know about their biological roots. They have organized to assert their right to know. This new militancy is having its effect on legislatures and courts. There is a discernible trend toward allowing adopted persons to see their adoption records or real birth certificate.

There is a triangle of sensitive feelings here, and so resolving the issue of adoptees' "right to know" has not been easy. An eight-year-old Maryland child wrote to her state senator saying, "I was adopted when I was three months old and I want to meet them." A woman in Maryland argues, "Why should the state separate an adult adoptee from his heredity? Did the adoption agency have the right to promise the birth parents that the child would not contact them during the child's entire lifetime? My birth parents' privacy was breached from the moment of my birth."

On the other hand, a thirty-five-year-old Florida woman told "Dear Abby": "I was fourteen when I gave up the child I had conceived by my stepfather. That part of my life was a nightmare. I suppose some biological parents would dearly love to be reunited with the child they gave up, but for me it would be traumatic.

"I closed a door I never want opened."

A woman in Colorado wrote to "Dear Abby": "When I left my child at the home for unwed mothers, they assured me that my records would forever be confidential and no one—and certainly not my child—would ever know who her biological parents were."

And then there are the rights to privacy of the adoptive parents. A study conducted by a University of California at Los Angeles psychiatrist found that although almost all adoptees and biological parents were pleased with their reunions after many years, only about a third of the adoptive parents were cooperative and understanding of their children's desires to meet their biological parents. A third of them were upset by the whole idea, and many others were just not told of the reunions to spare their feelings.

Most state laws say that the birth certificate of a child who is adopted will be altered to substitute the adoptive name. The original birth certificate is then sealed with the decree of adoption, to be opened later by the state registrar only under court order. These are the records that adopted persons wish to see. They want to know their heritage, to discover their natural parents, to learn their medical history, or simply to satisfy their curiosity.

Only five states allow adoptees to see their files. Alabama, Kentucky, and Kansas allow an adult adoptee to examine the original birth certificate and know the identity of the biological parents. South Dakota and Virginia laws allow an adoptee to see adoption records, not the original birth certificate, and these records usually include identifying information.

There are four places where you can try to get information about your biological parents. The public or private adoption agency that handled the adoption has this information, but only a very few agencies will disclose it without the consent of the biological parents. The hospital where you were born and the doctor probably have identifying information, but most will not release it without the consent of the parents. The state registrar of vital statistics has this information, but most states provide a criminal penalty for its release. (According to accounts of their searches, however, some adoptees find that careless clerks routinely provide them with original birth certificates.)

The last alternative is a court of law, and it is there that many adoptees have won access to their identity. If you can show "good cause," the court may grant you access. The need to know medical conditions that you may have inherited has been regarded as "good cause," and so has the need to determine whether you are entitled to an inheritance. A 1976 New Jersey decision seems to shift the burden of proof to the state, saying that if the state cannot show that harm would come to either the biological parents or the adopted person, there can be no denial of access. The court also agreed that psychological reasons alone were "good cause" for discovering original birth records; there need not be medical or inheritance reasons. Other adoptees have argued that to deny them access deprives them of the equal protection of the law, in violation of the Fourteenth Amendment to the Constitution, because all other persons have access to their birth certificates.

Organizations sprang up in the 1970s to aid adoptees in what they call "the Search." The three leading ones are Adoptees' Liberty Movement Association (ALMA), P.O. Box 154, Washington Bridge Station, New York, New York 10033, telephone (212) 581-1568; Orphan Voyage, Cedaredge, Colorado 81413, telephone (303) 856-3937; and Adoption Research Project, P.O. Box 49809, Los Angeles, California 90049. At least three prominent books have described the search: *The Search for Anna Fisher* by Florence Fisher, founder of ALMA; *The Adopted Break Silence* by Jean Paton, founder of Orphan Voyage; and *Finding My Father: One Man's Search for Identity* by Rod McKuen, the poet.

The Adoptive Parents Committee (APC), 210 Fifth Avenue, Suite 1102, New York, New York 10010, telephone (212) 683-9221, has been formed to oppose the opening of adoption records. Concerned United Birthparents Inc., P.O. Box 202, Newton Highlands, Massachusetts 02161, is composed mainly of biological parents who have surrendered children to adoption; it is devoted to "humanizing adoption."

A starting point for persons interested in access to adoption records is the National Center for Child Advocacy, Department of Health, Education, and Welfare, Washington, D.C. 20201.

Inevitably, someone has designed a computer service to match adopted children and biological parents. It collects the name, birth dates, sex, region of birth, hospital, name of doctor, and adoption agency on adoptees seeking their biological parents and similar information provided by biological parents willing to be discovered. The National Adoption Registry, P.O. Box 1554, Evanston, Illinois 60204, is run by an organization called Yesterday's Children.

A WORD ABOUT JURORS

Few obligations of citizenship are as important as jury service. It is a mandatory obligation as well. Yet jurors are subjected to outrageous invasions of personal privacy. Prosecutors and defense attorneys have access to records in public agencies, including the tax department, to form personal profiles of each person called as a potential juror. Judges allow lawyers to present potential jurors with extensive questionnaires asking about age, length of local residence, length and type of employment, education, home ownership, association memberships, newspaper reading habits, party politics, hobbies, marital status, spouse's and parents' employment and education, stock ownership, home town, race, physical or emotional problems, and previous jury service. Or oral questions about the same matters are asked in open court and the information becomes a part of the trial record, open to the public for years. A juror in a notable trial in San Francisco discovered that information about the mental treatment of her relatives became a part of the trial record. And she was only an alternate juror who didn't even vote on the verdict.

In large communities there are firms that dig up information of this sort for lawyers. They operate much like consumer investigative companies, but are subject to no restrictions at all.

Jurors are generally not able to prevent dossiers being created about them, or even to know the contents of the files. Jury service has become, not the honorable rite of citizenship that it should be, but just another excuse for gathering personal information about others.

15

Tax Records:
The "Lending Library"

Confidentiality was so lax at the Internal Revenue Service in the Nixon administration that Senator Lowell P. Weicker, Jr., of Connecticut called it "that lending library." He helped to tighten it up with legislation passed in the fall of 1976 restricting disclosure of tax information to outsiders. One use that was limited was disclosure of federal tax returns to U.S. attorneys and defense lawyers so that they could grill prospective jurors. Now the lawyers will be told only if a prospective juror has been the subject of an audit or tax investigation. There are no restrictions, however, on prosecutors' and defense lawyers' access to individual tax returns in most *state* tax agencies.

Despite the 1976 tax reforms, Americans have much to fear about the Internal Revenue Service's extensive collection of personal information and its heavy-handed treatment of individual taxpayers' rights to privacy. With records on 88 million individual tax returns in its computer system in the mountains of West Virginia, IRS is one of the nation's most significant information collectors. Your individual tax return includes your yearly salary and supplemental income and may reveal the amount of your savings and of your debts, your medical expenses and the identity of your dependents, your expenses at work and your political contributions, your union or association dues and your charitable contributions, your entertainment expenses at work and the extent of your personal automobile mileage. Second only to your canceled bank checks, here is a mirror of your life.

At the time Richard Nixon resigned, more than a dozen federal agencies were making use of taxpayers' private returns. Under arrangements with most states, tax data on more than 50 million persons were being exchanged between IRS and state tax authorities. The Commissioner of Internal Revenue at the time admitted that there was no way to know what the employees of these federal and state agencies were doing with this sensitive information. They may have ignored it or sold it to credit bureaus. They may have used it to catch tax cheaters, or they may have shared it with private investigators. A man in Baltimore claims that a female IRS agent told her husband about the man's tax return. The husband, who happened to be an old high school friend of the taxpayer, met the man on the street one day and confronted him with information about his income, alimony payments, and deductions.

The Congressional Joint Committee on Taxation reported, after an investigation of IRS in 1977, "a potential for widespread unauthorized disclosures. Because of these weaknesses and shortcomings, security safeguards could easily be penetrated—especially by IRS employees and others having access to the facilities." The committee reported weaknesses in computer room security so that outsiders could have easy access. Supervisors did not monitor requests for tax information and had no idea whether they were legitimate. Nonemployees were admitted to areas where sensitive information was stored, and there was inadequate screening of employees with responsibility for handling personal information. There was inadequate security for protecting microfilm, magnetic tapes, disks, and other computer materials—containing millions of private facts—as they were shipped to and from the IRS. (Generally the IRS provides the following to the states: name, address, and Social Security number, marital status, tax period, a number for locating the original documents at the IRS, a mail-file code, exemptions (by code), adjusted gross income, interest income, taxable dividends, and total tax. Details from a federal return are available to the states by request. Some states, of course, ask their taxpayers to attach their federal returns to their state returns. Those states have no need to exchange with IRS.)

The Internal Revenue Service has responded to this evidence of actual and potential breaches of confidentiality in a way only too familiar in Washington: it asked Congress for up to $1 billion to build an automated network that would make all of this individual information available through 10,000 computer terminals in district and field offices. The architects at the IRS had not done much thinking about the security in such a network. In 1977 cooler heads in the Carter administration told IRS to forget its grandiose plan, at least for now.

The Service already has its Integrated Data Retrieval System (IDRS), which includes, on about 10 per cent of taxpayers in the master file in West Virginia, each taxpayer's name, address, and Social Security number, adjustments and correspondence concerning the taxpayer, unidentified remittances, delinquency-investigation file reference (if any), and deferred payment schedules. Theoretically updated daily, the system allows employees at each of the IRS service centers around the country to answer telephone and mail inquiries promptly.

And there is the Discriminate Function Program, IRS' computer system for selecting returns for audit—averaging presently about one out of fifty returns.

That would seem to be adequate gadgetry to keep the folks at IRS busy for many years. But any good tax investigator will tell you that you can't confine yourself to tax returns when seeking out tax violators. In the early months of the Nixon administration the Service invented the Information Gathering and Retrieval System (IGRS), an attempt to collect miscellaneous materials on some 450,000 persons that might lead to a violation of tax laws. Many of those 450,000 were prominent entertainers, athletes, dissidents, and politicians. It was not until 1975, after Nixon had left Washington, that this intelligence-gathering operation was disclosed to the public. One component of this was called Operation Leprechaun. This was an ill-fated attempt to spy on the personal lives, including sexual and drinking activities, of taxpayers in the Miami area. Leprechaun agents also sought to entrap targets into embarrassing activities, and they engaged in illegal forms of snooping.

IRS had also set up a Special Services staff that spent much of its time harassing eight thousand celebrities and dissidents and three thousand tax-exempt organizations that had irritated the politicians in the Nixon administration. The John Birch Society, the Malcolm X Society, and the Unitarian Society were among the groups targeted for attention in this activity.

The Service claims to have ceased these last two surveillance operations. Its guidelines now read: "Compliance with the tax laws which the Service is authorized and directed to enforce cannot be determined solely by reference to the information on returns and documents filed with the Service. Therefore, the Service must obtain information from outside sources for the effective administration of the tax laws." Tax agents are limited to gathering information that is "directly tax related," that is:

–Personal expenditures or investments not commensurate with known income and assets.

–Receipt of unreported income.

–Overstatement of itemized deductions, business expenses, cost of sales, tax credit, etc.

–Improper deduction of capital or personal expenses.

–Failure to file required returns or pay tax due.

–Omission of assets or improper deductions or exclusion of items from estate or gift tax returns.

–Violations of conditions or requirements relating to tax-exempt status of organizations.

–Improper operation of a qualified employee plan or trust.

–Similar activities, in consideration of the taxpayer's wealth, occupation, tax returns, and prior inquiries. "Prudent judgment must be exercised. . . ."

This means that IRS agents may continue to monitor television game shows and collect the names and addresses of contestants who win big prizes. They may ask questions about housewives who moonlight as private nurses or domestics. They may check construction sites for skilled tradesmen declaring themselves independent contractors to avoid withholding taxes. They may rent mailing lists of medical societies and jockey associations to run against their computerized master file of taxpayers. They may scrutinize restaurant receipts in the personal accounts of credit card holders to detect tips that waiters failed to report. They may ask for the dry-cleaning bill of a suspected underworld gangster. They may take notes on improvements to your home. All of this, and more, the IRS investigators do in their searches for violators.

And once they find violators who do not pay up, IRS agents are granted broad authority to seize property and other assets held by the taxpayer "by any means." This is called a "jeopardy assessment" under the law. The IRS may seize bank accounts, automobiles, boats, airplanes, and just about anything else that may be found in an open area and would not require an intrusion to seize. To seize assets that would require an intrusion into the domain of the taxpayer, the Internal Revenue Service would probably require a search warrant, the United States Supreme Court hinted in 1977.[36]

For what it's worth, the Tax Reform Act of 1976 exempts from IRS seizure fifty dollars of a taxpayer's weekly salary, plus fifteen dollars for each dependent.[37] Further, the IRS within five days must inform the taxpayer of the information on which the jeopardy assessment is based; the taxpayer is then given thirty days to apply to the agency for a review. This does not get your assets back, but it does make individual IRS agents who made the assessment accountable.

WHAT CAN YOU DO?

That same Tax Reform Act of 1976 significantly restricted IRS access to your financial records held by a third party and the IRS' disclosure of tax return information to persons outside the Service. The act requires that the IRS provide you fourteen days' notice when it issues an administrative summons to see your records at a bank, savings and loan association, credit union, consumer reporting agency (as defined in Chapters 4 and 5), credit card company, securities broker, attorney, or accountant. (This requirement was also described in Chapter 2, about bank records.) After receiving this notice, you have the right to intervene in any legal proceeding with respect to enforcing the summons, and you may suspend compliance with the summons if you notify the IRS and the financial institution holding your records within the fourteen-day period. If you do so, a federal district judge will decide whether to enforce the summons. This right to intervene in court may be more illusory than real, because, as we discussed in Chapter 2, the Supreme Court has said that the customer has no expectation of privacy in his or her own bank records. And as we discussed in Chapter 11, the Court has also ruled that no confidential privilege exists between accountant and client. You could not, therefore, assert your Fifth Amendment privilege against self-incrimination and prevent your accountant from turning over tax records. But you may be able to resist the summons on other grounds, and you may have a Fifth Amendment right in information held by your attorney. And at least you have notice that records about you in the custody of a third party are being inspected by an arm of the government.

The Court may allow the IRS to waive this notice requirement in exceptional circumstances. The new law also requires the IRS to notify a court when it seeks the financial records of a class of persons under a "John Doe" summons without specific names. This was a direct result of the Internal Revenue Service's access to all customer records at the Kentucky bank mentioned in Chapter 2.

The Tax Reform Act of 1976 also reversed the emphasis under prior law that tax returns were *public* unless the President directed otherwise (contrary to popular impression). Tax returns are now *confidential* unless Congress declares otherwise. Exceptions to this general rule are (1) when the taxpayer consents; (2) upon written request of tax authorities in your state; (3) to the administrator of an estate or a deceased taxpayer's kin; (4) to committees of Congress; (5) to the Departments of

Justice or the Treasury for tax investigations (not jury analysis, surveillance, or curiosity); (6) to federal investigators in non-tax cases if they have a court order; (7) for statistical surveys; and (8) to track down parents who have failed to meet child-support obligations. The President is entitled to see selected individual tax return information, but only if the request is from the President himself in writing and if he reports to Congress each quarter with the names of individuals whose returns are involved. The President and heads of agencies are also entitled to know whether prospective appointees to major government positions are under suspicion of violating tax laws.

As federal records, Internal Revenue Service information is subject to the Privacy Act of 1974 discussed in Chapter 7.

Tax returns are regarded as confidential by law in the following states: Alaska, Arizona, Colorado, Delaware, Georgia, Kansas, Kentucky, Louisiana, Maine, Maryland, Massachusetts, Minnesota, Mississippi, Nebraska, New York, North Carolina, North Dakota, Ohio, Oklahoma, Oregon, Rhode Island, Tennessee, Utah, Virginia, Washington, West Virginia, and to a limited extent Wisconsin.

Wisconsin has a unique variation. State law allows disclosure of tax information to a newspaper "for purposes of argument" and "any public speaker . . . referring to such information in any address." For one dollar, residents of Wisconsin and residents of selected other states may know the net income or gift tax paid by an individual, providing the individual is notified of this within twenty-four hours. Legislators and local officials may see tax returns as part of their official duties.

In Massachusetts, anybody is entitled to know whether or not another person filed an income tax return, but nothing else.

There's a third party involved here, because more than half of all American taxpayers have someone else prepare their returns—either an income tax service, an accountant, a lawyer, or a member of the family. The Internal Revenue Service has issued regulations restricting disclosure of taxpayer information by a tax preparer—a person who prepares your taxes as a business, whether or not a professional.[38] Federal law prohibits a tax preparer from using information in your tax return for any purpose other than tax preparation. This means that a bank officer may not prepare your taxes and then inform the loan department that you will be a likely candidate for a loan before April 15. Nor may H. & R. Block use tax information to solicit mutual funds or insurance by sending its customers' names and addresses to a mail-order life insurance company with which it has a joint venture. (The nationwide tax preparation service did just that before the federal law limiting disclosure was passed in 1971.)

There are exceptions to the rule of confidentiality. The tax preparer may (and must) disclose information on your federal tax return under court order, may use it to prepare state and city taxes, and may disclose it to comply with other parts of the tax code. A lawyer who prepares your taxes may use the information to provide legal services to you, such as estate planning and litigation. An accountant may use the information to provide you other accounting services. A fiduciary institution like a bank may use the information to provide you related fiduciary services. The tax preparer may add your name and address to a list to solicit your tax business again, but may not sell or rent the list (except to someone who buys the whole business). The tax preparer may disclose your information to others who help in the preparation, such as an outside computer service. The preparer may keep a copy of your tax returns; in fact, he or she is required to keep a copy or at least a list of customers.

The tax preparer may request—but only once—that you give written consent for your tax return information to be used to send you advertisements about a non-tax service provided by the tax preparer, such as mutual funds or credit card services. Tax preparers are required to keep customer information confidential by state laws in Hawaii, Minnesota, and Vermont, among other states.

Two nonprofit groups that monitor the Internal Revenue Service and analyze tax policies in behalf of consumers are among the most effective public interest groups in Washington. They are Tax Analysts and Advocates, 2366 North Taylor

Street, Arlington, Virginia 22207, telephone (703) 522-1800;
and Ralph Nader's Tax Reform Research Group, P.O. Box
14198, Benjamin Franklin Station, Washington, D.C. 20044,
telephone (202) 547-6300.

16

Telephone Privacy:
Beeping Toms

May the telephone company charge you for an unlisted number? Do publishers of city directories and some government agencies have access to unlisted numbers? May the telephone company give out a list of the toll calls you have made? Can the police tell automatically your address and telephone number when you dial 911 in an emergency? Does the telephone company listen in on your telephone?

The answer to all of these questions is yes.

There isn't much privacy in using the telephone, but I suppose we always knew that anyway. From the beginning of telephone service, customers were aware that the local switchboard operator could listen to conversations. Just about all customers shared a "party line" with other telephone subscribers. We didn't demand privacy in our telephone calls and we didn't expect it. In fact, having a knowledgeable operator handling calls or a neighbor picking up the party line often helped in an emergency.

Telephone service has changed considerably since the early days. There are few, if any, shared lines and calls are switched by automatic equipment. Most of us still regard the telephone as an unsecure device for an intimate conversation (even though we often go ahead and share secrets by telephone anyway). The ability of others to intercept telephone calls has received considerable publicity, and we'll talk about electronic surveillance in Chapter 18. What is less commonly known is that there are so many other aspects of telephoning that are exposed to outsiders.

More and more telephone users want unlisted numbers, so that they are safe from suspicious strangers, estranged spouses, pushy salespeople, or debt collectors. In many parts of the country, you have to pay for this right to privacy. California telephone companies charge fifteen cents extra a month for not listing you in the telephone directory. Some companies charge more than one dollar. Bell Telephone Co. of Pennsylvania charges fifty cents a month. The telephone companies say the charge is necessary to pay operators who answer the additional calls for telephone information when a number does not appear in the telephone book and to pay for clerks to keep it out of the directory. Persons who want this convenience, not all telephone customers, should pay for it, they say.

A college professor in Pennsylvania has challenged all of this, saying he would be content to have his name appear in the directory with "unlisted" in place of his number. "They want everybody there, everybody accounted for," he says. "Privacy is terribly important to me and I don't want to be charged for it." He argued his case to the state public utility commission, but thus far no telephone company has been ordered not to charge for unlisted telephones.

More than 15 per cent of all telephone subscribers—and up to 40 per cent of those in urban areas—choose to stay unlisted. And they're not even getting what they pay for. Unlisted numbers have a way of getting around town, as any unlisted subscriber will tell you. Telephone officials solemnly say that the numbers are kept under lock and key. In fact, compilers of city directories often have access to all telephone numbers. These directories are commonly used by commercial organizations for solicitation. And they are used by debt collectors, private investigators, and news reporters.

The Pacific Telephone & Telegraph Co. admitted in 1976

that it routinely discloses Southern California unlisted telephone numbers to more than one hundred federal, state,
county, and city agencies, without ever informing subscribers.
The company said that it will confirm to a subscriber that the
number had been disclosed but will not volunteer the information. Among the agencies that regularly received unlisted numbers on request are the Federal Bureau of Investigation, Central Intelligence Agency, Border Patrol, Forest Service, Food
and Drug Administration, county probation offices, local police
and fire departments, Internal Revenue Service, county health
departments, county and city welfare departments, military
services, and volunteer "crisis" and suicide prevention centers.
Pacific Telephone provides about one hundred unlisted numbers a day to these agencies. New York Telephone Co. admitted doing the same thing, even to a cop on the beat in a
nonemergency. Telephone companies in all parts of the country have much the same policies.

Another instance of generosity on the part of telephone companies is their co-operation with government snoopers who ask
for a list of toll calls made from a particular telephone number.
Telephone companies provide these "telephone logs" freely to
the government without notifying the customer. The most notorious incident occurred in 1971, when the Chesapeake & Po-
tomac Telephone Co., in Washington, D.C., gave to the government a list of toll calls made by news columnist Jack
Anderson, the St. Louis *Post-Dispatch*, and Knight Newspapers. In 1974 the C. & P. Co. co-operated again, giving long-
distance records from the New York *Times* Washington bureau for the preceding seven months to the Internal Revenue
Service. The IRS thus had a list of 2,400 calls made by *Times*
reporters, to see whether an IRS agent might have talked to a
Times staff member. The telephone company also turned over
a similar log on the home telephone of a *Times* reporter.

These logs are useful investigative tools. They don't reveal
the contents of a conversation, but they can help identify con-
tacts and associates of a caller and lead investigators to sources
of information.

Since 1974 the Bell Telephone System says it has been requiring government investigators to present a subpoena or administrative summons if they want customer information. But subpoenas or summonses are commonly signed by a supervisor of the investigator, an underling in the prosecutor's office, or the investigator him- or herself without any regard for the necessity of the information and the individual rights involved. Subpoenas and summonses do not provide the protection that a search warrant does. Before 1974 telephone companies did not notify the customer when individual telephone records were sought and released. Federal courts in Washington, D.C., hearing news reporters' challenges to this procedure, have found it no violation of the Fourth Amendment to the Constitution.

Of course, there is a device that investigators can attach to a telephone line, usually at the central office, to record all outgoing numbers dialed on a particular telephone. This is called a "pen register." It does not record whether a call is actually completed, and for an *incoming call* it records only the fact that a call has caused the telephone to ring. Because it does not record the content of calls, courts may authorize a warrant for police to install a pen register—and order the telephone company to co-operate—without regard to the limitations in the federal wiretap law, discussed in Chapter 18.

When you call 911 in an emergency, some police departments will soon have a way of telling your telephone number and address without your saying a word. In a federally supported experiment in the Oakland, California, area, police dispatcher equipment automatically flashes the incoming caller's number and address on a video receiver. If the caller is unable to communicate for any reason, the dispatcher knows where to send help.

The value of this technology is clear, but it's an unfair invasion of privacy if callers are unaware of the device. If they are aware of it, some persons who wish anonymity may be reluctant to call 911 for emergency help. Remember, the names of complainants and witnesses are recorded in many communities' automated criminal justice information systems. To allay fears, some police departments may provide an auxiliary number for callers who wish anonymity.

For the computerized system to work, it must have in its storage all of the numbers—listed and unlisted—in the community by name. Still, a survey of residents in the Oakland area—listed and unlisted—showed that about 80 per cent approved of the scheme.

Calls to 911 are generally recorded, to aid police efficiency. The Supreme Court in the state of Washington has ruled, incidentally, that an emergency call to 911 is a "private conversation" under state law and so the tape of the conversation is not admissible in any court.

The disturbing aspect of the 911 experiment in California, of course, is that the technology will be employed by others in less benign circumstances, without our knowledge. The time when we can telephone a business establishment or government agency for information without being forever identified may be coming to an end. The telephone company already uses the technology to help long-distance operators know the origin of toll calls. When the operator asks you from which number you are calling, chances are he or she already knows.

And there are a few more things the telephone company knows. It says that by monitoring your line from afar it can determine the amount of power consumed on the line (when your telephone rings, for instance). This could lead the telephone company to suspect that you have four extension telephones hooked into your line when you have paid for only two. (It is also a means of discovering certain kinds of wiretaps that drain a detectable amount of power from the telephone line.) The Federal Trade Commission has ruled that you are able to buy your own telephones to use on the Bell System, but your telephone company feels otherwise. If you have what it calls "unauthorized equipment," it will inquire, then ask for the right to inspect your premises. You are not obligated to consent to this, except at a mutually agreed time. You need not grant access at all, but then you run the risk of losing telephone service.

The telephone company listens in on millions of calls a year.

This does not violate federal law against interception of electronic communications, because the law permits what is called "service monitoring" so that telephone companies may monitor the quality of their service. This allows the companies to seek out "phone freaks" who are cheating the telephone companies with toll-free calling devices. And it allows them to check on the quality of operator service and equipment. There are absolutely no limits on the extent and propriety of this surveillance, except the good faith of telephone companies and their employees.

Companies that operate their own switchboards—and which companies don't?—have used this "service monitoring" exception in the wiretap law to listen in on their own employees, to detect discourtesy or dishonesty. Courts have ruled that this sort of eavesdropping does not violate the law, even though employees are not informed of it. Companies whose employees deal with customers over the telephone do it regularly. The Avon ladies are overheard by their employer, and so are classified advertising sales staffs at major newspapers. Department stores regularly monitor their own telephones; so do airlines and insurance companies and the Department of Defense and the Internal Revenue Service. A judge in Philadelphia ruled in 1973 that if you quit in disgust over this practice you may be entitled to unemployment compensation.

The state of Georgia is alone in requiring companies doing this to label each monitored telephone and to register for a license with the state. The licensing list is publicly available, and so many companies have quit the practice in Georgia.

Eavesdropping with the consent of one party to the conversation (whether or not for "service monitoring") is generally legal. Four notable exceptions are California, Hawaii, Pennsylvania, and Washington, where the consent of *both* parties is necessary to comply with the law (with limited exceptions). A Federal Communications Commission "tariff regulation" allows the use of recording devices on telephones as long as the user warns the person at the other end of the line. The telephone company, under its tariff agreement with the FCC, is supposed to ensure compliance or remove telephone service.

Richard Nixon's automatic tape recording system on White House telephones obviously violated this requirement, but the rule has been changed since then to permit recording devices on White House telephones without a warning. Until 1978 anybody, except broadcasters, who used a recording device on a telephone was supposed to use a "beep tone" as a periodic warning. This requirement has now been removed. The Federal Communications Commission felt that the rule was unenforceable. The FCC still requires that both parties to a conversation be alerted if a telephone call is recorded.

While many Americans are dubious about the privacy of telephone calls, there is no comparable fear about telegraph service. Certainly the suspicions have subsided considerably since this warning in the New York *Times* in 1866:

> The popular idea that the secrecy of private communications sent by telegraph is always preserved is, we suspect, a good deal of a fallacy. It is true that laws of this State and probably of others make it a penal offense for operators to disclose the contents of communications intrusted to their care; but they have very little practical force and have come to be widely regarded as obsolete. It is always difficult to trace the betrayal of confidence to any responsible party, and an operator or other employee knowing this has but little scruple in yielding to the strong temptations that are constantly held out to disclose intelligence that may have come into his hands.

The telegraph company is still the custodian of a lot of personal messages, but either telegrams are not as vital to our lives any longer or we trust the company more.

At any rate, the Federal Communications Commission requires Western Union to preserve for six months a copy or computer record of each telegram sent, for possible access by the sender or receiver of the wire or by a law enforcement investigator with a subpoena.[39]

WHAT CAN YOU DO?

If you wish to remain unlisted and will pay the price, you might try telling the telephone company in writing that you do not consent to the disclosure of your number to any outsiders. Draft such an agreement for you and a telephone representative to sign, similar to the bank contract suggested in Chapter 2. If you wish to protect your telephone privacy and *not* pay the price, you may have your name and number listed, but not your address, for no charge. Or try getting telephone service in your first and middle name, so that you will be listed in the directory by your middle name. Or place a hyphen between your middle and last name and see what happens. This will not prevent strangers from calling, but it will prevent strangers from finding your number through your name.

You could always create your own organization and be listed in the directory under its name. But you will have to pay business rates, which are higher than residential rates. Or you can get a telephone answering service—for thirty or forty dollars a month—or an automatic answering device.

If you wish to be liberated from telephone logs, pen registers, and wiretaps, you'll have to use a random telephone booth. But don't use your telephone credit card.

Ask companies with which you deal whether they monitor calls to and from customers. I know of no cases in which a company has abused the contents of a customer call that it has overheard, but the potential is there. And it is an offensive practice when done without the knowledge of the employee and customer. For employees, there is the possibility that overheard conversations will be used for disciplinary action.

There are no restrictions on government access to telephone toll records or to billing information. A Privacy Protection Study Commission in 1977 and Senator Charles McC. Mathias, Jr., of Maryland have both proposed legislation that would require notice to the customer and legal process by the government whenever the government seeks such information.

The Bell System telephone companies say now they notify customers immediately, unless ordered not to, when customer records are requested or subpoenaed. The companies will also respond to your inquiries if you want to know whether your telephone logs have ever been requested by a government agency or turned over to the government. Write or call your telephone company and mention the promise made by American Telephone and Telegraph Co.'s press release of February 15, 1974.

Bill collectors may not use false pretenses to collect money from you, nor may they call between 9 P.M. and 8 A.M. unless you say it's convenient.[40] Once you have notified a bill collector of the name and address of an attorney handling your debt, the bill collector must deal only with the attorney, and not bother you. If your employer has a rule against bill collectors coming around, the bill collector may not go to your place of business looking for you. Bill collectors may not mention the fact of your debt when they ask others in the community for your whereabouts. Nor may they continually keep your telephone ringing as harassment. Nor may they place telephone calls "without meaningful disclosure of the caller's identity." False or misleading representations may not be made. The Federal Trade Commission says that bill collectors may not send you messages that look like telegrams if in fact they are not telegrams. Nor may they misrepresent the imminence or likelihood of legal action against you.

Anybody, whether bill collector or not, who makes repeated telephone calls solely to harass you is violating federal law.

PART III

The New Technology
and Your Rights

17

Computers

The other day, as I was paying my bills, completing my income tax returns, and filing a health insurance claim, it occurred to me how incredibly time-consuming has become the paper work necessary just to keep one's personal affairs in order: checkbooks, letters to schools, consumer complaints, insurance claims, civic organizations, retirement benefits, taxes, college admissions, employment forms, government benefits, travel reservations.

Computers have done nothing to lift this burden from individuals. Rather, the opposite has been true. Computer technology has increased the burden and demoralized the individual citizen.

All the computer benefits thus far have favored the *processors* of people—airlines, government agencies, billing offices, educational and health institutions—not the people themselves. Until consumers get their share of the technological "goodies," there will be no true acceptance of computers in this country.

Some examples:

–For a fee of twenty cents and within thirty minutes, a member insurance company can get from the Medical Information Bureau computer in Boston a record of other insurance companies' medical information about me. For me to get the same information, I must use the mails.

–The FBI's National Crime Information Center and its local counterparts transmit millions of messages on thousands of criminal cases instantaneously. Yet the individual can't use any of this computer power to post bond for a friend in a distant city, get an analysis of crime in his neighborhood, or avoid endless waits for duty as a juror or court witness.

–The Social Security Administration's computer network is linked with many government agencies and, as we have seen, with private insurance companies. Yet the individual is not able to use that computer power at the nearest Social Security office to speed a pension check or veteran's check on its way.

–Many members of Congress now use computers to process correspondence to and from constituents. But where is the member who has used his or her computer allotment to install a terminal in the member's district office so that constituents may have instant access to the representative's voting record? Voters need to make a long-distance telephone call to get this information.

–The Internal Revenue Service maintains a computerized master file on each and every taxpayer, but its tax assistance offices are horse-and-buggy operations. Nothing lends itself to computerization so well as the process of completing Form 1040 each year, yet this computer power is not made available to taxpayers.

We are always hearing about the wonderful things computers have done to make our lives easier. In fact, they have improved the lives of government and industry. They are marvelous for cataloguing information, for managing inventory, for running assembly lines, for transporting goods, and for tedious clerical chores. They are less successful for processing people— and facts about people. When they attempt to do that, computers have threatened our rights and liberties.

In order to regain control of our destinies, we must first figure out how computers work. What follows is my own layman's explanation of how electronic data processing works:

All of us are familiar with punch cards: utility bills are a common example. Notice the series of square holes on them. These cards used to say, "Do not fold, bend, staple, or mutilate," because a distorted card would not fit through a machine used to count all of the holes. In the early part of this century, the cards were fed into an electrical tabulator with tiny pins backed by springs. Where there was a hole in the card, the pin would spring forward, through the hole, to complete an electrical circuit on the other side, in much the same way as turning on an electric light switch. The connection would activate a counter, which increased the total by one for whatever category was represented by the hole. Where there was no hole, the pin would hit the card and not make an electrical contact. Later a combination of holes came to represent words. The first letter of a person's name, for instance, might be represented by a hole, two non-holes, a hole, and five non-holes in a vertical line on the first row.

Or the tabulator could be arranged in the opposite way. An uncompleted electrical circuit could tell the tabulator to count, and a completed circuit (through the hole) could tell it not to count. We see this principle in "electric-eye" doors. When we pass between two posts with lights facing each other, we break that electrical current and "turn off" the device that keeps the door closed. And so the door opens.

The first thing to remember about computers is that they are literal-minded. They don't make intuitive decisions (although scientists are working on this). If you pass your hand between the posts of the automatic door, you interrupt the electrical circuit. The door opens even though you don't plan to go through it—you are merely waving your hand in front of it. So, too, with computers. Primitive ones would record the name—like *Privacy Journal*—on a punch card along with the names of thousands of persons. Along the line, the computer would be designed to address mail to all of the names, and it would dutifully write "Dear Mr. Journal." This problem can be anticipated and the computer instructed not to do this. The instructions are called a *program*. But more about that later.

One thing about cards—they get dropped and shuffled. And so paper tape came to be used, with punched holes similar to those in cards. Tape kept the data in order, but it had its obvious disadvantages. The information from some other form—

your application for insurance, for instance—would have to be punched into the tape by a *key punch operator*. Lots of errors creep into a computer system that way. Punch cards, if they weren't mutilated, could be fed directly into the tabulator or sorting machine.

Paper tape also breaks easily, and so magnetic tape was developed.

Magnetic tape uses a variation on the principle of punch cards and tapes. Instead of a hole through which the pin—now an electrical impulse—can pass, plastic tape is coated with a layer of magnetic material. On one row of the tape, two magnetized spots and three nonmagnetized spots could represent the first letter of a person's last name, and so forth. The electrical impulse, then, is "bounced back" from the tape to make the circuit, instead of passing through holes in the paper.

Magnetic tape stores more information in less space than cards or tape. One reel of 4,800 feet of magnetic tape can store the equivalent of twenty pages of information about each person in the United States, according to Alan F. Westin, the Columbia University law professor who has conducted considerable research into information collection and its impact on privacy. And the data doesn't get shuffled if the tape is dropped. Magnetic tape moves faster, without breaking. It may also be erased and used again for recording new information. A magnetic stripe has been placed on the back of many credit cards so that its data may be read by a computer terminal at a hotel or restaurant.

Our bank checks with black numbers at the bottom demonstrate a combination of cards and magnetic characters. Each of the black numbers contains an arrangement of magnetic ink unique to that number. The checks can thus be sorted by machine, which recognizes each of the numbers. The magnetic arrangement tells the computer one thing: your bank account number. Notice on your canceled check that the amount of the check is also added in magnetic numbers, at the bank. This helps the computer to debit your account and to prepare your monthly statement.

Anybody who has taken a test that is corrected by machine is familiar with the dark pencil markings that must be made for the correct answer. The computer is programmed to expect an electrical circuit to be completed on whatever are the correct answers in a multiple-choice examination. If there is no pencil marking in the correct place, the computer tabulates an incorrect answer. The computer may regard stray pencil markings in the vicinity of the answers as an intended response by the test taker.

Remember, once again, computers are literal-minded. If a student answers a subtle question with the correct answer *in narrative form,* the computer regards that as an incorrect answer because the choice that the test authors considered the closest to the truth was not marked in pencil. Test takers used to have to use special pencils with magnetic particles in the lead. Computer equipment—called *optical readers* or *optical scanners*— can now pick up conventional pencil markings. Some scanners can now "read" typewritten letters.

The most common example of these characters for optical scanning is the "bar stripe" on most packages sold in retail stores. This is called the Universal Product Code. The arrangement of each black line tells the computer how to identify each product as it passes over the reader built in to the checkout counter. (Sometimes the reader is an electronic "wand.") The computer is instructed what price to calculate for the product. This is done by a *program,* whose content may be changed daily depending on the present price of a product. The stripe need not be altered each time there is a price change, only the computer file.

Mail is sorted by the Postal Service and by mail departments in companies handling large volumes, like book clubs, with similar bar code stripes on envelopes.

You can see now how computers get their information. They are making, in effect, millions of rapid "yes" or "no" decisions. Hole or no hole; magnetic particle or no magnetic particle; pencil marking or no pencil marking—there are only two possibilities. This is the principle of modern computing, called *binary coding.* Combined together in rapid-fire order, these two multiply to millions and millions of possibilities. A "yes" four times followed by a "no" once means something different from a "yes" three times followed by a "no" twice. Each number in the Arabic system, each letter of the alphabet, and countless other concepts have their own binary code for computer purposes. Words and concepts are simply reduced to *digital* form. The computer machine that processes all of these codes is, of course, a piece of *hardware*. The cards, tapes, and magnetic stripes that are fed into the machine are *input*. The program for the computer—or central processing unit (CPU)—and the written materials to guide the over-all computer system are called *software*. Machines that scan the magnetic characters or tabulate cards for the central processing unit are called *peripherals*.

Once you get the computer trained to accept a myriad of "questions" that can be answered simply "yes" or "no," there are virtually no limits to the various forms of input you can connect to the central computer for processing. A typewriter keyboard provides one form of input. When I type the letter *P*, this is translated into a certain "yes" and "no" combination (instead of pressing against a ribbon to make an image on paper). This translation is fed into the central unit. These keyboards are called computer *terminals*.

Traffic signals are an elementary form of computer input. Either the light is green or it is red (or red *and* green, equaling amber). A television picture can be digitized and fed into a computer. So can data from weather thermometers, barometers, and wind meters. Or X rays, smoke detectors, or radar devices.

Sound can be used as input. Either the computer hears a sound or it hears silence. Either it hears a sound of a particular frequency or it does not. Sophisticated computers can respond to the human voice. A Touch-Tone telephone, with each button making a slightly different sound, is a common form of computer input. Using a telephone, a bank teller can press a number code to "open the door" of the computer, press your account number, and then press a number code that activates the program that asks the computer, "What is the balance in this account?" The central processing unit, remember, has already processed the magnetic numbers on your checks and deposit slips and—if its powers of retrieval are any good—should be able to tell what the current balance is. That is exactly what the central unit does, relying on what it knows. "What it knows" is the *memory* of the computer system.

All of the information that a computer system processes may be stored in different formats. This storage could be no more than a roomful of many magnetic tapes that must be placed by hand on the computer—but in modern computer setups those tapes are automatically loaded as instructed by the program. Tapes, of course, take up a lot of space. And there's another drawback. To find your bank account, the computer would have to go through, in sequence, all of the bank accounts ahead of yours until it found the correct one. This is *sequential access*.

To meet this need, computer technologists developed magnetic disks, which resemble long-playing records. Flexible plastic platters are called *floppy disks*. When a particular piece of information is needed for processing (to debit your bank account) or as *output* (to give your current balance to the teller), the system doesn't have to plow through all of the data sequentially—as you have to do when you want to find a particular song on recording tape. Instead, it can locate and retrieve the needed data directly—as you can do, if you wish, with a needle arm placed at the appropriate place on a long-playing record. This is called *random access*. These paper-thin disks are stored in plastic packs that allow a user to transfer several hundred million characters of information to the central processing unit at one time. Imagine a large city storing all of its tax records in a *disk pack*. When an operator at the terminal indicates that you have paid your tax, the computer system instantly finds your record in the storage of disk packs, transfers it to the central processing unit to update the record, and then returns it to its proper place in storage. This does not prevent a second operator at a different terminal from updating the records of a different taxpayer. When you are told that an agency cannot retrieve your record because "it's in the computer," this means that its computer system does not yet have this rapid retrieval ability.

Random access by disk storage is fast, but not fast enough for a computer system that works in billionths of a second. A much faster method, called *core* storage, is now used. It is a configuration of magnetized rings of microscopic wire mounted on a grid. Thousands of electrical currents buzzing back and forth through the wires locate the information needed by the central processing unit and alter it accordingly.

The technology was further refined in 1970 with the development of a *chip*—a piece of silicon no larger than your smallest fingernail, on which are mounted wires in integrated circuits. This *monolithic* storage takes half the space of core storage and allows operations at still higher speeds. These tiny chips have made possible microcomputers—portable, cheaper, and easier to build. They are appropriate for personal use now, much like a hand-held calculator with an extensive memory.

Computer systems use all of these forms of storage. Data used regularly is stored in what is called *main memory* and information less frequently used is placed in *secondary memory*. It must be transferred to the main memory before it can be processed by the central unit. There is a process called *paging* that transfers data between main and secondary memory so smoothly as to virtually eliminate the distinction.

The central processing unit has two kinds of instructions that are superimposed on it. One indicates the action that must be done, and the other indicates where to find the data necessary for the job. These are computer *programs*. Programming a computer system is an art in itself, of course. The program must be altered to meet changing circumstances—as when a credit bureau decides to purge data after six years, not seven—or to meet unanticipated flaws—as when a computer letter is addressed to "Mr. Journal" or a billing system dates bills "March 1" each leap year instead of "February 29." A talented programmer can even place in the unit all the possible moves in a chess game in response to all possible moves made by a human opponent. And many programmers have done this.

It is common for a city or county government to have one

central computer system, with welfare records kept in one storage area, tax records in another, criminal records in still another. This is a *shared system*. The Federal Bureau of Investigation used to require that each police department participating in the National Crime Information Center operate an exclusive computer system. This is called a *dedicated system*. NCIC rules said that only systems dedicated to and operated by law enforcement could participate; there had to be a "cop at the top." The FBI's argument was that this is the only way to guarantee security of criminal information. But shared systems can be built so that one set of users has access only to the memory of its own data and other users have access only to the memory of their own data. The instructions for processing criminal data differ from those for processing welfare, tax, or other sorts of data. Different sets of instructions can be superimposed on one central processing unit. This is called *multiprogramming*. (If convicted felons start to receive welfare checks and poor families get stopped as criminal offenders, you can be sure that the computer programmer screwed up.)

The cost of buying separate central processing units would be prohibitive for many municipalities, and so the FBI has relaxed its rule, now that it is convinced that shared systems can be secure for each user. With federal money, some cities have built shared systems for all of their data, whether personal or nonpersonal. These so-called integrated municipal information systems keep all automated data in one computer unit. Multiprogramming instructs the CPU to mail tax bills and to analyze future tax revenues.

Among private businesses, some owners of computers find that the machines have much more capacity than one firm can use and so they rent computer time to other companies. This is called *time-sharing*. Each doctor's office in a community does not buy a computer for billing, but buys computer time from a time-sharing company. The terminals to the shared central unit can be connected by telephone lines, microwave, or cable.

We have not talked yet about the end result of all of this computer power. What comes out is *output*. The simplest form of output is a list of the data arranged according to the programmed instructions, with appropriate totals, printed on machinery attached to the central processing unit. These lists are called *printouts*. We all have seen them. Often they have holes punched on each side; these are to guide the paper through high-speed printers, at more than 2,000 lines a minute. A device can shave the holes from the printout, cut and fold it, and insert it into a computer-generated piece of paper that becomes an envelope. This is the way high-speed billing systems for doctors and others work. You can see how some computerization has actually increased the confidentiality of personal information. From the time a clerk typed your billing information on a keyboard in the doctor's office until the time you receive a sealed envelope in the mail, no other human eyes have seen the medical information.

A printout can appear in other altered formats. It may appear on cardboard, with the holes shaved off, then be folded in half and sent home as a report card. It can be an airline ticket.

Or the printout can be cut into several different pages, collated, stapled, and sold as a book. Some firms sell children's books that are produced by computers programmed to include in the text references to the child's own pets, family, and surroundings. Computers can be programmed to produce magazines with text and advertising custom-made for you, perhaps without your knowledge.

There are other forms of output. The computer can be plugged into a photocopy machine, instead of a printer, or into a television set, or a tape recorder, or an automobile engine, or an assembly line conveyor belt, or a traffic light, or a train switch, a fire alarm, a kidney dialysis machine, a mail sorter, a laser, or a TV camera.

A common form of output is the cathode ray tube (CRT) terminal that resembles a television screen. Instead of printing the data on paper, the computer flashes it on the screen. With the keyboard attached to the terminal, the user can alter the data in the computer. This is called an *interactive system*. Newspaper reporters in modern city rooms write their stories on these keyboards and see their words flashed on the screen. They can then edit the material as it appears on the screen.

And if they are interrupted, they can send the story into memory until they want to retrieve it with the press of a button. When the reporter completes the story, it can be retrieved from the central unit's memory by an editor. After that, the editor can instruct the computer to have the story printed. The computer's output will then be not a conventional printout but a strip of text with lines justified (uniform at both left and right margins). The computer will split words in the proper places at the ends of lines, based on a dictionary of such syllabication placed in its instructional program.

Credit, insurance, education, and health records are handled in much the same way. When you call a company, the clerk can type out an nquiry on the keyboard and see your records flashed on the screen. The clerk can then alter the data in response to your inquiry. Preventing clerks at other terminals—or strangers—from altering the data in these interactive systems is a major problem.

The CRT terminal, then, is a means of input and output.

A tape recording can be attached to a central unit as output. If the computer can tell a printer with twenty-six letters in it to spell the word *privacy*, then it can also tell a sound speaker with thousands of spoken words on bits of voice tape in storage to say "privacy." Thus, when the bank teller asks for your current balance by Touch-Tone telephone, the computer is programmed to activate the bit of tape saying "one hundred," the tape saying "fifty," the tape saying "dollars," and the tape saying "fifty cents." The computer has spoken "$150.50"—if you want to call that speaking.

The human being at the other end of the computer system may react to the computer's product merely by activating another machine. If your bank balance is a negative one, for instance, a clerk could activate a machine to send you a notice. But this can be done without human intervention by plugging the computer into the machine that sends overdraft notices. Instead of having an order clerk read an inventory printout, see that the stock is low, and telephone the wholesale distributor, why not have the computer automatically dial the wholesaler (from its stored memory of telephone numbers) and talk to the wholesaler's computer, which in turn will process the order? That is exactly what takes place. One computer "talks" with another in an automated network.

If a department store has closed your credit account as past due, its computer informs the computer at the credit bureau to add this information to its secondary memory. There is no human intervention. If the motor vehicles department computer has recorded an accident involving you, its computer can inform the computer at your insurance company to add this to its memory and alter your rates accordingly. Again, no human intervention.

The technology to link computers like this exists already. The only deterrent has been a concern that it's unfair for computers to gang up on humans. No one likes people talking behind his or her back. And no one likes computers doing it, either. This linking is, however, an efficient way to eliminate duplications, catch cheats, and save time. When perceived notions of good management clash with more general concerns about civil liberties, efficiency often prevails.

When computers pool their resources like this, the capacity for memory becomes virtually limitless. Each computer can search the memory of all other computers on the network. And each computer memory on the network is supplemented by the memories of other computers on secondary networks.

In this age of computer networking, it may not matter any more that a record about you can be retrieved by your name or Social Security number. A computer record about you may well be retrieved, by process of elimination, through disparate facts in these different memories that fit only you. If a government agency wanted to target you, its computer could ask one computer in another agency to search its memory for all persons of your approximate age, another computer's memory for all persons from your locale, a third computer's memory for persons with similar physical characteristics, a fourth computer's memory for all persons with your occupation, and so forth. What emerges is a list of persons with all of these characteristics—a list of one person, you. Such a system would not be covered by the definitions presently included in privacy laws that have been written; they speak of "systems of records from which information is retrieved by the name of the individual or some identifying symbol." What are the boundaries of a system of records? Are data that can be pooled to target a particular person "retrieved by the name of the individual"?

A primitive way of pooling data in different computers was to deliver a batch of input—cards, tapes, or disks—to another central processing unit and run a computer match. This is called *batch processing*. The results would then be returned to the requester. Now these computer matches are done by electronic connections—*on-line*, as the computer people say. The FBI's National Crime Information Center is an on-line system. A police department in a remote location can query the system in Washington, instantaneously, by bits and pieces. It doesn't have to deliver tapes to Washington. The response comes back electronically. Interestingly, Massachusetts puts its *conviction* records on-line, so that out-of-state police can retrieve them in this way. *Arrest* records, more sensitive, are not placed on-line. Many operators of computer systems don't understand the distinction and carelessly place all personal data on-line, regardless of its sensitivity.

A computer system like that run by American Express Co., or any of the other travel and entertainment credit card companies, is an ideal means of reconstructing where a card holder *has been* and what he or she *has done*. Bank records are the same in this respect, a means for after-the-fact surveillance. When these systems operate in what is called *real time*, then the system provides a means for *simultaneous* surveillance. A snooper can tell from a real-time credit card system where a card holder *is* and what he or she *is doing*—and can prevent him or her from doing it, too! An electronic system of banking, in real time, provides the means for a snooper to tell where you *are* spending your money, not where you *did* spend your money.

The means for a credit card company to operate a real-time system, by the way, is a special Touch-Tone telephone called Transaction Telephone. When a waitress or shop owner inserts your credit card into the telephone and presses the telephone number of the credit card company's computer, the telephone reads data about your account from the magnetic stripe on the back of your plastic card, sends it to the central computer, and receives back an impulse that will light up a red or green light on the telephone. A green light means that the charge is valid, a red light tells the merchant to seize the card. In advanced systems, this telephone can be used to make direct deductions or charges on an account stored in the central computer.

Similar "point-of-sale" devices are a part of cash registers in retail stores. They are used to tell a central computer unit in the store to deduct the item you purchased from inventory and to add the price to your monthly charges. The same equipment can be linked to your bank to deduct the amount of purchase from your account directly, without ever having to fuss with paper work. Don't panic and think that this can be done now without your authorization. You will probably have to provide a personal identifying number to authorize the deduction. In the early years of this electronic funds transfer system, you'll be able to choose to use a check or cash. But later, the technology may well force all of us to participate in the system whether we want to or not.

Computers are able to place telephone calls to you, as well as vice versa. Marketing companies use computers automatically to call telephone numbers—programming the computer to retrieve the telephone numbers from memory or to call all numbers in sequence. When you lift your telephone—in some systems, when you activate the computer with your "Hello?"—the computer begins a tape-recorded advertisement. Or the computer may turn the call over to a human being who has been alerted to your demographics—income level, racial composition of neighborhood, magazine subscriptions, and the like. The computer can be programmed to take your order, if you're fool enough to buy over the telephone from a machine. And it can be programmed to call back if it gets no answer or a busy signal. Bell Telephone Laboratories has developed an antidote —one of the few technological developments that may be a direct asset to the consumer. By making use of the * and # on the Touch-Tone telephone (buttons currently used by computer operators when the Touch-Tone is a computer terminal), a telephone subscriber could activate a do-not-disturb signal. This would tell callers that they may return the call later, or, with another new device, your telephone would automatically return the call when you are ready.

Here are some of the other jobs computers are now performing, using the principles we have discussed:

Bartending lends itself perfectly to computerization. The CPU stores the inventory of different liquors and brands, along with an instructional program of recipes for hundreds of drinks and their cost. The customer presses buttons with the right code for a martini, another code for the brand of gin, a third for on-the-rocks or straight, a fourth for dry or regular, a fifth for a double, a sixth for olive or lemon twist, and seventh for cash, credit card, or hotel room number. A clever drinker could perhaps tell the computer to have his bar bill directly debited from the account of the National Security Agency. At least, he could try it on the first one or two martinis. After that, he might end up getting vodka and beer mixed and debiting the computerized weapons system in the Kremlin.

Many city hotels use a computerized security system whereby the guest who enters a room promptly inserts a magnetic-coded plastic card into a slot in the room. The computer has been programmed to accept only that card in that room. If another card or no card is inserted in the slot, the computer rings an alarm. If the card is lost or the guest checks out, the computer is instructed to recognize a new code for that room. Georgetown University uses a variation on this theme in its dormitories, as was mentioned in Chapter 12.

A computer narrows down the search through thousands of mug shots for a suspect matching a particular description. Through a process called "pattern recognition," the computer sorts out profiles that resemble anthropological measurements from a police artist's sketch. The same technique has been used by government spy satellites to locate fields where marijuana or opium is growing.

Computers can produce the equivalent of full-dimensional X rays by reconstructing 25,000 different readings sent to it by a scanner.

Computers can monitor the inventory and the coins available in thousands of vending machines around a city—and sound an alarm if someone tampers with a machine.

Computers calculate raises and measure the progress of workers.

Computers search the card file of the Library of Congress' periodical and book collections. Computers can search texts of legal and medical publications that have been previously entered into the memory storage. By entering a key word, the user can receive a computer list of all mentions of that key word in the medical or legal literature. Likewise, computers scan all of the clippings of ten years of the New York *Times* and sixty other periodicals.

Computers keep track of the stops and starts of bills in state legislatures and in Congress. Some machines can measure the impact of proposed legislation on different portions of society.

One of the most common tasks for computers is to match persons—or animals or objects—of particular characteristics: teachers with students, foundations with grantees, adopting parents with adoptive children, steers with cows, people driving cars with people needing rides, roommates with roommates, job seekers with job openings, needy people with public services, and of course, boys with girls and girls with boys, and, in some cities, boys with boys and girls with girls. Computer matches may narrow down the field, but they rarely substitute for human intuition. Often the computer presents its beneficiaries with more than they ever want to know about a subject, more choices than they can possibly use. The computer, above all, is literal-minded. It may match a boy who likes the Cleveland Indians with a girl of Sioux background; an unemployed disc jockey with a job opening at Hialeah Race Course; a patient suffering from water on the knee with the Water Department; a patient with athlete's foot with the Department of Recreation; a person in shock with the Public Utilities Commission.

Using a television camera as input, a computer can reduce an image to computer-readable form and transmit it across the country to a photocopy machine.

Using a heat or light sensor as input, a computer can produce a graphic display of air pollution and its flow across a city.

And computers catalogue, channel, select, and reject people. In that sense, the machines affect our destinies.

WHAT CAN YOU DO?

Don't be shocked if things go wrong.

Everybody has an individual approach for dealing with computer snafus. Here's mine:

Allow a reasonable time for the error to be corrected. Then try a telephone call at first. Always identify yourself by name and learn the identity of the person with whom you are speaking. Describe your problem in a dozen words and ask, "Who can help me?" Don't be shocked if you are transferred to another person. You can tell later whether this is a brush-off, but three or four transfers in most American companies or government agencies are not rare. Repeat the process. Get progressively firm with each new person, asking that you not be placed on hold without advance warning. Have your account number in front of you. Smart companies and agencies don't need this information, but most of them aren't smart. If you are promised a solution to your problem, make sure you have the name of the person who makes the promise. The person may think that you want the name to say nice things about the one who helped you, but you need it to raise hell if your problem is not solved.

If your problem is not solved, deal only in writing after that. Write either to the same person, to the name indicated on your computer record, or to the head of the company or agency.

Some computer forms have a place for you to check if you have included a message. Use it. Otherwise, draw a line through the information that human eyes would most likely focus on, and lead those eyes to your message.

I often write on the back of my check, above where the endorsement is placed, a note similar to this: *Letter from Robert*

Ellis Smith acknowledged. Later, your canceled check is evidence that the company had notice of the complaint enclosed with your payment.

Your problem will soon get complicated, but avoid making it sound like a hopeless mess. If you do, the people on the other end will do the same.

Be knowledgeable about your rights, in advance. If you speculate on what went wrong in the system, that may help. Anticipate trouble. An erroneous overdraft is going to cause a ripple effect with merchants to whom you have written checks. Inform them. Dunning letters, even if inaccurate or challenged, will still result in notices to credit bureaus and bill collectors.

If you have a professional affiliation that will attract attention, throw it into your complaint. But don't make threats. The organizations are bigger than you. Write the kind of letter that would motivate you, if you were on the receiving end, to stop what you are doing and straighten out another person's problem immediately.

Once you have gotten satisfaction, make sure that backup files have been altered appropriately, and that erroneous information has been erased from computer memories. Make sure that corrections have been sent to other computer systems.

Anticipate computer logic and its ludicrous end results. Alter the input you provide—whether an application form or a verbal recitation—so that the end result is what you want. If you have had confusion over your name or status before, anticipate that it will occur again in other computerized systems.

If you wish not to provide certain information on a form that will be fed into a computer, try not to leave areas blank. But don't lie. Where numbers are requested, fill in zeros. Where letters are requested, write "Not available" or "Unknown," or "N/A" or "Unk."—whatever fits in the little boxes.

Allow enough advance time in applications you file so that you can bargain on privacy. Submit a form with the minimum amount of personal information. If it gets bounced back, provide a little more information. Or do without the service. Or start to raise a fuss. In place of personal information that will become part of a computer's memory, often you can provide alternative evidence that is less sensitive to you.

Don't ever accept computer-printed materials as gospel. They are no more credible than the verbal expressions or handwritten notes with which they originated. Ask questions about how the computer system works. Know exactly what becomes of the information you provide. Ask for an example of the computer's product.

Some companies and agencies have "ombudsmen" to help. Make use of radio, television, and newspaper "Action Line" services. The news media love computer horror stories; exploit that weakness.

For an elementary knowledge of computing, get a helpful fifty-page book called *More About Computers*, available free from IBM Corp., Armonk, New York 10504, or your local IBM office.

Whenever you can, take a tour of the computer facility where you work, where you bank, where you have medical treatment, or where you attend school. Where possible, follow your records through the system and act as your own efficiency expert. The efficiency experts hired by a company or agency—called *systems analysts* in computer operations—are concerned about the smoothness of the operation, not its impact on you and your welfare. Your perspective is a different one.

Do not be impressed solely with precautions taken for the *security* of the data. This is very important, but it is just one aspect of *privacy*. You are interested also in having individual access to your own data so that you may verify the facts. You are concerned about the *authorized* uses of your data (as well as the *unauthorized* uses that security precautions are designed to prevent). You are interested in accuracy. And you are interested in a log being maintained to show later when and where information about you has been used or disclosed. Computer managers call this an *audit trail*. These components of fair information practices go beyond the physical and electronic security of the records.

Somewhere close to you is a friend or colleague who works

with computers. Exploit that person's knowledge just as surely as you would any other expert who's not costing you money.

Like it or not, our personal welfare is dependent on computers and their caretakers.

In the early 1980s, 20 per cent of all Americans will need knowledge of computers to keep their jobs. And 65 per cent of the jobs will be dependent on computers. Get ready.

18

Electronic Surveillance

Wiretapping was best described in 1928 by Supreme Court Justice Oliver Wendell Holmes as "dirty business." Justice William O. Douglas said forty-five years later that it had become "a disease that has permeated our society." And so it has.

Wiretapping—the interception of wire conversations by electronic means—comes in five varieties. The largest number of overheard conversations are with the *consent* of one party to the conversation. Second, there are federal and state *law enforcement wiretaps*, pursuant to a warrant approved by a judge and based on probable cause of criminal activity. Next, wiretaps are conducted by government agents *without a warrant* for criminal, political, or other reasons. These are illegal. Fourth, there are wiretaps by federal agents to gather *foreign intelligence*. These are permissible with the approval of a special court in Washington, or if installed in embassies and other facilities of foreign governments, with the approval of a federal security agency. Lastly, there are a significant number of wiretaps installed *by one private party* on another's telephone. These taps are also illegal. They are commonly used in cases of marital discord, industrial espionage, or political chicanery. (There's a sixth category that we don't know much about: eavesdropping by the Soviet Union and other foreign governments in this country.)

Except in California, Hawaii, Pennsylvania, and Washington, wiretaps with the consent of one of the parties to a conversation are legal. Anybody may wire his or her own telephone with a recording device and record his or her *own* conversations on that telephone, without violating the law. The police may wire their own phones, dial your number, and record the call. A regular beep tone to alert you is no longer necessary.

The law clearly allows telephone companies to monitor any telephone calls they wish, in order to check the working order of equipment. The telephone employee rarely cares about the content of the conversation or knows the identity of the callers. The telephone companies also use this authority to detect people who are defrauding telephone companies by using devices that avoid toll charges.

The consent concept in the federal law has been extended to authorize users of telephone equipment to monitor their own lines, even though each individual employee has not provided consent, or even knows about the eavesdropping. Federal law says that this monitoring is legal, without a warrant or individual consent, to check on "the rendition of . . . service." "Service monitoring" is discussed in Chapter 16. Eavesdropping to detect employee dishonesty has been regarded as legal under this provision of the law. However, it is not valid for one member of a household to consent to electronic eavesdropping in behalf of the other members of the household.

The best-known category of wiretaps includes those installed by law enforcement officers, with a warrant approved by a judge in advance under federal or state law.[41] The warrant must be specific as to the targets and the location of the surveillance. The judge may order the wiretap if satisfied that there is probable cause for belief that an individual is committing, has committed, or is about to commit a particular crime—espionage, sabotage, murder, kidnapping, extortion, bribery, gambling, jury tampering, obstructing justice, theft from interstate shipments, counterfeiting, drug dealing, bankruptcy fraud, illegal union activities, conspiracy, or other *violent felonies*.

There must also be probable cause to believe that electronic surveillance will provide good evidence. The judge must certify that other investigatory techniques have been tried unsuccessfully and wiretapping is a last resort. The authorization may last only as long as is necessary to gather enough evidence, and no longer than thirty days unless additional thirty-day extensions are granted. Law enforcement agents must minimize interception of conversations that are innocent or irrelevant. The judge then decides what use will be made of the tape recordings. Within ninety days the judge must inform the targets of the wiretap about the surveillance. Even if the application to tap had been denied, the judge must inform the potential target within ninety days that the government wanted to tap him or her.

There are about 600 of these court-ordered taps reported each year by state law enforcement and about 125 by federal investigators.

The overwhelming majority of court-ordered wiretaps are used by the federal Drug Enforcement Administration and a few local prosecutors against narcotics offenders and by federal and state investigators against syndicated organized crime, much of it in the New York City metropolitan area. Studies have shown that, by and large, prosecutorial wiretaps do not gather evidence that leads to convictions. "It's more disruptive than suppressive. You disrupt the commission of criminal acts," says one law enforcement agent. "The key word is *disruption*," says another. One major bookmaker was quoted in agreement: "You can't work without a telephone. Federal wiretaps are going to put us all out of business."

Wiretapping is an expensive business, and it ties up valuable manpower, usually with very little yield in the way of criminal convictions. The warrant requirements of Title III of the Omnibus Crime Control Act of 1968 are cumbersome, and judges often disallow the use of wiretap evidence that was secured with a slight deviation from the requirements.

The following states—and the District of Columbia—allow nonconsensual wiretapping by police only in circumstances similar to those under federal law: Arizona, Colorado, Connecticut, Delaware, Florida, Georgia, Kansas, Louisiana, Maine, Maryland, Massachusetts, Michigan, Minnesota, Nebraska, Nevada, New Hampshire, New Mexico, New York, Oklahoma,

Oregon, Rhode Island, South Dakota, Virginia, and Wisconsin.

In the balance of the states, the only legal nonconsensual wiretapping is conducted by federal agents under federal law.

In states like Illinois and Texas where there is no authority for nonconsensual taps, there have been instances of police installing listening devices in violation of law. In 1975 the chief of police in Houston said that his officers had engaged in illegal electronic surveillance.

With tightly written statutes like Title III and its counterparts in the states, law enforcement agents from time to time take short cuts and authorize their own wiretapping, in violation of the law. About all of the seventy members of the Special Investigations Unit in the New York City Police Department (in New York State there is authority to wiretap with a court order) were found to have engaged in illegal taps in the early 1970s. The SIU was founded in 1969 in response to public demands that narcotics abuses be stopped. The SIU went overboard and, according to the U. S. Attorney's office in New York, paid for much of the unauthorized wiretapping from funds confiscated from the hoods whom the unit arrested on narcotics charges. After the officers started to line their own pockets in addition to underwriting wiretapping, they got caught.

Federal grand jurors in Washington, D.C., and New York City determined in 1977 that assorted FBI agents installed illegal wiretaps in their enthusiasm to chase after antiwar radicals in the late 1960s. No federal agent has ever been convicted of wiretapping in violation of law, even though there have been documented instances in the FBI and Customs Service. FBI reports and local police reports usually attribute the information received from wiretaps, whether authorized or not, to "a confidential informant" or "a reliable informant." (The FBI doesn't say "informer." It prefers "informant.")

At the time of the Watergate disclosures about government abuses of power, there was ample evidence of federal government wiretapping without warrants. The warrantless wiretapping that is legal was conducted under an exception to the requirements of the federal wiretap law: "Nothing in this chapter . . . shall limit the power of the President to take such measures as he deems necessary to protect the nation against actual or potential attack or other hostile acts of a foreign power, to obtain foreign intelligence activities . . . or against any other clear and present danger to the structure or existence of the government." Under this authority, the federal government maintained about 150 taps each year, most of them on the embassies of foreign countries in Washington. The Nixon administration sought to use this warrantless authority to wiretap organizations based in this country that constituted what was perceived as a domestic threat to the United States. The U. S. Supreme Court, however, ruled in 1972 that wiretapping of such groups and persons requires a warrant. President Nixon used the same authority to order warrantless wiretaps of present and former members of the staff of his national security adviser Henry Kissinger and of Washington news reporters. Because the Nixon Administration stretched the definition of a threat to the national security, Congress in 1978 amended the 1968 wiretap law to require a warrant for just about all government wiretaps. Even though a warrant is now required, the application for a court-ordered "foreign intelligence" wiretap does not have to meet the high "probable cause" standard required in a criminal case.

"The CIA may not engage in any electronic surveillance within the United States," according to President Carter's Executive Order 12036, issued January 24, 1978.

The most sordid aspect of this "dirty business"—and the most widespread—is outside of government, when one person wiretaps another in violation of federal, and often state, law. Here are some examples:

A thirty-two-year-old Florida man connected to his bedroom telephone a hidden tape recorder that would automatically start and stop as the receiver was lifted and replaced. He purchased the automatic on-off device for twenty-five dollars, along with installation instructions. A similar device was installed in the bedroom of the governor of Alabama, George C. Wallace, in 1977. Wallace and his wife and the Florida man and his wife were on the verge of divorces.

A couple in Texas placed a wiretap on the telephone of their daughter between 1967 and 1973 to monitor her drug use.

Suspecting that a $62 million loss was caused by embezzlement, two sons of the late billionaire H. L. Hunt hired two private detectives who tapped the telephones of associates at HLH Products in Texas in 1969 and 1970.

A Connecticut man hired a New York City private investigator in 1972 to look after a pharmacy he owned in Washington, D.C., because there had been serious financial losses. The investigator, apparently without the knowledge of the owner, was charged with installing two tiny transmitters on the store telephone lines to overhear the employees.

Wiretaps were discovered on the telephones of three lawyers representing clients with reported ties to organized crime in New Jersey. An anonymous letter said that federal prosecutors placed the devices, but the prosecutors said that the organized-crime personalities themselves installed the electronic surveillance so that they could blame it on the government and get cases against them dismissed.

Officials of a textile firm in South Carolina bribed an operator at a motel to connect the telephone in the room where labor organizers were meeting to the telephone in another motel room rented by the company. Before the meeting, eavesdroppers then propped up the receiver of the first telephone with a popsicle stick, a paper clip, and two paper matches. They returned to their room to overhear the conversation in the labor leaders' room. Not surprisingly, the labor men discovered the peculiar tilt of their telephone receiver, and the company snoopers were prosecuted.

Employees of a private hospital in Illinois, under instructions from a patient's doctor, surreptitiously used an extension telephone to overhear the patient's conversations with her lawyer. As in the previous instance, such eavesdropping on telephone calls is illegal even though no special devices are used.

An Alabama man installed a device on the telephone lines in

his home and recorded conversations between his wife and a man who was making advances. The wife resisted, but not firmly enough for the husband. He played the tapes to family members and neighbors. The couple was divorced shortly after. One private investigator, who says that 80 per cent of his work involves husbands spying on wives, describes a special "ten-day blitz" he recommends. The blitz includes telephone taps, car and room bugs, voice-activated tape recorders, and an automatic camera, all of which could be purchased for private use for about $500. If nothing is uncovered within ten days, he tells his client to forget worrying about the other spouse playing around.

In seven out of ten instances, these illegal wiretaps among private parties involve situations within families, usually marital discord. Often a private investigator is hired to gather evidence of adultery or inadequacy as a parent. Eighty per cent of the devices that telephone companies discover each year are in residences.

Some businesses wiretap telephones used by employees to detect dishonesty. Some companies suspect that they themselves are wiretapped by competitors trying to steal trade secrets. Politicians and both sides of labor-management squabbles have been known to wiretap opponents. The FBI receives about seven hundred complaints of violations of the law by private individuals each year, of which fewer than fifty pan out to serious cases. The American Telephone & Telegraph Co. reports that fewer than 2 per cent of the complaints its affiliates receive about eavesdropping produce any evidence of actual wiretapping.

Of course, many people are unaware that the law has been violated when they discover someone else eavesdropping. Many more are even unaware that someone is listening in. The cases have their comic—and tragic—aspects, and the most notorious one of all changed the course of recent American history. That was the ill-fated attempt by agents of President Nixon's re-election campaign to place wiretaps on the telephones of the Democratic National Committee in the Watergate building in 1972.

What is a wiretap and how does it work? The simplest form is an extension telephone that is attached to the wires (enclosed in a cord) leading from your telephone to public telephone lines. This has its drawbacks, because it is easy to detect.

A listening device, such as a microphone, cannot send sound directly to a speaking device, such as a loudspeaker, unless the sound is amplified. An amplifier is a necessary part of any system that transmits sound, and an amplifier requires electrical power in order to operate. That electrical power can come from a wall socket, from batteries, or from the telephone line itself. A telephone line carries a small amount of electrical power in it to operate the tiny amplifier in the receiver—and to ring the bell and light the small lights, if any.

An extension telephone thus drains a detectable amount of electrical power from your telephone lines. So does a set of earphones. The power loss could even reduce the volume level on the telephone you are using when overheard. The challenge for electronic snoopers in the past twenty years, then, has been to design listening devices that drain the least amount of power from a telephone line and that cannot be detected by the naked eye. They have met the challenge.

Here is how the National Lawyers Guild described law enforcement wiretapping in a 1977 book called *Raising and Litigating Electronic Surveillance Claims in Criminal Cases* (San Francisco: Lake Law Books), a good guide for laypeople who want to know how wiretapping works and the current law affecting it:

> In the area of phone tapping, law enforcement agencies have the advantage of a working relationship with the local telephone company. . . . The usual procedure starts with a call to the telephone company vice president. The agency presents a warrant (it is not known what procedure is followed if no warrant has been issued) and informs the vice president what number it wishes to monitor and when it wants the initial connection to be made. The matter is then put in the hands of the telephone company's Chief Spe-

cial Agent. The Chief Special Agent issues an order to
the switching office which serves the number to be
monitored. A technical employee then connects the
appropriate line to a sophisticated monitoring device
known as a "blue streak."

The "blue streak" is powered by phone company
battery power and is silent in operation. It is electronically isolated and filtered so that it will not intro-
duce any hum, clicks, or noise into the tapped line.
The blue streak device allows a law enforcement
agent to call a certain number (a different number
than the one belonging to the tapped line) and automatically be connected to the tapped line. The agent
can install a voice activated recording gear at a remote
location and thus insure that all calls made on the
tapped line will be recorded.

Another type of interception is installed at the terminal box
found on a telephone pole near your premises or in a closet in
your apartment house or office building. Your line can then be
routed to any other line in town. This is what is done if you authorize an answering service to pick up your calls. This requires
the installer to climb the pole or locate the coupling box elsewhere—usually with the co-operation of the telephone company. This type of installation was used at the Georgetown
home of Washington columnist Joseph Kraft. President Nixon
ordered White House agents to install a tap on his telephone
in 1972.

This is regarded as by far the most effective kind of tap, but
new technology has made possible more covert means. Modern
devices are much like miniature radio stations, with a microphone to pick up sound, an amplifier, and a tiny antenna to
transmit radio signals through the air to a remote receiver. (A
motorist passing the Watergate office building on the night of
June 17, 1972, could well have picked up on an FM radio voices
from the tap being installed at the Democratic National Committee.) These devices use transistors, instead of the larger and
less reliable electron tubes that were used in television and

radio sets before the 1970s. These transistors are connected by a complex network of wires. The small transistors and wiring have been further reduced in size to integrated circuits, which consolidate the complex circuitry on a chip (made of silicon) almost as tiny as a ladybug. This same kind of miniature circuitry has revolutionized computers, as we saw in Chapter 17. An integrated circuit that takes audio input, converts it to a radio signal, and transmits it several blocks away costs fifteen dollars or less. The power source can be a tiny battery, the telephone line, or (rarely) a wall socket. The snooper who installs the device must get access to the premises by invitation, pretext, or trespass.

Electrical signals radiate from telephone wires as they travel along, and so a listening device need not even be attached directly to a phone line, only close enough to pick up the radiated signals. A disadvantage of these devices is that they pick up extraneous sounds near the wires as well as sounds radiated from the wires.

Eavesdropping devices that intercept communications transmitted orally, not by wire, are called bugs. They are not commonly used by law enforcement because installation requires an entry into the premises, either with permission, with a warrant, or with a break-in. Bugs can often be detected. They must be plugged into a power source or their batteries must be changed periodically. To secure a warrant to install a bug, a law enforcement officer would have to persuade a judge that incriminating conversation will occur at *a particular location,* and that is difficult to show. In addition, bugs pick up all of the conversation in a room, not just the conversation of the targeted person, as a telephone tap does. Some bugs are simply microphones that use existing telephone or electric lines.

For a police officer to wire him- or herself with a hidden device and enter your premises to transmit the conversation does not require a warrant. This differs very little, said the U. S. Supreme Court, from a police officer's taking detailed notes of the conversation after it has occurred, except that it is more accurate.

A laser beam bug has had limited use overseas. The beam is aimed at the outside of a window of a room that is being monitored. From across the street, it detects ever-so-slight vibrations on the window caused by the conversation in the room and then translates the vibrations into audio sounds for the eavesdropper.

There are devices that when attached to a targeted telephone can pick up conversation in a room. The investigator merely calls your telephone number from somewhere else—even long-distance. Your telephone does not ring, but the investigator is now able to hear whatever sounds in the room are transmitted by the tiny microphone attached to your telephone.

A bug can be disguised as an aspirin pill and swallowed or—yes—even as an olive in a martini. It can be attached to an automobile or to your luggage. It can be installed behind the plate covering a light switch in your home or office (where there is a constantly available source of electrical power and little possibility of detection). It can be attached to the opposite side of a wall to overhear conversation in a room (like an adjacent hotel room or adjacent apartment). This bug is called a "spike mike." Except for the spike mike, these more bizarre bugs are not in common use because their ability to transmit over long distances is not very reliable and they soon run out of power.

Reduced in size, produced without external wire connections, and draining little power from a telephone line, these electronic surveillance devices have been almost impossible to detect.

Modern computing has further enhanced the state of the art. The sounds from a listening device can be fed into a central processing unit—a microcomputer—that eliminates all extraneous noises. Or a computer that responds to the sound of the human voice can screen all recordings made from a wiretap for preprogrammed key words—like "heroin," or "gambling," or "missiles," or "bombs." The computer can store the relevant tapes by subject matter for later scrutiny and discard the irrelevant conversations. This eliminates one of the current deterrents to widespread electronic surveillance: it usually ties up too much manpower listening to extraneous conversations. Conceivably, the computer could be programmed to listen for persons whom it can identify by their voice characteristics (see Chapter 22) and catalogue conversations involving only those persons in whom the investigator is interested. Or it could analyze relevant conversations for stress in the voices, which some investigators feel is an indicator of truthfulness (see Chapter 20).

Thus the technology exists for listening to thousands of telephone and room conversations, recording them at a remote location without detection, screening the conversations for key words and for particular individuals, and determining whether or not the words are spoken under stress—all without human intervention!

Still, the National Lawyers Guild advice is enduring:

> In connection with this area, [we] should further be aware of the human factor and human limitations involved in electronic surveillance. It is easy to be intimidated or over-awed by the capabilities of some of the newest electronic surveillance devices. It is true that ultra-miniaturization has made the eavesdropper's task far easier and has simultaneously increased the difficulty of detection. Recent advances in integrated circuit technology [extend] almost to the fantastic. However, an important lesson was learned in Vietnam. The United States used the most technologically advanced surveillance devices known, but the technology failed to work. The "electronic wall," consisting of thousands of electronic surveillance devices spread across the countryside, was almost a total failure. Various electronic devices placed in foliage, dropped by aircraft, and hidden by roadsides were intended to relay information on Vietcong troop movements to remote U.S. listening posts. Through a variety of tactics, including common sense, destruction of devices, and electronic countermeasures, the electronic surveillance plan was foiled. For example, one of the tactics

involved fastening a discovered listening and trans-
mitting device to an animal and turning it loose to
roam through the jungle.

WHAT CAN YOU DO?

The most difficult question I have to answer is a frequent one:
"How can I be sure I'm not wiretapped?"

If you suspect that you are the victim of electronic surveillance you have to employ the same strategy as the Vietcong.

The first rule of caution is "Don't flatter yourself." The people who worry the most about electronic eavesdropping are
those who, in fact, are not being overheard. There is one indis-
putable fact about electronic surveillance: the overwhelming
majority of citizens in the United States are not being wiretapped or bugged. Installing and maintaining the devices is expensive, if the devices themselves are not. In an average year,
perhaps 2,500 nonconsensual wiretaps are installed in the
United States by state and federal law enforcement, national
security agencies, and private parties.

The chances that a listening device is attached to your telephone are slight, but the chances that you have been overheard
on someone else's telephone that is wiretapped are higher. One
tap intercepts an average of seventy conversations a day, according to Herman Schwartz, professor of law at the State University of New York at Buffalo. Assuming an average duration
of twenty-six days, as in the case of court-ordered taps, that
would mean a total of more than 4 million conversations overheard in known wiretaps in an average year in the 1970s.

If you suspect that your telephone is being monitored, make
sure that you can find a motivation for someone to do this to
you. Is there family disharmony? Are you involved in political
action? Would you be perceived as a threat—using the broadest
possible stretch of the imagination—by a government agency or
a political opponent? Do you belong to an organization that interests the FBI, the Department of Defense, or local police?

Would your employer suspect you of leaking information or cheating?

Next, try to prove that information learned by someone else could have come *only* from telephone conversation on your telephone. One way to do this is to talk deliberately about false (but believable) information on the telephone you suspect is being monitored. Then watch where the information surfaces. If you continue to do this, you may have much more fun than discovering the physical evidence of the surveillance.

Don't spend excessive time worrying about wiretaps on your telephone unless (1) there is a strong motive for someone to overhear you and (2) you have a strong suspicion that information learned by someone else could have come only from an overheard telephone conversation.

If you still suspect a wiretap, check the classified section of the telephone book for private investigators who specialize in countersurveillance. For a fee, they can "sweep" your premises for evidence of a tap or bug. They may find physical evidence of a listening device (obviously installed by an amateur) or a slight drain of electricity from your telephone line. With a special instrument, they can detect radio signals being transmitted by a hidden device in your home or office. The reliability of these investigators—some of whom also work the other side of the street and install taps—varies widely, and you may not get what you are paying for. Most of these investigators say that their searches rarely turn up evidence of eavesdropping.

Telephone companies will perform this service for you, usually without charge. They are not exactly neutral parties, because they may have helped install a government tap in the first place. (The wiretap law authorizes courts to order the telephone company to provide assistance.) Members of the telephone company security department co-operate closely with local and federal law enforcement; many of them are FBI or police alumni. Telephone company policy is to inform the customer if no evidence of eavesdropping is discovered. Otherwise, the company will inform the customer only that a device has been found and that further inquiries should be addressed to the proper law enforcement agency. This is done whether the device is a legal one authorized by a court or an illegal one. If a telephone employee discovers a wiretap on his or her own initiative, the customer is not advised if the tap is legal but is advised if the tap is illegal, according to company policy. The telephone company is required to report to law enforcement any evidence of illegal taps. On the other hand, federal law prohibits any person from disclosing the existence or contents of applications and orders for court-approved wiretaps without the permission of the judge handling the case.

Experts say that the following are usually *not* evidence of electronic eavesdropping: other conversations faintly overlapping your own, an echo or "hollow sound" on long-distance calls, buzzing, clicks, static, or single interrupted rings of the bell. These may be evidence of a telephone operator listening in on a call, because telephone companies do this legally thousands of times a day, presumably to monitor service.

A hum on your line or a delayed "play-back" of your own conversation may be evidence of eavesdropping.

There are some countermeasures you can take against eavesdropping. Music or other extraneous noise will frustrate a room bug every time. Or simply tune your FM radio to a place between stations and leave it playing static noise. Or playing an all-news radio station next to a bug you suspect is connected to a voice-activated recorder would wear down the bug's battery before long. You can reduce the chances of being monitored by installing more than one line with different numbers in your home or office. Each line would require a different tap if someone wanted to be sure of catching all of your conversations. This would tie up a lot of equipment. Also, devices to scramble your telephone conversations are available.

Federal law prohibits the advertising or sale of electronic equipment whose primary purpose is the surreptitious interception of wire or oral communications. Most of these devices, obviously, can be used with the consent of one party to the conversation, which is legal in most states. Manufacturers claim, for this reason, that the devices are legal. Their credibility is doubted, however, when they sell the equipment in states that disallow eavesdropping even with consent and sell it to police departments that have no wiretap authorizations in their state laws. Many of these devices are paid for by local police with funds provided by the Department of Justice Law Enforcement Assistance Administration itself. Well-known manufacturers of electronic equipment—including Bell & Howell Co.—are involved in this "dirty business" of making and selling devices that are commonly used for improper eavesdropping.

There are two ways to determine whether the federal government has tapped your telephone. The wiretap law requires that a federal judge notify you within ninety days of an application for wiretap approval submitted by the government even if the application was rejected. (Extensions of this time period are commonly made by the court.)

Under the Privacy Act of 1974 discussed in Chapter 7, you are able to inspect records about yourself held by federal agencies, unless the records are part of an active criminal investigation. You may request a federal agency to send you information about any wiretapping used against you. Other files about you in a federal agency may indicate that the source is "a reliable informant." This can be a clue that you were wiretapped. The FBI says it maintains a record called the Elsur Index listing the names of persons overheard and the subscriber to the telephone service overheard. If you did not identify yourself by full name when you called someone else's telephone that was tapped, you probably will not find your name in that index.

If you are indicted for a federal crime, the government is obligated to reveal to you any information in its files that tends to exonerate you. This would include wiretap authorizations and contents.

19

Fingerprinting

Who wants your fingerprints? The military services. Banks, securities dealers, and other employers. Local police when you are arrested. Mental hospitals. Agencies that issue gun permits and licenses. State universities. Federal agencies involved in national defense. Even the FBI wants the fingerprints of tourists visiting its headquarters in Washington. The fingerprints from all of these sources eventually find their way to the FBI's library in Washington of more than 160 million prints on 88 million persons. There they would sit, until a police department would seek to confirm the identity of a known suspect, or an occasional innocent citizen would seek to verify his or her identity to collect an inheritance or other benefit.

Comparing fingerprints was a tedious chore, done by myopic FBI clerks laboring under green eyeshades. They could not possibly go through even a portion of the 160 million prints to find those that matched prints found at the scene of a crime. The best they could do was establish a match once the prints of a known suspect were secured.

No more. The FBI's massive fingerprint file is an automated library now, with computerized techniques for narrowing down the search to a half dozen possible fingerprints. The new FBI system is called AIDS, Automated Identification Division System. It files into computer memory the name, date of birth, sex, and other characteristics of individuals, plus a digitized ver-

sion of their fingerprints. The latter task is performed by an optical character reader like those discussed in Chapter 17. This
one is called FINDER II. (FINgerprint reaDER, get it?) It
scans the tiny characteristics of each print, called *minutiae* and
ridges, and passes the data directly to a small computer that
classifies the fingerprint characteristics according to categories.
Some of us have different types of swirls on the fingertips from
others. All of this is stored in a computer memory capable of
storing one third of a trillion bits of data—with 15 million
fingerprints *on-line*. An FBI operator can then query the computer system for all the prints fitting a certain category of print
taken from an arrested suspect, from the scene of a crime—or
from a bad check. If the sex or age of the suspect is known,
that, too, can be included in the inquiry. The computer
searches its memory for all of the fingerprints whose digitized
codes fit that of the fingerprint on the inquiry. It converts these
few possible matches into "hard copy" facsimiles of fingerprints
for a clerk to compare with a filmed image of the known fingerprint. The clerk signals the computer to produce identifying information and arrest information, if any, with the fingerprint
that matches the known print. The data are then rushed
directly by computer to the police department that made the
inquiry. Some police departments rely on mail delivery; others
will soon use domestic communications satellites to transmit
these data. If the fingerprint submitted to AIDS for matching
includes identifying information about an individual and if
there is no match, then the fingerprint will be entered into the
system for future reference.

Before long, a criminal investigative team may query AIDS
through a computer terminal at the scene of a crime, and receive a response within seconds. Currently, the greatest use of
the system is in rapidly comparing the ten-finger inked print
cards taken by police at the time of booking with prints stored
in Washington. Prints found at the scene of a crime—called *latent prints*—present difficulties because they are not always
complete or clear enough. FINDER II can enhance the quality
of these prints, however. Another technique is to display an en-

larged image of the latent print on a television screen and have an operator use what's called a graphic pen to touch the image at each minutia of the print and to trace its general flow. The pen is connected to the computer system so that the various locations it touches are entered into the computer. With this technique, an incomplete print may be adequate to establish a match.

The fingerprints required of aliens applying for naturalized citizenship are checked by the FBI in this way. Each alien must carry an ID card with a fingerprint on it, but copies of these prints are not sent to the FBI's collection.

A lot of persons concerned about crime think that it's a good idea to have fingerprints on file for every American. After all, what do law-abiding citizens have to lose?

William De Palma of Whittier, California, can tell you. As he was washing his delivery truck in his driveway one day in 1967, he was arrested and handcuffed by four detectives who charged him with robbing a savings bank. De Palma knew he was innocent; he had never been in the place. But the police said they found his fingerprint at the scene. On the basis of this evidence—which juries will believe more than eyewitnesses—he was convicted and sentenced to fifteen years in prison. In fact, an eyewitness said later she saw a known bank robber in the vicinity of the savings bank when it was robbed. But De Palma was denied a new trial three times. He hired a private investigator, who discovered that the fingerprint expert who certified De Palma's print at the trial had none of the credentials in criminology that he had testified to. Upon more digging, the investigator discovered that the "expert," who ran the crime lab in the Buena Park police department, had used cellophane tape to lift De Palma's fingerprint, which was on file at the police department, from a photocopy. He placed it on a "lift card" allegedly holding the print taken from the savings bank at the time of the robbery. The expert had done the impossible. He had forged a fingerprint to frame a suspect. Even the specks of dust surrounding the print on the phony "lift card" were identical to specks of dust surrounding the original image of De

Palma's print on file at the police department. That was extraordinary, to say the least.

And where did the forger find De Palma's fingerprint, why did the police department have it on file? Because De Palma was arrested on a misdemeanor charge ten years earlier and prints were routinely taken when he was booked at the police department.

The statute of limitations saved the fingerprint "expert" from prosecution, but he was sentenced to one year in jail for perjury in an unrelated case. After more than two years in prison, De Palma was released in 1973 and exonerated, but left deeply in debt.

The FBI, though, is enthusiastic about its new computerized fingerprint matching. The process has been employed thus far only in law enforcement. As the FBI said in 1975, "it takes little imagination to foresee its extended application to other areas requiring high-speed identification of persons, such as security access control and commercial credit transactions."

Naturally, the company that sold FINDER II to the FBI is now marketing an identical system, called Fingerscan, to companies that need tight security around their facilities.

The Educational Testing Service requires a thumbprint from each young person who takes the Law School Admissions Test, to deter a smart kid from taking the test for a dumb kid. ETS policy is that "refusal will not bar anyone from taking the test," but students are not generally aware of this. A person who refuses to provide a thumbprint will be asked to provide positive ID at the end of the examination.

Many stores ask for a thumbprint on the back of any check presented by a customer. They try to sweeten this offensive practice by making the ink colorless. Or they give their methods euphemisms like Identaseal, Touch Signature, "personal seal," or Thumb Signature Endorsement. The latter plan, used by some banks, tells the customer, "You may be asked to personalize some of your banking transactions with a new kind of endorsement. It's a fast, clean, simple procedure, virtually foolproof in helping to fight bank fraud." It's also a fingerprint

—one that must be affixed to the back of your check, but you're not told that directly. One purpose of the system is to provide proof of the identity of a person who passes a bad check or forges a check. But the larger purpose is to lead us all to think that our fingerprints will catch us if our checks bounce.

The practice is offensive, of course, because we associate fingerprinting with criminal activity. And we shouldn't be fooled into thinking that the print can create no harm because it is returned with our canceled checks within a month. It is, but a copy remains on microfilm at the bank for five years, under the Bank Secrecy Act discussed in Chapter 2.

WHAT CAN YOU DO?

Shop elsewhere.

20

"Lie Detection"

Here is a letter that a young woman wrote to the governor of Florida in 1974:

Dear Sir:

Upon applying for a job at ____ Bank, I was told that I would have to submit to a lie detector test. Refusal to submit will mean that you are not permitted employment at said organization. Therefore, much against all my beliefs in the American system, I took the lie detector test feeling very much like a criminal. One must realize growing up in America, the first time one sees a lie detector test is normally on a detective show on television, where the gangster, who is normally lying, is screaming—"I'll take a lie detector test!"

At 11 A.M. you go to the [security] company. The man there then says he's going to try to put you at ease as he then commences to ask you a lot of questions such as do you have any hidden motives for applying for this job, have you ever drunk to excess, have you ever smoked marijuana, or taken any merchandise or money for $5? Have you ever been arrested? Have you ever used any other name? Have you ever been dismissed from a company where you previously worked? Did you have to leave your hometown be-

cause of delinquent bills or any other reason? The
questions go on through two pages.

Then, now that you are supposed to be relaxed, he
tells you to turn the chair around. This is so you are
not facing the machine. He puts something around
your arm as if a doctor was taking your blood pressure, a chain around your waist, and two small bands
around two fingers of your right hand. Your arm is
then placed on two sponges and you are told to close
your eyes and keep them closed. This alone is scary!

Then he continues to ask you about ten questions
pausing fifteen seconds after every question. Of
course, unless you are stupid or completely in some
kind of euphoria the question that you await is,
"Have you ever stolen anything?" Whether you have
or have not, this makes you feel as if you have. Therefore, although you are broke, you go home feeling like
a thief!

Tom Hemmert didn't *have* to take a "lie detector" test. He's
a member of Local 31, Retail Clerks International Union, in
Lima, Ohio, and its contract with his employer, Allied Food
Mart, prohibits requiring an employee to submit to a test. One
summer, after a $1,000 shortage in funds was discovered, all
employees at the market were asked to take polygraph tests.
Hemmert knew he was innocent and had nothing to hide, and
so he volunteered to take the test.

What Hemmert didn't realize, however, was that he had
some subconscious suspicion that persons outside of the store
were responsible for the shortage. His suspicion nearly cost him
his job.

As the polygraph operator rattled off a series of easy questions, he suddenly asked Hemmert, "Do you know who took
the money?" The young clerk hesitated, then answered in the
negative. The polygraph caught the hesitation. The examiner
and Allied security personnel assumed Hemmert was hiding
something and he was immediately suspended.

Through a Local 31 grievance action, Hemmert has now

been reinstated with full pay and seniority. And he now knows why the Retail Clerks insist on a no-polygraph clause in all of their labor contracts.

A Georgia man wrote the following to a member of Congress:

> As a former employee of a small milk store chain, I had to take these tests every three months. Before taking my last test, I told the tester I had drank [sic] some soft drinks and milk without paying. I was asked to take the test anyway and the tester used abusive language to intimidate me while attempting to make me estimate a larger amount of beverages consumed without paying. Since then I've read up on polygraph machines and, along with my personal experience, I am convinced of the farce the "lie detector" can represent if only the tester is willing to be unethical. A lie detector, I suggest, is the newest form of torturing the wanted confessions out of citizens.

After spending two years investigating "lie detectors," the House of Representatives Committee on Government Operations concluded in 1965, "There is no 'lie detector,' neither machine nor human. People have been deceived by a myth that a metal box in the hands of an investigator can detect truth or falsehood." A decade later, the same committee took another look at the polygraph and its uses. In 1976 it said, "The clear import of the hearings upon which this report is based leads to the same conclusion as was reached in 1965."

Aside from the obvious political liabilities, a congressional committee might reach the same conclusion about Santa Claus. But that does not mean that a good many people would not go on believing in Santa Claus. In the case of the polygraph, their belief is misguided.

What is a polygraph? It's a machine developed after World War I to measure three physiological changes in human beings: breathing pattern, blood pressure and pulse, and skin resistance to external current (called galvanic skin response). Breathing is measured by a rubber tube placed around the individual's chest. A conventional cuff placed around the person's arm measures blood pressure and pulse. Electrodes attached to the fingers measure skin response. These three indicators are wired to pens that chart the ups and downs in a person's responses on a roll of paper.

The first theory of the machine is that these indicators will change as a person experiences stress. An operator who is supposed to be trained in the technique (and who in many states must be licensed) asks the individual questions—some of them innocuous and some of them significant—and analyzes the results on the paper. The examiner is not necessarily looking for an increase in breathing or a decrease in pulse. It's change in either direction that is supposed to be a measure of stress.

The second theory of "lie detection" is that stress reveals lying—or, as the polygraphers call it, deception. The first theory may have validity; the second does not. Through the years the machine has been used in three ways—as an investigative tool in criminal cases, as a device for screening employees or detecting dishonesty among employees, and as a means for a person whose veracity is questioned but who feels strongly that he or she is truthful to prove that truthfulness. Its only effective, and benign, use is a limited one: namely, to detect stress in persons seeking psychiatric care or counseling.

A private investigator who believes strongly in polygraphing offers this helpful explanation:

> The polygraph is an instrument which measures certain bodily reactions, and in this respect it doesn't make mistakes any more than a medical diagnostic instrument will. Lie detection is not a machine, but a system which uses the polygraph. In the hands of a competent, properly trained specialist, it is very difficult to beat. Conversely, it's very rare when it accuses somebody falsely of lying. This is a human thing, it isn't an exact science, and any time you can have mistakes. A lot of it is just intelligent interrogation. A good polygraph expert has got to have some

insight into people; he's got to be able to formulate
the right questions.

Not all polygraph believers are as straight-talking. As a matter
of fact, for a profession that purports to detect deception, it is
more full of deceivers than any other profession I know. Examiners must try to convince the subject that the machine is infallible (and that's a lie). Examiners often use falsehoods to elicit
information from a subject.

What this investigator is saying is that he specializes in detecting when people are telling the truth and that a machine
helps him in his work. If he were to testify before a jury truth-
fully, he would have to say that his credentials for judging
truth or falsehood are simply his years of experience as one who
does this sort of work. That kind of expertise is not good
enough to decide whether a person on trial is guilty or innocent. Just about all courts in the nation do not allow the results
of a polygraph examination to be admitted into evidence. The
standard for determining whether a certain type of scientific evidence is to be admitted at trial requires that the "theory from
which the deduction is made must be sufficiently established to
have gained general acceptance in the particular field in which
it belongs," according to the leading case on this matter.[42] At
that time the polygraph was in its infancy, and the court disal-
lowed its use. Now, more than fifty-five years later, courts still
do not feel that the machine has sufficient acceptability in its
own scientific field to merit its use in court.

I have found only three exceptions to this rule. In 1972 the
federal court in the eastern district of Michigan allowed the use
of polygraph results by a defendant in a perjury case. But the
results were never used at trial because they were inconclusive.
A year later the U. S. Court of Appeals for the Fifth Circuit
found the Michigan decision unpersuasive and rejected polygraph results in another case. In 1974 the Wisconsin Supreme
Court (if both sides agree) and the New Mexico Supreme
Court ruled that the tests are admissible.

Courts have not been impressed with the statistics on the
reliability of the technique. No proponent of the device of

whom I am aware has systematically compared the results of the polygraph with independent facts to determine the machine's ability to detect when an individual is lying. Just about all of the reliability tests have involved "make-believe" situations in which some of the subjects in the experiment were told to lie and the rest were told to tell the truth. Even then, the most enthusiastic proponents claim an accuracy rate of no more than 90 per cent. Most studies show a reliability rate of 50 to 75 per cent.

Flipping a coin to decide truth or falsehood would produce an accuracy rate around 50 per cent. Scrutinizing the outward behavior of a suspect would be accurate probably more than that.

This is why courts reject polygraph evidence, even after fifty-five years. But there are other reasons for rejecting it in the criminal justice system and in employment. This is what I said in testimony before the Subcommittee on the Constitution of the Senate Judiciary Committee in October 1977:

> The qualifications and objectivity of those administering the tests are highly questionable. There are few, if any, objective and fair testing situations. Most examiners will tell you that a "successful" test depends on their convincing the subjects that the machine is infallible. Most examiners use untruths to lead a subject into admissions. Many persons are temperamentally unsuited to the test and a habitual or pathological liar can "beat" the machine.
>
> But even if polygraphs were regarded as totally reliable, I would still oppose their use as lie detectors, just as I oppose the use of wiretaps. Wiretaps, after all, are totally reliable, but they still violate individual privacy.
>
> For a person to decline to subject himself to a polygraph test should not be considered evidence of guilt, nor of concealment. Persons with nothing to hide have much to fear about a polygraph examination, including the indignity of it all. Refusal to submit to a

polygraph test is a sign of awareness, not suspicion.

Polygraph testing seeks to penetrate the inner domain of individual belief, thereby infringing on an individual's rights of free expression, guaranteed by the First Amendment. One's belief, as opposed to one's conduct, should remain inviolable against inquiry by government or employer.

The polygraph test seeks to compel an individual to disclose information about himself despite the guarantees of the Fifth Amendment, which assures the right against self-incrimination, the right to remain silent. Damaging personal information that one normally would not reveal is exposed—even information totally irrelevant to job performance. This results from the coerced and programmed nature of the questions and from the subject's defensive willingness to elaborate on answers. (The subject has been led to believe, after all, that the machine is infallible.) No polygraph test is truly voluntary. A person is faced with the alternative of not being employed, or of being fired, or of not receiving a security clearance, or of arousing the hostility of his employer.

The Sixth Amendment assures the right to confront one's accusers. As Senator Sam Ervin used to say, it's hard to cross-examine a machine. And that's one of the key reasons for its inadmissibility in courts.

The use of a polygraph arguably constitutes an unreasonable search under the Fourth Amendment, when a test investigates a person in a deeply probing manner through a wide range of questions. It would be ironic if, under Fourth Amendment law, we limited an employer's right to search a worker's desk or purse or home, but not his or her mind.

Polygraphs can also result in an unreasonable seizure under the Fourth Amendment when the results are revealed to third parties, including other employers, credit companies or the police. It has been suggested that polygraph machines be linked to computers so that the results may be analyzed automatically, stored for long periods of time and retrieved from long distances.

Further, the Supreme Court has recognized that various constitutional guarantees, taken together, create a constitutional right to privacy. An individual's sense of personal autonomy and reserve—his personal privacy—are lost when he must place his innermost thoughts at the mercy of a large black box with a moving stylus. Thousands of persons must do this, simply in order to get work serving hamburgers, driving a cab or waiting on tables.

There is, in American criminal justice, a strong traditional presumption of innocence. This same tradition prevails in enlightened sectors of the business world. But too many polygraph experts justify their testing by proclaiming that it provides an opportunity for persons *to prove their innocence.* They should be told that in most of American society, no individual has that burden. Nowhere is it written that American citizens are obligated to have an electrical appliance measure their sweat in order to clear their names—in a court of law or in the workplace.

I was arguing in favor of a federal law to prohibit the use of polygraphing and similar techniques as a condition of employment. That is the law now in seventeen states.

The Constitution, as we have seen, protects a criminal suspect from going to jail for "failing" a lie detector test or declining to take one, but what protects a person from losing gainful employment for the same reason? In thirty-four states there is no protection.

A University of Minnesota psychologist who favors careful use of the device in criminal investigations, David T. Lykken, pointed out the unfairness of using it for employment screening in an article in the March 1975 issue of *Psychology Today:*

If we assume that the test is valid 90 per cent of the

time, the mathematics of the situation go something like this. Suppose fifty of a company's 1,000 employees are pilferers. The lie detector will assess forty-five (90 per cent) of them as guilty. It will also correctly identify 855 (90 per cent) of the 950 innocent workers. But the remaining ninety-five (10 per cent) will fail the test. This means that more than two out of three of the 140 persons who flunk the test will be innocent. It is plain that too many innocent persons suffer when lie-detector tests are used to screen employees.

Yet, faced with increasing losses because of embezzlement, shoplifting, drug abuse, and other unsavory employee behavior, many companies rely on polygraph testing to screen employees. They ask all job applicants to take a test, administered by a private investigator whose credentials the individual never sees. Applicants are asked about past job performances, and about any prior stealing or drug use. In the warm-up or control questions to measure usual rates of embarrassment, the probers often ask about sexual activities, family matters, or other intimate facts that are nobody else's business. The applicants are then sent away, with no idea what becomes of the results. If they are rejected for employment, they are never told why. Many of them are left out of work thinking that there is something in the dark reaches of their subconscious that marks them as liars.

Some companies require their workers to submit to periodic polygraphing—twice a year or so—to deter them from pilfering. On these occasions they are asked about any stealing by their co-workers. Other companies use the machine only when there is money missing from a store or other evidence of dishonesty.

McDonald's Corporation, for instance, says it asks only supervisory workers over eighteen years of age to submit to polygraphing if there is a loss of $500 or more. No employee is compelled to take the test, according to company policy. Only relevant questions discussed in advance with the employee may be asked. And an employee may call off the questioning at any point, the company claims.

Other companies are not so discriminating. To drive a cab for a company in Richmond, Virginia, you must sign the following:

> I further agree and request to voluntarily submit from time to time to a truth test based on polygraph, or such other similar procedures as are utilized, releasing and indemnifying my employer, Truth Incorporated [the polygraph examining company], and any persons in any way connected therewith of any and all liability with respect thereto. I understand that such tests shall be limited to occurrences subsequent to the date of my signing of this agreement, and shall at no time involve matters except those directly related to my employer's business and the fidelity of its employees. I further understand that as a part of the preventive nature of these services it is my employer's present intention to conduct periodic tests of all employees and that the taking of such tests and the signing of this agreement shall not in itself reflect upon my fidelity as an employee.

The most frequent users of polygraph tests are fast-food franchises, chain drugstores, young people's clothing stores, auto rental firms, airlines, retail chain stores, taxi companies, restaurants, and bars.

The main victims are youngsters entering the job market for the first time, often to be paid at the minimum wage rate or below it. They are nervous about beginning work and distrustful of many employers. They are unaware of their rights and usually have no labor organization to support them.

Let there be no doubt that polygraphing in employment is a matter of class status. Even though the dollar losses are greater, you rarely hear of a company compelling a traveling executive to explain expense-account reimbursements under polygraph examination or a vice-president of sales to explain sudden drops in income. Bank tellers take polygraph tests; bank presidents do not. Drugstore clerks take polygraph tests; store managers do not.

Even though the polygraph, which measures three bodily changes, has not gained scientific acceptance, we have moved into the second generation of "lie detection" with devices that measure only one bodily change. The voice analyzer records changes in the vibrations of the human voice, on the theory that when a person is under stress these vibrations change. A similar device, called the psychological stress evaluator, measures changes in the inaudible frequency modulation of the human voice. These devices have been with us only since 1970, but business managers desperate for a short cut to truth have shown interest in them because they can be used without the knowledge of the subject. The machine fits into a briefcase. No obtrusive rubber hose around the stomach, no cuff around the arm here—a hidden microphone will do. Some users claim that the machines work on telephone or tape-recorded voices. They have even used the technique on the voices of persons long since dead to tell us who really killed President Kennedy. Clearly these devices are less reliable than even the polygraph because they measure only one bodily change. A study for the U. S. Army Land Warfare Laboratory in 1974 reported that the machines were not nearly as reliable as not only the polygraph but also the tried-and-true method of simply observing a subject's behavior. Accuracy rates in this test of voice analysis for the Army, the most recent pertinent research, ranged from 19 to 33 per cent. The technique is less successful, in fact, than mere chance. The Department of Defense and the Central Intelligence Agency, whose pursuit of new investigative toys is well known, have both found voice analyzers and psychological stress evaluators wanting. Neither agency relies on them.

They are thought to be rarely used. Throughout the federal government there were fewer than a dozen machines in 1974, and the companies that make them are far from candidates for *Fortune*'s Top 500 (or 5,000) companies. But because they can be used behind the back of an individual—or long after the subject has uttered words—who can say where or when they are used? An entrepreneur in the northwest United States has reduced the device to a black box with red lights that flash for a lie ("deception") and green lights for a truth. Sitting on the desk of a job interviewer, the device looks like a box of cigars or a fancy clock. At last report, the man hustling this one was working on a voice analyzer boiled down to resemble a wristwatch.

There are still newer techniques, which claim to work on a person who doesn't even answer a question. The subject can be drunk or drugged or unco-operative, but not asleep. One methodology involves a conventional retinoscope that an optometrist uses to peer into a person's eye. The developer says that the retina color, pupil size, and eye focus change when an individual is under stress because of a particular question, whether or not he opens his mouth. Another inventor claims that a camera can capture on videotape the split-second facial expressions that an individual makes only when lying.

Drugs that are supposed to induce an individual to disclose truthful information—so-called truth serums—have not reached the level of scientific acceptance necessary to make the results of such tests admissible at trial, whether or not favorable to the defendant.

The Weizmann Institute of Science in Israel has developed still another "lie detector," using a microwave beam bounced off a person's stomach. The microwave detects vibrations of a person's stomach caused by changes in breathing rates. This "respiration monitor" can also be used without the individual's knowledge, but its reliability has not been thoroughly tested.

In an age of rapidly progressing technology, it should not be surprising that inventors are rushing to find a machine that will prove beyond a shadow of a doubt what St. Jerome wrote in the fifth century: "The face is the mirror of the mind, and eyes without speaking confess the secrets of the heart."

WHAT CAN YOU DO?

The following states prohibit the use of polygraphs or similar devices as a condition of employment: Alaska, California, Connecticut, Delaware, Hawaii, Idaho, Maryland, Massachusetts, Michigan, Minnesota, Montana, New Jersey, Oregon, Pennsylvania, Rhode Island, Vermont, and Washington. New York bans the use of the psychological stress evaluator. Except for Idaho's, the laws cover government, as well as nongovernment, employment. Minnesota's prohibits an employer from even requesting that you take a "lie detector" test. In the other states a request that you are freely able to decline without hurting your chances for getting hired or retained would not violate the law. Applicants for employment in Maryland and Michigan must be told that mandatory polygraphing violates state law.

Many states require that polygraph operators be licensed, and some of these licensing requirements cover operators of "similar devices," like the voice analyzer. In Arizona an examiner in a pre-employment test may not ask you about religion, labor activities, sex, or politics. In New Mexico the examiner may not ask about sex, race, creed, religion, or union activities unless you have previously agreed in writing.

The Retail Clerks International Union and other labor organizations include in their contracts a prohibition against polygraph tests, and they wisely advise their members never to agree to one. Labor arbitrators just about always condemn the practice.

In the seventeen states that disallow the practice in employment, you should report any violation to your local prosecutor. Penalties are not stiff, unfortunately (for example, $200 in Rhode Island and Massachusetts; $1,000 and one year in jail in Alaska and Hawaii).

If you are required to take a polygraph test in a criminal investigation or employment situation, you should seek the advice of a lawyer before agreeing to anything. If asked to take the test to qualify for a job and there is no state law to help you, try giving the boss a copy of an article by David T. Lykken in the March 1975 issue of *Psychology Today* called "The Right Way to Use a Lie Detector." It convinced me that polygraph tests in employment are useless and unfair; perhaps it will persuade the boss.

If you are required to take a "lie detector test," the best advice is to look elsewhere for a job, no matter how hard it hurts. Companies with good labor relations don't use the device. Tell the employer that you know that the reliability rate of polygraphs is not impressive, that there are private thoughts (irrelevant to the job) that you choose not to reveal, and that you find the whole idea an insult to your dignity. Ask that there be no permanent notation made of your choice not to submit to the test.

If you find yourself compelled to sit still for a test, try at least to get a look at the results, with a full explanation. Ask to see the credentials of the person administering the test. And demand to know what becomes of the results. If you are adversely affected by polygraph results, you may have a right of appeal within the company or agency. Chances are, however, that a company that treats its employees so shabbily doesn't have a worthwhile employee grievance procedure.

Want to know how to "beat" the machine? I don't know for sure because I have never taken a test and don't intend to, ever. The House Committee on Government Operations had this to say about "beating" the machine: Get extremely nervous or fatigued. Stay up late the night before or drink gallons of coffee. Move around in your chair whenever you answer a question. If the examiner objects, move a part of your body that is out of sight. Or tighten a particular muscle like the one in your big toe. Concentrate on a particular location in the room and think about little else. Control your attitude so well that you are apathetic in all your replies. Think about something exciting, like a sexual fantasy. Get tested on a day when you have a cold or a toothache or a headache or a severe pain. Practice a Western style of yoga by separating yourself from outside stimuli or maintain a totally abstract frame of mind.

The House committee report in 1965 said, "The experts are in agreement that the test can be rendered nearly or completely invalid if a person's physical or mental makeup involves any of [these] conditions." Beat the experts at their own game.

21

Surveillance Devices

I have tried in this book to write about what is and not (with a few exceptions) what might be. The current reality is bad enough. We have succeeded in painting ourselves into a corner with the technology we have developed. We have established a complex of machinery that keeps tabs on us to such an extent that surely we would not have let it happen had we realized what was happening. We are unaware of what an automated spider's web we have created.

It is one of the ugly aftertastes of war. Much of the technology that threatens us today was designed to wage the war in Vietnam. When the war activity lessened in the early 1970s, zealous salespeople had to find civilian uses for the electronic devices that taxpayers had financed to fight the war in Southeast Asia. The technologists fell into the "paint-it-blue" syndrome. They took the equipment created for the Vietnam War, now no longer needed there, slapped on some blue paint, and sold it to local police. Money from the Department of Justice paid for it. Organizations outside of government followed suit. Factories, universities, nuclear power plants, the hotel and travel industry—all had their graduates of the Vietnam experience. All had their executives who felt threatened by increased crime and by unfamiliar faces on the premises.

Let's take a look at surveillance technology. This is not literary fantasy. Each of these devices is currently employed or currently in use in experiments.

The Army and Air Force claim to be able to see in the dark, and they are right. The Army has purchased a device that amplifies 50,000 times whatever light is available—from the moon or a cigarette—and projects an image of what it sees through the darkness on a screen. The device does not emit infrared rays that can be detected by others. It does not require that the user—the driver of a tank, for instance—peer through a viewer. The Air Force Security Police use a similar hand-held device for nighttime surveillance of Air Force bases or other sensitive areas. Civilian police may soon be able to use the device to check dark alleys—and dark dwellings. Dutch police have an infrared viewer that sees through solid walls.

The Drug Enforcement Administration, border patrols, and some local police use tiny "bumper-beepers" that attach by magnet to the underside of a vehicle. No warrant is needed unless government agents attach the device in a place where you have an expectation of privacy—your garage, for instance. The device transmits a signal back to a remote location (much like the voice transmissions of a room bug discussed in Chapter 18). Law enforcement agents can then track the travels of the vehicle, whether it is a car with illegal aliens about to cross into the United States, a hijacked cargo truck, or a private airplane transporting illegal drugs.

Chicago's expressways have tiny electronic sensors buried in the concrete at half-mile intervals. They are there to measure traffic flow, but if every automobile had a tiny transmitter, the computer system could conceivably track every car through the expressway system and identify speeders.

An experiment in Southern California used transmitters placed in lampposts around town to activate a radio system on a specially equipped truck as it passes by. The radio sends a coded message to the trucking firm headquarters confirming its location. If a hijacker forces the truck off its route, the dispatcher is immediately alerted. The dispatcher can even tell if the truck door is opened or if the driver leaves his seat because there are pressure-sensitive devices on the door and under the driver's seat.

The U. S. Law Enforcement Assistance Administration paid for that one, as they paid for a prototype "wired city system," whereby each citizen would carry a wristwatch-type transmitter. If the pedestrian is attacked, he or she could activate the device to send a signal to a tiny receiver posted on a nearby wall or pole in the city. The receiver would in turn signal police with the exact location of the trouble. Each user would have a unique identifier as part of the system.

Dallas and St. Louis police already use systems that electronically pinpoint the location of squad cars on a map back at district headquarters.

Another way of locating vehicles is by satellites. The vehicles are equipped with transmitters that allow the satellite to follow the movements of an automobile—within a few hundred feet— from coast to coast.

That's not all satellites can do. They can transmit fingerprints or mug shots, as we have seen. And they can transmit credit records or insurance records or intelligence data. The owners of the domestic communications satellite company are key forces in the personal information market: IBM Corp. and Aetna Life and Casualty Co. It's possible that Muzak canned music will soon be transmitted by satellite so that people in every corner of the world may dance—or eat or work or travel— to the identical beat. Would you believe that the idea for Muzak came out of World War I, just like the idea for "lie detection"?

Remote sensors on satellites in space are able to locate oil deposits and other valuable mineral resources on earth. From a height of nearly six hundred miles, they can locate good fishing locations in the Gulf of Mexico. Satellites send back photographs, too—of crops, air and water pollution, erosion, uncharted wilderness, and military installations in foreign nations. Satellites don't yet probe or photograph every American's back yard, but that's not because the technology is inadequate. Remember how we talked in the very beginning of this book about the ease with which the fence we use to protect the privacy of our premises could be penetrated?

Back on earth, the technology and law enforcement coalition has found potential ways to limit our freedom of movement. In Minnesota, one municipality connects a computer to a gasoline pump to tally automatically the number of gallons pumped to individual users of city-owned cars. The computer provides individual totals each day and month. It could feed the data into a larger computer system to monitor each individual's allotment. Each driver must insert his or her own plastic ID badge into the gas pump to activate it.

Some bureaucrats keep insisting that the country would run a whole lot more smoothly if we all were compelled to carry a unique, counterfeit-proof plastic identity card. They seem to forget that a large portion of our population—or their parents— came to the United States to escape obnoxious requirements that you always carry "your papers" with you. The U. S. Passport Office has taken the first step by reducing the passport to wallet-size, in response to foreign nations' requests for uniformity. Now that the passport fits into a pocket, there is less excuse for not carrying it. The passport will soon be read by an optical scanner attached to Customs and Immigration computer systems.

The reason that the authorities are enthusiastic about a computer-readable passport is that they can signal the computer memory to lift your credentials next time you pass through Customs. This is the same technology employed at the college dormitories discussed in Chapter 12 and by the Transaction Telephones discussed in Chapter 17.

In 1976 the U. S. Immigration and Naturalization Service began issuing machine-readable alien ID cards to the first of more than 5 million resident aliens. Each card includes the person's photograph, signature, fingerprint, and the mysterious magnetic stripe. In this case, the stripe tells the computer the identity of the individual, plus place of birth, date and place of admission to the States, initial of mother's maiden name, and current immigration status. Each border point will eventually be equipped with computer terminals—probably wands—to read the cards and match the data directly with computer memory on-line in Washington, D.C. Because there is great concern that illegal aliens are taking jobs away from others here, the Immigration Service would like to equip large employers with computer terminals on the system so that they could query the Washington computer memory about an individual's alien status.

The folks who run the food stamp program in the Department of Agriculture are looking at the immigration system with great envy. You can see what they have in mind. And you can see the inexorable trend—a national ID card required of each and every American. The card would be necessary to get a job, buy food stamps, qualify for welfare, vote, get a driver's license, enter or leave the country, visit the White House, cash a check, register at a hotel, board an airplane or train, borrow a library book—and before long, walk the streets of your neighborhood.

Perhaps we could ask visitors to our home to present the ID card to us to insert into a "Transaction Telephone" to establish the identity of our callers. The federal Privacy Protection Study Commission reported in September 1977 that if all of the nation's more than 120 million telephones were converted to Touch Tone, "there would be theoretically a capability in nearly every household to dial into a computer system and to input digital data into it (without additional hardware devices), as well as to receive computer-generated spoken instructions or responses from it. . . . If such activities were to become sufficiently economical—they already are technically feasible—and were permitted to occur without control, record keeping would take on new and vastly enlarged dimensions."

The capacity of telephone lines to handle all of this information traffic is less and less a limiting factor. Telephone companies have begun experimental use of "fiber optics"—strands of glass as thin as a piece of human hair that carry messages on beams of light, not electrical currents. Thousands of simultaneous messages can travel along these fibers in a fraction of the space taken up currently by the spaghetti of copper wires that is choking our cities. The traffic on fiber optics is supposed to be immune from lightning, airplanes, or anything else that may strike telephone wires these days. And wiretappers will have to develop a whole new way of intercepting telephone conversations because their methods will become obsolete. This breakthrough in telephone technology appears to be as significant as the breakthrough of integrated circuitry in electronics.

Fiber optics may propel the use of cable television in American communities (fiber TV?). Much ballyhooed since the 1960s, cable TV has never lived up to its promise of providing each home with *an interactive system* for shopping, choosing entertainment, playing games, receiving counseling, voting, and all manner of other activities. If we do move to such a "wired city," the implications for individual privacy will be immense. Such a system will centralize a tempting amount of information about the customer's buying tastes, and even perhaps his or her voting habits. This has been done already in Columbus, Ohio. Such cable systems provide the means for commercial firms to monitor the television viewing habits of the family, although this is not being done as far as we know.

Cable could be a two-way street. As an "interactive" system, it can provide the means for the customer at home and the merchant in town to ask and answer, buy and sell, charge and bill. Once that occurs, unauthorized snooping into the domain of the cable customer becomes possible.

There is another development in television that threatens individual privacy and autonomy. That is "subliminal perception" advertising that flashes a message—like "Buy it" or "Drink cola"—for a split second four times on the screen. The experts say that this subtle technique induces the viewer to buy the product. It was once said that flashing the word "popcorn" on a movie screen like that would immediately cause half the audience to head for the candy counter in the lobby. There is no law against this type of advertising on television, although the Federal Communications Commission has said it will take a dim view of it if the practice catches on. But how will we know?

You can always escape from your home if you covet privacy. But rushing downtown might not help. Some communities, like Mount Vernon, New York, have set up closed-circuit television cameras atop lampposts and roofs to monitor city streets around the clock. And going off to work won't do much good either, as we'll see in Chapter 25.

22

Voice Comparison

Spectrographic analysis is a fancy term for the technique of comparing the voice of a known individual with the voice of an unknown individual to see whether they match. The theory is that no two human voices are alike.

Speaking involves the lungs, trachea, larynx, throat, oral and nasal cavities, tongue, teeth, jaw muscles, and lips. Speech is shaped by breathing, age, family, geographical region, personality, and education. As a person speaks, factors about the voice are plotted mechanically on a graph. The graphic reproduction becomes that person's "voice print." This spectrogram is then compared with a comparable reproduction of another voice—such as one recorded on a threatening telephone call or a demand for kidnap ransom. If the prints are identical, this is supposed to verify the identity of the unknown voice.

Proponents do not claim that this comparison is as foolproof as fingerprint comparison. No one has yet claimed close to 100 per cent accuracy. Fingerprints do not change with the sex of the owner or with attempts by the owner to disguise them. A head cold does not distort fingerprints.

The technique should not be confused with voice analysis, discussed in Chapter 20. The latter purports to detect stress in the human voice, not to identify the speaker.

Voice comparison has been used to verify the identity of persons seeking to enter a secure facility, such as a nuclear power plant or a computer room. A small group of law enforcement officers is pushing to make it acceptable evidence of identity in a criminal trial. Only state courts in Florida, Massachusetts, Minnesota, New Jersey, and Pennsylvania have responded favorably, as well as the U. S. Court of Military Appeals and the Court of Appeals for the Sixth Circuit, which sets policy for federal courts in the states of Kentucky, Michigan, Ohio, and Tennessee. These courts have ruled that voice comparison evidence is acceptable only under very limited conditions.

The U. S. Court of Appeals for the District of Columbia in 1974 expressly rejected spectrograms as evidence because "whatever its promise may be for the future, voiceprint identification is not now sufficiently accepted by the scientific community as a whole to form a basis for a jury's determination of guilt or innocence."

There are other forms of identity that have not reached the point of usage where they have even been considered by courts. These include comparing the "hand geometry" of a known individual with someone else. The theory, discovered by the Air Force in fitting gloves for recruits, is that the length of the five fingers and the web of flesh between each finger is unique to each individual's hand. This method of identity is quicker and cleaner than fingerprinting.

Another theory holds that the pressure an individual applies to a pen is unique to that individual, regardless of what is written. A special pen attached electronically to a computer can create a digitized version of an individual's pen pressure. When the individual writes a message on a similar device at a later time, the computer will compare the pressure then with the pressure quotient stored in its memory.

Handwriting analysis—determining a person's character by his or her style of writing—is not used in courts, but it is used in criminal investigations and employment screening.

If perfected, voice comparison will be a great help in solving crimes. Of the various techniques, it necessitates the least intrusion into the privacy of the individual.

PART IV

Physical Privacy

23

Sexual Privacy

When Jimmy Carter told federal employees in 1977 to get married if they were "living in sin," the President was acting in an old tradition. Governments, and their heads of state, have always tried to regulate the sexual behavior of their constituents.

"Political repression begins with sexual repression," says University of Iowa historian Herman Rebel. "Sexual activity defies the state, because it is the ultimate act of anarchy. Sex is what two persons decide to do." Couples engaged in sexual activity experience the "joy of letting go." They care not a whit about who's President, or what bills need paying, or even where the children are.

The landmark "Kinsey Report" on *Sexual Behavior in the Human Male* (Philadelphia: W. B. Saunders & Co.) noted in 1948: "The human animal usually demands a certain privacy which is not always available when intercourse or other outlets are most desired; society tries to restrict all sexual activities to monogamous relations; and moral codes put a taint on many sorts of sexual gratification. It seems safe to assume that daily orgasm would be within the capacity of the average human male and that the more than daily rates which have been observed for some primate species could be matched by a large portion of the human population if sexual activity were unrestricted."

Because of the potentially anarchic aspects of sex, those who seek social control—government, employers, or others—have sought to circumscribe sexual activity. One way to do that is to limit sexual privacy, either by lessening the physical opportunities for sexual intimacy or by ballyhooing to the whole community who's doing what to whom in whose bedroom.

The FBI, for instance, has long been preoccupied with the sexual affairs of the persons it reports on. In the late 1960s the Bureau began "investigating the love life of a group leader for dissemination to the press," according to the first of thousands of documents released since 1974 about the so-called COIN-TELPRO counterintelligence program of FBI "dirty tricks." FBI-watchers suspected that the leader targeted was Martin Luther King, Jr.

COINTELPRO agents were also preoccupied with the alleged sex preferences of active feminists in the Women's Liberation movement. The Black Panther party has gained access to records showing that the Chicago FBI office sent an anonymous letter in 1969 accusing two leaders of the party of being perverts and, therefore, an embarrassment to the party.

In all societies, privacy appears to be a prerequisite for sexual activities. This is true even though sex is the least private of acts. As Rebel says, we are most vulnerable when engaging in intercourse—the one time when before another human being we have no privacy at all, no masks to camouflage our innermost desires.

It didn't always take place in the bedroom, of course. In fact, men and women in colonial America often retreated to the woods for intimate relationships. There was very little physical privacy in their homes then; cottages were filled with children and in-laws. Domestic relations court records of the period are filled with accounts like the one about a couple making love "among the mosterd topes and other wedes." In winter, the barn was the next best refuge—dark, remote, and relatively cozy. One woman was convicted of lying with a gentleman in a barn, according to David Flaherty, author of *Privacy in Colonial New England* (Charlottesville: University of Virginia Press). Undressing and bathing in view of relatives and friends of the opposite sex was not uncommon, because it was unavoidable. Married couples sometimes had a curtain hung around their bed and had the benefit of total darkness, but little else, to shield them from others during sexual intercourse. Sharing beds with others—including visiting strangers—was not uncommon at all. Sleeping space, and heat, were scarce.

"Married couples learned to accommodate themselves to these limitations on their privacy and took preventive measures," says Flaherty. ". . . Illicit sexual activities often occur with relative lack of privacy."

Women tend to prefer sex in the dark; men, in a lighted environment, according to Kinsey. Researchers of different cultures have confirmed what the colonists discovered: if there is a possibility for seclusion, intercourse will take place indoors; otherwise, it will be outdoors.

The Russian equivalent to our "Kinsey Report" says that intercourse in the presence of other family members is commonplace in state-built housing in the contemporary Soviet Union. A 1973 study in Canada found that modern couples, at least in North America, value privacy in sex. Husbands and wives had different reasons for ceasing intercourse for long periods, but the one reason both men and women agreed on was a perceived lack of privacy. The study team suspected that this was merely a convenient rationale covering up the real reasons for quitting intercourse—marital discord, illness, unemployment, decreased sexual interest, and so forth.

For rural Americans who worked alone in the fields during the eighteenth and nineteenth centuries, finding solitude during the day was the least of their worries. But in cold weather, and at night, privacy presented a difficult challenge. "Very often an entire family of a dozen, male and female, adult and child, slept, cooked, ate, lived, loved and died—had its whole indoor being—in a single room," wrote W. J. Cash in describing parts of the nineteenth-century United States South in his *The Mind of the South* (New York: Alfred A. Knopf).

As the country became more industrialized and urbanized, the desire for physical privacy increased. At the same time, Americans began to worry about large-scale information dissemination—by telephone and telegraphy, by mass-circulation newspapers. Employers wanted to know all about workers, including who was sleeping with whom.

The urge to know "mode of living" has been used to this day to justify thousands and thousands of insurance investigations into the private affairs of men and women. A woman living with a man without benefit of marriage is denied auto insurance coverage in many instances. A person living with another of the same sex may be denied life insurance or charged higher rates on the supposition that the two are homosexuals and on the further supposition that homosexuals have shorter life expectancy. Insurance companies admitted this in testimony before a federal Privacy Protection Study Commission that issued a report in 1977.

"Mode of living" is also the catchall phrase used to justify government snooping into the homes of welfare recipients. At one time a welfare application form in South Dakota asked women with illegitimate children, "When and where did intercourse first occur? Frequency and period of time during which intercourse occurred? Was anyone else present? If yes, give dates, names, and addresses. Were preventive measures always used?"

If there's a "man in the house," welfare payments are usually cut off. And there's only one way to find out—send a social worker or investigator unannounced to the home of the recipient. Get caught in bed making love in colonial times and you might suffer ridicule and gossip. Get caught nowadays and you lose public assistance or auto insurance.

The Supreme Court ruled in 1972 that such "visitations" are not unreasonable searches in violation of the Bill of Rights, because the welfare mother could always refuse entry—and do without public assistance. In contrast, just four years earlier the Court had ruled that a city inspector needed a warrant before he could enter a residence or a commercial warehouse, because the proprietor would be in jeopardy of paying a fine if he refused entry.

Justice Thurgood Marshall, in dissenting to the majority opinion in the welfare case, pointed out, "For protecting the privacy of her home, Mrs. James lost the sole means of support for herself and her infant son. For protecting the privacy of his commercial warehouse, Mr. See received a $100 suspended fine."

In Marshall's view, the Supreme Court was being selective in its recognition of the right to privacy. A look at privacy decisions by the Court since the mid-1960s bears him out. Before that, the leading privacy cases involved tort actions, usually by an individual who had been damaged by press or commercial exploitation of personal information about him- or herself. But in 1965, in *Griswold* v. *Connecticut*, the Court recognized a constitutional right to privacy.

The 1965 case voided Connecticut's law prohibiting the sale or use of contraceptives, because there was only one way to enforce such a statute: "allow the police to search the sacred precincts of marital bedrooms for telltale signs." *Griswold* involved a married couple's right to use birth control devices, and the opinion was written by Associate Justice William O. Douglas, who, despite his inability to sustain a long marriage, had a legendary respect for the sanctity of the institution. "Marriage is a coming together for better or worse, hopefully enduring, and intimate to the degree of being sacred. It is an association that promotes a way of life, not causes; a harmony in living, not political faiths; a bilateral loyalty, not commercial or social projects. Yet it is an association for as noble a purpose as any involved in our prior decisions," said Douglas.

Because of this language and because Douglas' formulation of the right to privacy has never had the support of a majority of the Court, it should not be surprising that in the eyes of the men on the Supreme Court sexual privacy has been a right mainly for married persons. Three of Douglas' liberal colleagues agreed that Connecticut's law was unconstitutional, but stressed, "It should be said of the Court's holding today that it in no way interferes with a State's proper regulation of sexual promiscuity or misconduct." It did not matter to any of the judges that the only way to enforce such laws was to allow the government to snoop into the premarital, extramarital, or homosexual bedroom.

In the eight years following, this right to privacy in *Griswold* was used to justify the Court's decisions allowing unmarried persons the right to use contraceptives, allowing an unmarried woman to terminate a pregnancy, and allowing a man to watch dirty movies in the privacy of his own home.

But the current Court has drawn the line—apparently at sodomy. In 1976 the Court upheld a three-judge decision from the northern district of Virginia that a state law punishing sodomy between consenting adults is not an unconstitutional invasion of privacy. The case involved homosexuals.

Then, a couple of months later, the Court refused to consider a Fourth Circuit Court of Appeals decision that allowed Virginia to punish a married couple for engaging in oral-genital sex. This left standing Virginia's criminal conviction of the couple—even though they had had their sexual relations within the "privacy" of their own home. Thus individuals have the right to watch all manner of sexual goings-on in a movie within the home, but not to engage in those very same sexual activities themselves within the home!

The woman in the Virginia case performed fellatio upon her husband and a second male "swinger" in their home, while someone took photographs. Some of the photos got into the hands of the couple's teen-aged daughters. When one of the girls displayed a nude photograph in school, authorities secured a search warrant and uncovered many more erotic photos in the home. The couple was charged under a Virginia law prohibiting sodomy. "Once a married couple admits strangers as onlookers, federal protection of privacy dissolves," said the Fourth Circuit. "If the couple performs sexual acts for the excitation or gratification of welcome onlookers, they cannot selectively claim the state is an intruder."

Hogwash, said three members of the court in dissent. An abortion is not an isolated private event; the fetus, the doctor, and others are involved. Yet an abortion has been held legal under the individual's right to privacy. "We conclude that secrecy is not a necessary element of the right," said the dissenters. What would not normally be punishable (sexual adventures by a married couple in private) cannot become punishable because of the presence of a third person, they said.

The dissenters further recognized that sexual activity between married persons "can never be made criminal"—even if done in public—unless it violates some other criminal offense such as lewdness, indecent exposure, or disorderly conduct.

One of the dissenters was J. Braxton Craven, Jr., a respected Harvard-educated jurist who thought that the right to privacy is not limited to what goes on in private, contrary to popular impression. "This freedom may be termed more accurately 'the right to be let alone' or personal autonomy, or simply 'personhood,'" he wrote. Craven's credo was: "An individual should retain the right to engage in any form of activity unless there exists a countervailing state interest of sufficient weight to justify restricting his conduct. This is the essence of personhood; a rebuttable presumption that all citizens have a right to conduct their lives free of government regulation."

The Supreme Court's limitation of the privacy right to "matters relating to marriage, procreation, contraception, family relationships, and child rearing and education" represents one trend in the law of privacy.[43] Craven's concept of "personhood" represents a strong countertrend. It would balance an individual's "right to do his own thing" against the needs of an ordered society. In Craven's words: "All would agree that there is a 'right' to wear a bathing suit on a public beach. Controversy begins as the suit diminishes. The proper question is not whether a person can or must wear a suit (who would say he must in his own bathtub?) but whether the state's interest in decorous and moral behavior is of greater weight in the particular instance."

A federal judge in Massachusetts in 1975 found the state's interest of greater weight than the right of individuals to bathe without clothes at the Cape Cod National Seashore. The judge upheld Department of the Interior regulations barring nude bathing at the federally protected beach. "Long before the creation of the Seashore in 1959, nude bathing by individuals or small groups was an established and accepted practice along the Atlantic beach,' said District Judge Frank H. Freedman. But by 1974, 1,200 men, women, and children were swimming without clothes each day, to the irritation of nearby homeowners. It was the crowd, not the nudity, that concerned the Department of the Interior, which assigned its regulation writers to define nude bathing:

> . . . a person's intentional failure to cover with a fully opaque covering that person's own genitals, pubic areas, rectal area, or female breast below a point immediately above the top of the areola when in a public place. . . . This regulation shall not apply to a person under 10 years of age.

The judge said those who want to swim in the nude are not exercising a right of free association protected by the First Amendment to the Constitution, but he recognized they do have a "right to be let alone." The right to swim in the nude, however, is not as fundamental as the right to hold a job or to vote or to speak, and so the regulation was upheld as a valid response to the environmental threat posed by 1,200 nude bodies.

Up in Boston, back in 1757, there was reported a great uproar because of "many persons washing themselves in publick and frequented places to the great reproach of modesty and good manners." And so the town meeting "voted and ordered that no person whosoever above the age of 12 years shall in less than an hour after sun-set undress themselves and go into water within ten rods of any dwelling house in this town, at that time inhabited, nor shall any person being in the water, swim to such parts of the town, as to be plainly within the sight of any dwelling house," according to an account of town records in David Flaherty's *Privacy in Colonial New England.*

Kinsey asserted that the British and the Americans are the most concerned of all peoples about keeping their bodies covered. The residents of colonial Boston and of contemporary Cape Cod both discovered that the Anglo-American culture will tolerate nude bathing only if it's impromptu, in small numbers, and unknown to others. Once the nude enthusiasts grow in number, the "state's interest" in protecting the rights of others enters into the situation.

No state yet recognizes the rights of persons to swim in the nude or sets aside areas for this activity. There are many unofficial nude beaches in the country, but, more often than not, local police have the option of arresting people without swimming suits for public lewdness or indecent exposure. A typical state law reads as follows:

> Public Indecency—A person commits public indecency when he performs any of the following acts in a public place and upon conviction shall be punished as a misdemeanor:
> (a) An act of sexual intercourse;
> (b) A lewd exposure of the sexual organs;
> (c) A lewd appearance in a state of partial or complete nudity;
> (d) A lewd caress or indecent fondling of the body of another person.

Just about all courts, when pressed, are ruling now that "mere nudity in public does not constitute lewdness." In the summer of 1978 the National Park Service, which has jurisdiction over federal recreation areas, proclaimed, "There is no federal policy regarding nude bathing. We leave it to the discretion of local superintendents. It's not our job to keep jails full. Our job is to protect the environment and insure maximum happiness for users." The regulation at Cape Cod has not been enforced, mainly because the large crowds have disappeared. Local police occasionally arrest bathers with no clothes and levy a small fine or drop the charges, and so their authority to do so has not been challenged frequently.

To apply the law in a selective way means that people really don't know where their rights to privacy end and the state's compelling interest begins. For instance, the Meade County Independent School District in South Dakota fired a teacher because her boy friend lived with her at home and because the teacher made no effort to hide that fact. The school board thought such private conduct set a bad example for the kids, and so did several parents who showed up at a hearing on the teacher's dismissal. The federal district court in South Dakota supported the school board's position.

But, not 350 miles west of Meade County, a Wyoming divorcee won more than $40,000 in damages when the U.S. district court in Wyoming agreed that her privacy had been invaded in similar circumstances. The woman's principal had wanted to know, among other things, why there was a light burning in her bedroom on certain nights when her children were away, and she was fired.

As these two cases show, employers seem to be greatly fascinated by persons who are living together "without benefit of wedlock," even though the practice is no longer rare. The number of persons admitting cohabitation has doubled in the past years, to about 1 per cent of all American households, according to census figures. Among those under age forty-five, there has been a fivefold increase in the past five years.

Federal employers, like the FBI, have occasionally suspended or fired employees who were "living together." In 1977 an FBI agent caught living with an unmarried woman was suspended without pay, placed on probation, and transferred away from Washington, D.C. Neighbors had complained about him to another FBI agent who lived nearby. At a hearing he was asked about his relationship and he responded, "With all due respect, it's none of the Bureau's business." But a U.S. district judge in the northern district of Virginia ruled that the FBI could lawfully discipline the agent for what the FBI considered immoral conduct.

The FBI claimed that, by "living together," the FBI agent and his friend were violating the law. The Bureau was right. Cohabitation, defined as any persons living together as man and wife without being married, is a misdemeanor in Alabama, Alaska, Arkansas, Florida, Idaho, Illinois, Kansas, Massachusetts, Michigan, Mississippi, Nebraska, New Mexico (no penalty), North Carolina, South Carolina, Virginia, West Virginia, Wisconsin, and Wyoming and a felony in Arizona. Fornication, defined as voluntary sexual intercourse by an unmarried person, is a misdemeanor crime in Florida, Georgia, Hawaii, Idaho, Illinois, Massachusetts, Mississippi, North Carolina, Rhode Island (ten-dollar fine), South Carolina, Utah, Virginia, West Virginia, Wisconsin, and the District of Columbia.

It is probably not a violation of any state laws for two persons of the opposite sex, unmarried to each other, to share a hotel room. Many hotel clerks think this is a violation, and hotel policies on this vary. No one seems to mind if a couple lies and registers as man and wife.

Good sources of information about the legal and financial aspects of living together are *Living Together, Married or Single: Your Legal Rights* by Nora Lavori (New York: Harper & Row, 1976) and *Living Together: A Guide to the Law for Unmarried Couples* by Barbara B. Hirsch (Boston: Houghton Mifflin Co., 1976).

A couple of years ago the FBI reprimanded two of its clerical employees who were living together. "They called us in separately and asked us if we have been spending nights together," said the male partner, who was reported to the FBI by an irate (male) roommate.

"The man asked me if we'd had sexual relations. I said yes. His questions were really quite personal. I couldn't understand what business it was of his. He said that we would most likely be put on probation and that if we hadn't been engaged, we probably would have been fired." The couple was eventually married, but shortly thereafter quit the FBI.

In 1974 a young lawyer in Washington was turned down for a job in the Department of Justice because he was living with an unmarried woman. A postal clerk was fired in San Francisco on the same grounds, but he fought the Postal Service in court. The federal court in the northern district of California in 1970 ruled that firing the postal employee because of his private sex life violated his right to privacy under the U. S. Constitution. The Civil Service Commission had informed the man that he was unsuitable because his home situation constituted "immoral conduct," but the court upheld his right to privacy under the Ninth Amendment.

Insurance companies, as well as employers, keep information about cohabitation. The result can sometimes be denial of coverage or increased rates—more commonly against women than men. The practice has caused some backlash against insurance companies. New York State's Attorney General, for one, has stated that to deny a person insurance or to increase rates because an unmarried couple is living together violates his state's insurance law.

But companies that investigate applicants for insurance carriers—like Equifax, Inc., of Atlanta, which dominates this industry—still report on cohabitation, often drawing unfavorable inferences. Equifax says that it collects this information because it may be of help to some of the companies it serves. Those companies, like Nationwide, say that cohabitation between persons of the opposite sex can create an unstable condition relevant to insurance underwriting, or who the beneficiary of a policy may be, or what other persons will be using an insured automobile.

"The stability of a relationship is an underwriting judgment," says a Nationwide insurance official. "Our underwriters must make these judgments and background checks." By contrast, according to a spokesman for Kemper Insurance, "we take no negative recognition of the insured's choice of sexual lifestyle, unless it operates to directly increase the hazards of the actual operation of the insured automobile." Royal-Globe Insurance says cohabitation is "not germane." But all of the companies defend their right to have information of this sort.

Courts generally agree that what happens between married people in the home is entitled to privacy protection, even if they often find that there is a countervailing state interest. But what about sex-related activities that occur outside the home? In a time when government regulation and litigation affect just about every aspect of life, it shouldn't be surprising that these activities have also drawn the attention of courts and regulatory agencies. Here again, the record is mixed, with selective application of standards of conduct. A few random examples:

A Federal Highway Administration rule once prohibited more than one person from using the sleeper berth in the rear of long-haul truck cabs. The berths were installed to allow one driver to rest while the other drives. The highway administration felt they were unsafe for two persons at once. Word finally got to Washington—thanks to eight persistent California couples—that many husband-wife teams operate interstate trucks. And so, in January 1975, the federal government caught up with reality and relaxed its regulation.

Many hospitals draw the line on marital togetherness at the delivery-room door. They won't allow the husband to come into the delivery room during the birth of his child or, if he wishes, to participate in the delivery. One rejected new father, a graduate of the LaMaze training course, called LaMaze a more beneficial obstetrical procedure than traditional practices that deny the right of the father to participate. He sued Porter Memorial Hospital, a public facility in Valparaiso, Indiana, saying his "right of marital privacy" had been infringed, but the U. S. Court of Appeals for the Seventh Circuit said the hospital could bar husbands, for medical reasons. The opinion in 1975 was one of the last by Circuit Judge John Paul Stevens before his promotion to the U. S. Supreme Court.

Two boys at a California Youth Authority training center asked a state judge to keep female guards out of the boys' dormitories. "They allege," said the judge in 1976, "that female employees supervise their showers, latrine use, and the sleeping quarters in which they change clothes. They allege that female employees conduct 'skin searches.' They also allege that female staff members have been present to supervise the dressing, shower and toilet areas of the school, gymnasium and swimming pool." Forty-one trainees sent a letter to the judge saying that they were satisfied with the arrangements and that the embarrassed boys "should be more than happy to have women around them."

The law of privacy, said the judge, "encompasses the individual's regard for his own dignity: his resistance to humiliation and embarrassment; his privilege against unwanted exposure of his nude body and bodily functions." This is true in prisons, he said, even though other rights of privacy are not accorded inmates, like confidential use of the mails and telephone. The judge ordered the youth facility to reassign more than one hundred female guards In a similar situation, female inmates at New York's Bedford Correctional Facility filed suit to stop the assignment of male guards to their housing units. In New York and California, the guards had been reassigned as part of a plan to end sex discrimination in employment.

Strip searches are a gross invasion of the individual's privacy, and they have been upheld only where probable cause and circumstances warrant. But that doesn't authorize a police officer to take advantage of his or her position, as three Chino, California, officers did back in 1958. One of them asked a female complainant to undress and pose for his camera in indecent positions. Two colleagues helped to make prints of the film and circulate them to friends in the police department. The Ninth Circuit Court of Appeals in condemning the officers said, "The desire to shield one's unclothed figure from view of strangers, and particularly strangers of the opposite sex, is impelled by elementary self-respect and personal dignity."

On the other hand, if taking off your clothes is your thing, the government may not deny you a job, as it tried to do to a Maryland nudist who wanted to be a police officer.

Even the pros and cons of prostitution have been argued before the courts, as civil liberties lawyers seek to push the courts toward a more relaxed view about the offense. Statutes against other pre- or extramarital activities such as fornication, sodomy, and adultery are also now under increasing attack. In the words of the federal district court in Maryland, "There is indeed a changing attitude in this country toward policing morality where consenting adults are involved."

As long as government chooses to pass laws regulating morality both inside and outside the bedroom, our sexual privacy is not safe. As long as the laws exist, those in authority can enforce them selectively.

Since the contradictory rulings of the courts have not clarified where the individual's rights end and society's rights begin, some legislatures are trying to do it themselves by changing or eliminating sex laws. More than one third of the states have decriminalized sodomy between consenting adults: California, Colorado, Connecticut, Delaware, Hawaii, Illinois, Indiana, Iowa, Maine, Nebraska, New Hampshire, New Mexico, North Dakota, Ohio, Oregon, South Dakota, Washington, West Virginia, and Wyoming. New York and Pennsylvania exclude married couples from prosecution under sodomy laws. Kansas, Texas, and Arkansas exclude heterosexuals from prosecution under sodomy laws. The National Gay Task Force says that enforcement of these laws has been almost exclusively against homosexuals, even though studies show that two thirds of all heterosexuals violate such statutes. Florida's sodomy law used to punish "the abominable and detestable crime against nature" until a state court said it was too vague to be constitutional. (All states punish forcible sex as a felony.)

As of 1978 the following cities had passed ordinances prohibiting discrimination in housing, employment, and public accommodations on the basis of sexual preference (homosexual or heterosexual): Alfred, New York; Amherst, Massachusetts; Ann Arbor, Michigan; Austin, Texas; Berkeley, California; Bloomington, Indiana; Champaign, Illinois; Chapel Hill, North Carolina; Cleveland Heights, Ohio; Columbus, Ohio (housing and public accommodations only); Detroit, Michigan; East Lansing, Michigan; Iowa City, Iowa; Madison, Wisconsin; Marshall, Minnesota; Minneapolis, Minnesota; Palo Alto, California; Portland, Oregon; San Jose, California; Seattle, Washington; Tucson, Arizona; Urbana, Illinois; Washington, D.C.; and Yellow Springs, Ohio.

The following cities prohibit discrimination against homosexuals in city employment: Boston, Massachusetts; Cupertino, California; Detroit, Michigan; Ithaca, New York; Los Angeles, California; Mountain View, California; New York, New York; Pullman, Washington; San Francisco, California; Santa Barbara, California; and Sunnyvale, California. Pennsylvania prohibits discrimination on the basis of sexual preference in state-government employment.

The following counties prohibit discrimination against homosexuals county-wide: Santa Cruz County, California; Howard County, Maryland; and Hennepin County, Minnesota.

There are competing forces at work in the United States of the late seventies Many people are publicly asserting their rights to control their own bodies and "personhood" with regard to abortions, homosexual rights, less restrictive dress and sexual behavior, and fewer inhibitions in language. At the same time, Americans are asserting their rights to keep sexual activities private—inviolate against intrusions by employers, government, parents, and neighbors.

A classic example of this schism is the gym teacher in California who was threatened with expulsion for an off-duty activity. He appealed, saying he had a right to privacy off hours. His off-duty activity was posing nude for a national magazine, *Playgirl*.

"It is a very odd definition of privacy," said William F. Buckley, Jr., the conservative writer, in his syndicated column of March 18, 1975. "To expose one's private parts to the public is to move in the other direction of privacy."

The teacher called it "privacy" as a legal theory, but what the teacher was really seeking to protect was his right to personal autonomy in his sex life. And, in the end, many individuals are able to do this regardless of who is President or Chief Justice. Powerful organizations, says New York Senator Daniel Patrick Moynihan, "must confront the fact that the great decisions of the world are made by solitary couples—male and female—and are made in bed to boot." And they are made without regard to government policies on tax deductions or anything else, as Vice President Mondale and others have observed.

The best that we can hope for is that society increasingly sheds its concerns about certain unorthodox individual activities and that we don't run out of space in which to do them. In an increasingly crowded environment, we will be forced to tolerate and respect one another's rights to be let alone.

24

In the Mails

"Gentlemen do not read each other's mail," said former Secretary of State Henry L. Stimson in 1946. The word never reached the Federal Bureau of Investigation, the Central Intelligence Agency, the U. S. Bureau of Customs, or the U. S. Postal Service.

Federal laws and regulations say that no federal agent may *read* any first-class mail, except with a search warrant approved by a federal court. But federal agencies claim a right to *open* certain mail, if not to read it. Once mail is opened, is it logical to expect that it won't be read?

Parcel post, printed matter, and other non-first-class correspondence may be opened and inspected by postal agents without prior permission or consent. Most persons who use the mail know that. But they expect confidentiality in first-class letters.

Without warrants, the Bureau of Customs opens about 270,000 pieces of first-class mail from overseas each year, to search for goods on which a duty is owed or for contraband such as illegal drugs or weapons. Federal law permits a Customs agent "to search any trunk or envelope, wherever found, in which he may have a reasonable cause to suspect there is merchandise which was imported contrary to law."[44] What gives one of the five hundred mail openers in the Customs Bureau "reasonable cause"? Certainly, an X ray that detects contraband in a first-class package. Certainly, a bark from one of the detector dogs that sniff mail for drugs. Customs also claims, however, that "the weight, shape and feel of the mail article or its contents" can be probable cause for suspicion.

Customs doesn't sift through the 1 billion pieces of mail that arrive here each year from overseas. It designates particular countries from which it is interested in screening mail—Denmark, perhaps, for pornographic literature or Thailand for drugs. Bags of mail from these nations are set aside for Customs mail handlers to check, by X rays, detector dogs, or human intuition. If no improper contents are found, the envelope is resealed, rubber-stamped (saying the mail was opened by Customs), and sent on its way. If there are goods on which a duty is owed, the Postal Service collects the proper amount. If contraband is found, it is seized and the rest of the correspondence may be sent to the addressee. Or, if it is a significant shipment, the Drug Enforcement Administration will take the case for investigation and possible prosecution.

Of the 270,000 pieces it opens each year, Customs turns up about 48,000 envelopes with improper materials—roughly 15,000 items of pornography, 5,000 packets of marijuana and other drugs, and 28,000 imports on which duty is owed.

All of this does not violate the Fourth Amendment to the U. S. Constitution as long as the Customs agent has reasonable cause to believe that the envelopes contain dutiable goods or contraband, according to the U. S. Supreme Court in 1977.[45] The Court made clear that this authority does not include the right to read any of the mail (unless there is a search warrant to do so). To think that the mail is not read defies elementary notions of human behavior. A congressional investigating team in 1977 found that Customs inspectors were unaware of the prohibition against reading mail and made no distinction between the first-class mail they open and parcel post. One Customs dog handler was caught reading a letter at the Customs mail room in New York City. A Customs agent for a full year read incoming mail addressed to a person in Tennessee. The agent had no warrant. The suspicion? The correspondence was in Chinese. Another Customs agent read mail addressed to the

Consulate of Chile in San Diego. Assorted others read mail out of idle curiosity.

The latest word from the Department of Justice is that reading mail requires a warrant. (The U.S. attorney in the southern district of New York claimed that the restriction applied only to sealed mail and that the Customs had already unsealed the mail and therefore the restriction wasn't applicable.)

A Customs Bureau official told Congress in 1977 that other federal investigating agencies laughed at Customs when told they couldn't read mail that was opened. From 1953 to 1973, in violation of federal statutes and the Constitution, the Central Intelligence Agency conducted an extensive program of opening and reading first-class mail passing in and out of the country through Hawaii, San Francisco, New Orleans, and New York City. The Federal Bureau of Investigation got to take a look as well. Mail to and from the Soviet Union was automatically suspect.

Under this institutionalized nosiness (code-named HTLINGUAL and SRPOINTER), the CIA copied at least 215,000 letters and distributed them to other federal agencies for leisure-time reading. The CIA took down the names of every person mentioned in the correspondence—1.5 million persons in all—and stored them in its computer data bank in McLean, Virginia. Among those whose mail was read and photocopied were John Steinbeck, author of *The Grapes of Wrath*; Jane Fonda, film actress and political dissident in the early 1970s; Senator Frank Church of Idaho, whose mother wrote to him from Moscow; a sociology professor at Amherst College who notified two colleagues at Moscow State University about an academic conference; an American exchange student in Moscow writing back home to his father; and an American woman who wrote to a Soviet dissident whom she had met on a trip to Russia. Can the United States adequately crusade for the freedom of dissidents in the Soviet Union if American agents themselves are reading the mail of the Soviet citizens?

The CIA claims to be able to read mail without even opening the envelope. It uses a chemical to decipher the writing inside, according to secret testimony in 1975 by William E. Colby, then director of the CIA. But as long as postal authorities allowed the CIA to read mail in the States, there was no need to use the special potion in the United States.

The CIA's routine reading of mail within the United States was said to have stopped in 1973, and the Postal Service said in 1975 that it no longer permits CIA agents to get a look at the mail. The FBI somehow does get hold of mail, most of it from overseas, and reads it. Until 1977 it even had a special office behind the Capitol in Washington, D.C., for translating when necessary. Most of this mail is personal correspondence between American families and friends in Russia or China.

The extent to which federal agents open and read domestic mail is not known. About two hundred times a year, court orders allow federal authorities to do so. Federal agents are not supposed to do so without warrants.

The FBI makes use of the Postal Service's change-of-address records. FBI documents about a friend of mine showed that the Denver Field Office reported to headquarters the new address to which my friend had asked the Post Office to forward his mail. (The FBI also received the co-operation of a Denver moving company to find out where my friend was shipping his furniture.)

In addition to opening and reading mail, federal agents also use "mail covers," the interception of mail to a particular address to copy down all information on the outside of the envelope. About three hundred postal inspectors conduct the monitoring. Return addresses and the date of the postmark are copied and forwarded to the agency that requested the cover. Sometimes a fugitive will disclose his or her whereabouts by placing a return address on correspondence to the family. A mail cover on a company suspected of mail fraud may turn up the addresses of victims who could provide evidence for prosecution. The Postal Service takes the position that such surveillance does not violate the Fourth Amendment and requires no warrant, because the mail is not opened. The service will monitor mail only for law enforcement agencies and only to protect the security of the nation, to locate a fugitive, or to obtain evidence of criminal activity. The service does this about five thousand times a year, and at any one time there may be up to three hundred mail covers in effect.

All of this is done manually, but as automated equipment is used increasingly in mail handling, mail covers could easily be automated. Currently most mail is sorted according to zip codes by clerks who activate computers to channel the mail appropriately. Some large companies—such as book clubs—and the Internal Revenue Service use bar codes on the outside of envelopes for automated sorting within their own organizations. A scanner reads the code and sorts the mail to the proper office, in the same way bank checks are sorted. The bar code identifies the particular addressee, just as the bar codes on groceries identify the price of an item. Before long, the Postal Service may sort large mailings in this way, with the bar codes identifying the zip code, postal carrier route, and street address. Return envelopes supplied by a department store or utility, for instance, could be printed with the proper coding. To arrive at the right destination, they would not even need to have an address typed or written on them. Some optical character readers can read typewritten letters as well, but variations in style and spacing make this scanning less dependable.

To get ready for this, the Postal Service seems to be moving to an eight-digit zip code. The additional three digits would designate your postal carrier route so that the mail could be automatically sorted into the mail deliverer's bag. When the carrier routes change, the computer could be reprogrammed to make the necessary adjustments. By adding a few more digits, the Postal Service could provide each person who receives mail with his or her personal "zip code."

As the electronic coding of addresses becomes more precise, the Postal Service will be able to institute computerized mail covers with no difficulty at all. It will no longer have to be limited to five thousand or so a year.

Firms that send large amounts of information around the country—especially among their own regional offices—are resorting to "electronic mail." These firms deliver computer tapes or disks or chips to an independent company in the same city, and that company transmits the data by telephone, microwave, or satellite to its affiliates in other cities. The affiliates then send the data to the addressees, either by hand delivery or electronically.

Individual correspondents have a similar message service available to them. Western Union's Mailgram service takes your message over the telephone and transmits it to the city of destination. There it is converted into "hard copy"—a computer printout that looks like a telegram—and included in the next day's mail.

Current restrictions on mail snooping may not provide adequate protections in electronic mail. The current wiretap law, for instance, does not prohibit the interception of *data* communications, only communications that may be *listened to*.

The federal law preventing strangers from snooping into our mail was written in 1825. It says:

> Whoever takes any letter, postal card, or package out of any post office or any authorized depository for mail matter, or from any letter or mail carrier, . . . before it has been delivered to the person to whom it was directed, with design to obstruct the correspondence, or to pry into the business or secrets of another, or opens, secretes, embezzles, or destroys the same, shall be fined not more than $2,000 or imprisoned not more than five years, or both.[46]

The same law prohibits postal employees from detaining or delaying mail, but this has not deterred the Postal Service from its mail covers.

Strictly speaking, it's a federal crime for someone even to pick up a letter belonging to someone else merely to examine its envelope, unless the person believes by mistake that the mail is his or her own. Unsealed mail is entitled to the same protection as sealed mail.

When delivered to the addressee or someone authorized to receive it, a letter leaves federal custody and ceases to be a postal matter, according to Roy D. Weinberg, a lawyer who specializes in this subject. Letters left in a mail receptacle or dropped through mail slots onto the floors of locked offices remain in federal custody until picked up by the addressee. Mail placed on the desk of the addressee is regarded as out of federal custody.

At that point, however, many state laws protect the confidentiality of correspondence. New York's, for example, says:

> A person is guilty of tampering with private communications when:
> 1. Knowing that he does not have the consent of the sender or receiver, he opens or reads a sealed letter or other sealed private communication; or
> 2. Knowing that a sealed letter or other sealed private communication has been opened or read in violation [of the law], he divulges without the consent of the sender or receiver, the contents of such letter or communication, in whole or in part, or a resume of any portion of the contents. . . .

This presumably protects communications whether or not sent through the U.S. mail—like a hand-delivered love note or business document, a locked diary, or a sealed birthday card.

There is an additional protection—the law of copyright protects whatever you write from use or copying by others (whether or not you formally register it with the Copyright Office in Washington, D.C.). "Common law copyright," said a federal court blasting the CIA for its mail openings, "was never solely concerned with the financial interests of authors." It protects "a non-pecuniary interest in the privacy of letters," including letters that are not formally published. "Common law copyright protects an author's privacy as well as his pocketbook."[47]

The same court said:

> The law has recognized, for practical reasons, that the recipient, too, has an interest in the letter and certain rights pertaining to it. Were this not so, the addressee

of a letter would be unable to exercise the normal kinds of control over his or her mail, including the power to discard a letter once it has been read, or the right to show the letter (except where a breach of confidence might occur). . . . Under some circumstances, the recipient has even been deemed to have a right superior to the author's, enabling him to publish a given letter over the author's objections.

This means that the writer of a letter probably has no right to restrict its publication or disclosure *by the recipient*, unless the former is able to show a serious breach of confidentiality or invasion of privacy. However, the writer or the recipient probably has a right to prevent *a third party* from using or disclosing their correspondence willfully and maliciously.

Mail to and from prisoners may be opened by correctional authorities, according to the U. S. Supreme Court, but it may be censored only for matters that threaten the security and discipline of the institution. This does not include inflammatory political comments or derogatory remarks about the prison or its staff. These may not be censored.

25

In the Workplace

In earlier days, privacy in the workplace could be taken for granted. Most rural work is done alone, as is household work, and even much factory work afforded more solitude than a person wanted. But as twentieth-century work has moved to crowded assembly lines, office complexes, and large retail establishments, privacy for the working person has nearly disappeared. Because of this, there seems to be a revival of interest in privacy as a working condition when it's time to renegotiate labor agreements. Workers in crowded environments are realizing that their efficiency, their concentration, their peace of mind, and—most of all—their dignity require a measure of privacy. Here are some of the issues they are raising.

Disclosure of personal information. Many companies are discovering that not all workers welcome a public announcement of a promotion or other work change; nor does everybody like to have news of his or her latest illness posted on the bulletin board without permission. IBM Corp., for instance, now asks for consent before releasing such information about an employee. In one sense, the essence of privacy is control over information about ourselves. In this regard, an individual has the right to consent before the company discloses personal information, regardless of how innocent that information appears. This should include the release of salary information to the placement officer at one's former high school or college, or the release of employee information to a government investigator. A particular bone of contention is the use of lists showing salary level and prior contributions, in order to beef up employee giving to charity campaigns such as the United Way. Ohio Bell Telephone Co. suspected that some employees were making inflated pledges to keep supervisors and fellow workers off their backs and then submitting reduced or canceled pledges. The company circulated a computer printout of these pledge changes to supervisors and union leaders for "review." Ironically, or perhaps not so ironically, when a Cleveland news reporter asked the business executive who headed that city's United Way Services to reveal his personal gift to the drive, he refused, saying it was a "private matter."

Surveillance. Retail clerks work in an environment that is normally surveyed by closed-circuit television cameras. Labor arbitrators have ruled that the TV cameras may be used for store security, but not for catching employees goofing off on the job. About five years ago, factory workers in Cleveland discovered that their boss had concealed a microphone in the ladies' washroom and connected it to a speaker in the front office. The boss also adopted a shop rule that employees had to notify the plant foreman before using the rest room. Workers suspected that the owner wanted to monitor workers' gossip about upcoming labor negotiations. He was known around the plant as the "crapper tapper."

Some department stores use two-way mirrors or peepholes in customers' dressing rooms. The intention, clearly, is to reduce shoplifting. Many workers insist on guidelines preventing the use of such devices to spy on store employees themselves.

The law does not protect workers who are subject to wiretapping by their bosses. The telephones, after all, belong to the company and, under the law, if one party to the conversation consents to the wiretap it is not illegal. Federal law also permits electronic eavesdropping by the "operator of a switchboard . . . for mechanical or service quality control checks." That implies that the wiretapping must be for the purpose of *equipment* quality control, but a federal court in San Francisco has ruled that Macy's Department Store there did not violate the law when it tapped its own phones in order to catch employees who were pilfering merchandise. Preventing pilferage, the court decided, was "quality control."

Peace and quiet. At the drop of a hat, experts will tell you that Muzak and other forms of programmed music give a lift to workers and customers alike, give you something to look forward to, break the monotony, eliminate excessive talking, increase productivity, and, most important, inspire more purchasing. But how about the minority of people who find such noise irritating and distracting? For workers in an environment where piped music or announcements are necessary to promote sales, shouldn't the employer provide a place where the staff may enjoy a respite from the noise pollution during break time?

And aren't hourly workers entitled to rest rooms, changing rooms, and lounges that afford the maximum amount of physical privacy during breaks? American business provides a higher measure of physical privacy during break time to its high-level executives than to its hourly workers. The executives, actually, have less need of it because, like the rural workers of an earlier day, they already have a large measure of solitude during their worktime. Business provides very scant physical privacy during work breaks to hourly workers, whose duty hours are often spent in a crowded, noisy, and unprivate environment. And, of course, it's the hourly workers who would also be less likely to enjoy much privacy in their commuting to and from work or in their own homes. Driving to and from work in their own cars is the only privacy many people have. Commuters on public transportation don't enjoy even that bit of privacy.

After hours. Some companies make sure that telephone calls are made to employees' homes during off-duty hours only if the calls are essential. Some workers get overtime pay for receiving calls at home that involve work-related problems. That seems to limit telephone calls to essential business, but other firms are not even sensitive to this further invasion of privacy.

As we have seen earlier, some companies worry excessively about employees' behavior, political beliefs, and modes of dress when off duty. The main victims of this off-hours harassment lately have been employees of energy utilities who campaign for effective controls of nuclear energy development. There are other victims: employees are often punished for unorthodox religious practices, for the misdeeds of a relative, for being "controversial," and for union activities. For an individual, each of these matters, in the classic privacy sense, is "none of your business."

Plant security. Corporate security systems are assuming awesome proportions, even when the company is not involved in sensitive work like weaponry or nuclear power. Nabisco, Inc., requires each employee at corporate headquarters to carry an ID card with the person's photograph, ID number, level of security-zone clearance, and the distinctive measurements of the employee's right hand. To get into the building or into one of the thirteen security zones, an employee places the ID card in a computerized reader and simultaneously places his or her hand on an authenticator for comparison. As we discovered in Chapter 12, graduates of the University of Tennessee will already be accustomed to this procedure. In an apparent attempt to catch the "Cookie Monster," Nabisco has closed-circuit television monitors at each of the building's entrances, as well as overlooking its computers, vault, and payroll office. Cameras that perform in low light or in darkness and that can pan, tilt, and zoom keep track of employee movements throughout the building, in the parking lot, and even around a nearby pond.

At Texas Instruments in Dallas, Texas, you can't get into the building without words of greeting to a computer, which compares your voice with the characteristics of the voice it has identified previously as yours and stored in its memory. The computer also reads and verifies employees' company badges and opens the appropriate doors. At one point in corporate headquarters, the hallway floor is actually a scale that measures the weight of each employee. If your identity matches that of an authorized employee *and* your weight matches as well, you may enter. If you are an impostor, or if you have had a weekend of heavy eating, you are out of luck.

This security "overkill" brings to mind the arrangements in George Orwell's *1984*:

The television received and transmitted simultaneously. Any sound that Winston made, above the level of a very low whisper, would be picked up by it; moreover, so long as he remained within the field of vision which the metal plaque commanded, he could be seen as well as heard. There was of course no way of knowing whether you were being watched at any given moment. How often, or on what system, the Thought Police plugged in on any individual wire was guesswork. It was even conceivable that they watched everybody all the time. But at any rate they would plug in your wire whenever they wanted to. You had to live—did live, from habit that became instinct—in the assumption that every sound you made was overheard, and, except in darkness, every movement scrutinized.

As we saw in Chapter 21, the new technology has now pierced even the darkness.

Big Brother in 1984 knew that a person can never truly possess the right to privacy if that right disappears between the hours of nine and five.

26

In the Community

Your place of employment and the streets of downtown may not be the only places where your every move is monitored by electronic surveillance or computer data collection. I was shocked to come across the following article in *Law Enforcement Communications* magazine in October 1976, but I suppose I should have anticipated that our mania for security would bring us to this:

> All Saints Episcopal Church in Atlanta has been able to leave its welcome mat out—and its front door unlocked—since installation of a low-light-level closed-circuit television system this year.
>
> "The number of visitors to our sanctuary has increased surprisingly since we installed our closed-circuit TV system in May," comments W. Edward Prewitt, vestryman and chairman of buildings and grounds for the church. "People who are interested in history come to see our Tiffany windows. Others visit just for the solitude. And, we're very pleased to see all of them here."
>
> During the first month the system was in operation, thieves also attempted to enter the church. But those attempts, and all subsequent attempts, have been detected and thwarted by the camera.

For ten years, crime forced the vestry to keep the church's main front doors locked. Numerous break-ins occurred on the church grounds in the years before the "closed door" policy was instituted. "However much we wanted to keep the doors open, we felt that we had to safeguard our church," Prewitt explains.

The camera can "see" throughout the sanctuary, including the areas immediately below the camera [which faces the altar]. Contact-type alarms were also installed in the main entrance door frames. They are designed to send a silent alarm when the door is separated from its frame.

When a visitor enters the church, a sounding device in the office 100 feet away receives a signal. A church employee, stationed there, is alerted to the fact that someone is in the sanctuary for religious, aesthetic, or criminal purposes. He checks activity on a small CCTV monitor.

"We are trying to develop an eye for suspicious behavior," Prewitt said. "We noticed that [thieves] were nervous, secretive, and apparently were not here to enjoy the peace and solitude."

Thus, the CCTV cameras are helping to keep citizens on their best behavior in the church as well as in the community.

Peace the All Saints Episcopal Church may have. But solitude clearly it no longer has.

I read this news item to an undergraduate college class I teach about the right to privacy. Half of the students thought that the TV surveillance in a church was an outrageous invasion of personal privacy and religious freedom. The other half felt that the camera surveillance was preferable to keeping the church locked or threatened by burglaries.

Since biblical times, prayer has been regarded as a private matter. This is a good example of a time when an individual seeks privacy, not to hide something, but to concentrate, to dwell on private thoughts.

Jesus taught in the Sermon on the Mount (Matthew 6:5–6):

> And when thou prayest, thou shalt not be as the hypocrites are: for they love to pray standing in the synagogues and in the corners of the streets, that they may be seen of men. . . . But thou, when thou prayest, enter into thy closet, and when thou hast shut the door, pray to thy Father which is in secret; and thy Father which seeth in secret shall reward thee openly.

Churches, of course, have joined the computer age just like other organizations. Many religious denominations co-operate with banks so that parishioners' regular contributions may be deducted directly from their bank accounts or charged to their credit-card accounts. When the transfer of funds becomes electronic, church members will be able to contribute varying amounts each week by pushing buttons on a computer terminal at the church. And the computer will link the church office with banks in the community. Many church organizations—mostly the large nationwide evangelical movements—couldn't do without computers to keep track of their contributors and followers. Among those using computer systems for processing members' accounts are the Reverend Ike's United Christian Evangelical Association, the Seventh Day Adventists, the Voice of Prophecy, Billy Graham's crusades, and Rex Humbard's church organization.

The Roman Catholic Church and the Church of Jesus Christ of Latter-Day Saints (Mormons) keep track of their ecclesiastical personnel by computers. At any given time, the Catholic Church's computer system can ascertain the number of priests, nuns, students, and hospital beds under Catholic auspices within the United States. The Mormon Church monitors its tithing by computer, and printouts are sent out regularly to local officers. Genealogy plays an important role among Mormon believers, and so the Church since 1970 has been converting its 35 million genealogical records to a computer data bank under a mountain near Salt Lake City.

The Divine Light Mission operates a large data bank in Denver to keep track of its members' backgrounds, talents, spe-

cial interests, language fluency, and other skills so that the
Church may draw on them. Its guru believed, "All technology
was created for man to make use of and computers are valuable
tools in bringing the Master closer to his disciples."

If the Church is not sacred, what is? Certainly not the mar-
ketplace. Auto dealers in some parts of the country have been
known to place hidden microphones in their showrooms. The
salesperson leaves to "take a phone call." He listens in a back
room to a prospective couple's conversation to determine each
one's vulnerabilities. The salesperson returns with a custom-
made sales pitch and knows exactly where to aim it. Many department stores have two-way mirrors to prevent shoplifting in
customer changing rooms. Customers are rarely informed of
this invasion of their bodily privacy.

If you're not being watched, you're being recorded. When
your child signs up for the Ronald McDonald Birthday Club,
his or her name ends up in a computer in Baltimore. To handle
more than 100,000 applications each month, McDonald's codes
each kid's birthday so that he or she gets one of eight possible
free food offers.

There are hidden cameras, two-way mirrors, or snoopers hiding behind the ventilation screens in the rest rooms of some retail stores and transportation terminals. Many schools have had
to install video machines in their lavatories to deter vandalism,
violence, drug use, and abuses of other students.

A researcher who studied the habits of construction workers
reports that the right to be a Peeping Tom has become somewhat of an employee fringe benefit. He said that construction
workers regularly "watch the windows" of nearby apartments,
offices, and hotels. They regard the avocation as harmless. On
occasion, the men get permission to take a break to go window-
watching, and so the voyeurism has become a fringe benefit
that they expect.

Few personal facts are as sensitive as an individual's taste in
reading. This is recorded on computer in some communities.
The East Brunswick Municipal Library in New Jersey checks
out books with a wand that reads data from the book and from

the user's library card. It enters the information into a computer system that automatically mails overdue notices. And the system can tell the librarian each month which types of patrons like which kinds of books and which titles are getting frequent or infrequent use.

The American Library Association has an unequivocal policy that circulation records and anything else that identifies a person with specific materials should remain confidential. Libraries should insist on a court order or subpoena before revealing this information and should resist compliance unless the order is valid and based on good cause, according to the association. The use of computers by libraries may make this an impossible standard to meet. The individual circulation records for the East Brunswick library, for instance, are stored in the town's data processing center next door.

This mass processing causes embarrassment. The Mountain View, California, library threatened to turn over one borrower's overdue account to a collection agency. The borrower happened to be a second-grader whose six children's books were overdue. Her parents switched to a library that does not use a collection agency for fines.

I don't mean to imply that someone else—or a machine—is watching you everywhere you go and that a computer is recording your every transaction in the community. I do mean to imply that the technology for such a closed society has existed for a couple of years now. And I do mean to imply that there are no organizations that have decided that their relationships with their clientele are such that TV cameras, computers, and electronic surveillance have no place. I do mean to imply that we must draw the line somewhere. We must either limit the types of organizations that may employ this technology or decide as a community that there must be a few nonautomated, nonintrusive sanctuaries left. Just as states have created wildlife sanctuaries where humans may not hunt the animals, so we need sanctuaries for human beings where automation may not stalk us.

A WORD ABOUT SEARCH AND SEIZURE

The Fourth Amendment to the U.S. Constitution reads:

> The right of the people to be secure in their persons, houses, papers, and effects, against unreasonable searches and seizures, shall not be violated, and no Warrants shall issue, but upon probable cause, supported by Oath or affirmation, and particularly describing the place to be searched, and the persons or things to be seized.

The law of search and seizure is a precise and changing one; lawyers have built careers specializing in it. Here are some general rules that may provide some guidance, but there are many nuances you must check before relying on this simple guide.

Remember that the Constitution and its amendments are restrictions on actions by the government, not by private parties. To claim a violation of the Fourth Amendment, you must find evidence of *state action*—by a federal agent, a local police officer, a public servant, a governmental body, a tax-supported institution, a court, an elected official. Searches by private parties may invade your privacy but they do not violate your constitutional rights unless the action is taken in behalf of the state. Searches by the managers of a privately owned sports arena, by an airline, by a hotel manager, by a landlord, or by a neighbor do not raise constitutional issues under the law.

Under the Fourth Amendment, a search may be conducted by a representative of the government only if it is reasonable or pursuant to a search warrant based on probable cause of criminal activity.

A police officer may always search your body or premises with your consent, as long as the consent is given freely, clearly, explicitly, without duress, and with the knowledge that you need not consent if you do not wish to. One cynical non-lawyer once said, "I didn't know what a consent search warrant was. [Some lawyers] said, 'Well, that's when two policemen go to a house. One of them goes to the front door and knocks on it, and the other one runs around to the back door and yells, "Come in." ' " That story was told by Jimmy Carter in 1974.

If an officer shows up at your front door and announces that he or she wants to look around and you agree, the courts often find that kind of consent invalid because it was by implication coercive.

An officer may search your person incident to an arrest—for contraband, the fruits of a crime, and other evidence. An arrest may not be used simply as an excuse for a general search, nor may the officer search for evidence of a crime different from the one for which the arrest was made.

The U. S. Supreme Court has permitted the search of the driver of an automobile stopped for a minor traffic offense. The search is allowed to protect the arresting officer, to prevent escape or suicide, or to prevent the destruction of evidence. The officer may use force if necessary and may seize just about anything. Officers are also permitted to "stop and frisk" a suspicious person on the street, only for purposes of "patting down" the person for possible weapons. If the officer comes across evidence of a crime—illegal drugs, for instance—the officer may seize the evidence.

An officer may search your premises if there is no time to get a warrant because there is an emergency, if he or she is in hot pursuit of a suspect, if there's reason to believe that evidence will be destroyed or removed, or if an arrest occurs within the premises. Viewing your premises by binoculars, flashlights, or similar, electronic devices is not a search, as long as there is no expectation of privacy where you are.

There is no need to get a warrant to search a vehicle, in most cases, because it can easily be moved beyond the reach of the officer.

In all cases of warrantless searches, there must be probable cause to believe that a person has committed, is committing, or is about to commit a crime.

All other searches must be conducted with a valid search warrant approved by a local or federal judge or magistrate, based on affidavits of facts—a tip that another person has drugs on his or her person, a suspect's confession that a weapon is hidden in a basement, a tip that a person took a stolen television set into a garage. The warrant must be specific and accurate as to the place or person to be searched and the facts on which it is based. In all cases, whether with a search warrant or not, an officer who has legitimate authority to search may seize whatever he or she finds "in plain view." A search warrant to find a gun allows the officer to seize illegal drugs or stolen property found in plain view in the course of the search.

If an illegal search is conducted, the victim has two remedies: to sue the government for deprivation of constitutional rights (or invasion of privacy) or to prevent the evidence seized from being used in a criminal trial. Courts will not permit evidence seized illegally to be used in a prosecution; this is called the "exclusionary rule."

School officials or police may generally search a pupil's desk or locker without consent or a warrant. Courts say that the school principal assigns and controls desks and lockers and may "consent" to the search, even if the desk or locker contains a student's personal effects. Most courts have also upheld the validity of police or school officials' search of a pupil's person, without consent or a warrant, *on school property*. The National Association of Secondary School Principals recommends that principals search a student's clothing, desk, or locker only if the student gives permission freely and is present, except under extreme circumstances. Students should realize that they are extremely vulnerable with regard to in-school searches and should not store anything at school that they would not want police or school authorities to discover.

The management at privately owned sports arenas and stadiums often announces by loudspeaker or signs that you are subject to search as you enter. If you choose to attend the event anyway, you are presumably giving your implied consent to be searched. You cannot be sure that criminal evidence discovered will not be used against you. With or without consent, searches at privately owned facilities are probably valid. The owners of private amusement parks do not violate your Fourth Amendment rights by searching you on the premises, but you may have a civil claim against them. Searches at publicly owned facilities require implied consent.

Searches at border crossings are not considered "searches," and so no probable cause nor warrant is needed.

A WORD ABOUT DOOR-TO-DOOR SALES

Each year thousands of people succumb to the charms of fast-talking door-to-door salespersons, and as a result many people are left holding bills for appliances, brushes, encyclopedias, or other products they do not want or cannot afford. With these problems in mind, the Federal Trade Commission in 1974 established rules for a "cooling-off period" for door-to-door sales.

Under the rules, the sales representative must give the buyer a receipt for the products bought or ordered, and a form captioned "Notice of Cancellation." Both forms must be dated by the salesperson and must show the complete name and address of the sales company.

If the buyer decides within three days after the sale that he or she does not wish to follow through with the agreement, all he or she needs to do is date and sign the notice of cancellation and mail it to the company. The sales company has ten business days after receiving the notice to return the customer's payment, return any property traded in, or return any supplementary contracts signed by the buyer.

These rules apply *only to sales of twenty-five dollars or more* and have no bearing on telephone sales or on transactions solicited by the buyer—insurance sales or telephone company repairs, for example.[48]

A WORD ABOUT A WOMAN'S NAME

Does a married woman have the right to retain her birth-given maiden name, to adopt the surname of her husband, or to use a hyphenated combination of both? Yes, she may do any of the three alternatives, according to courts in Connecticut, Maryland, North Carolina, Tennessee, and Wisconsin and an administrative opinion in the District of Columbia. The general rule throughout the United States is that no court petition is necessary for any adult to select a name. Petitioning a court to change your name is simply an alternative procedure. A person may select any name he or she wishes as long as there is an intention to use it consistently and exclusively and without fraudulent or improper purpose.

There is a contrary court opinion in Alabama, upholding the Alabama Department of Public Safety's requirement that a married woman apply for a driver's license only in her husband's name. The U. S. Supreme Court affirmed this decision, but mainly because Alabama common law had traditionally favored the husband's name.[48] A court in Tennessee said that a woman is not denied equal protection of the law if she is forced to use her husband's name to get and keep a state civil service job. In many states, licensing agencies and other governmental offices still require a woman to register in her husband's name or to petition a court for a name change.

In short, there's no law that says a woman has to use her husband's name or can't go back to her maiden name, but everyone assumes there is. "A name is a person's identity," says a woman fighting to change the tradition. "Traditionally women have been denied this small portion of self-identity."

Two groups that are working to change this are the Center for a Woman's Own Name, 261 Kimberly, Barrington, Illinois 60010, telephone (312) 381-2113, and Women's Legal Defense Fund, 1010 Vermont Avenue, N.W., Suite 210, Washington, D.C. 20005, telephone (202) 638-1123.

A WORD ABOUT THE PRESS

When you agree to press coverage, you are consenting to the publication of the information you provide. You may, however, revoke that consent later if you discover that the information will be presented in an entirely different way from what you had expected when you consented.

You have little claim against a news publication or broadcast station that discloses information about you, even private facts, if you have become a matter of legitimate public interest, voluntarily or involuntarily. This is true because, under the First Amendment's protection of free speech, courts want to avoid unduly limiting the breathing space needed by the press for the exercise of effective editorial judgment. The current standard in an invasion of privacy claim against a news organ is:

> In determining what is a matter of legitimate public interest, account must be taken of the customs and conventions of the community; and in the last analysis what is proper becomes a matter of the community mores. The line is to be drawn when the publicity ceases to be the giving of information to which the public is entitled, and becomes a morbid and sensational prying into private lives for its own sake, with which a reasonable member of the public, with decent standards, would say that he had no concern.[50]

As long as the press can show that publication was not done with actual malice or reckless disregard for the truth, it is protected from lawsuits for invasion of privacy.

Courts will rarely even listen to a suit against the press for invasion of privacy in the first place unless you claim that the public portrayal held you *in a false light*, that information about you or a photograph was used grossly out of context. There is an exception to this. The protection of the press is far less if its public portrayal of you was so complete that it deprived you of something of monetary value—like a circus performance that is filmed in its entirety on television without consent or perhaps a photo display and description of an exhibit for which you charge others to see.

If you are suing a person or organization that is not engaged in news dissemination, you do not have to meet the high standard of proof necessary in privacy cases involving speech protected by the First Amendment. In these non-news-media cases, the standards are those described in Chapter 1.

27

In the Home

"My wife objects that I'm always going into another room to read," a man complained to a counselor. "Believe me, I would if I could. Wherever I go she follows me. If I want to go for a walk, suddenly *she* wants to go for a walk. If I decide to work in the garden, *she* decides to work in the garden, too."

A woman elsewhere has the same problem. "It's reached the point where I have to get in the car and drive around the streets if I want to be alone." But a second woman has the opposite problem: "My husband works late every night, and then on weekends he says he has to be left alone to relax."

Each of us needs moments of solitude regardless of how much we are loved by, or love, another. It's necessary to give your spouse—or roommate—some breathing space. There's a balance between love and respecting another's right to be let alone. This can be done by managing the home in such a way that one family member doesn't crowd out another and each member of the family has at least a small amount of personal space.

Psychologists don't know why one person needs more privacy than another, according to counselors Marcia Lasswell and Norman Lobsenz, in an advice column in *McCall's* of August 1977, entitled "Love vs. Privacy." "They think it can be traced to childhood situations. But they can't agree whether the desire for aloneness is the sign of a neurotic 'loner' or the hallmark of a well-adjusted person. If one spouse wants some time alone, the other often feels resentful or rejected. In turn, the one seeking privacy may feel guilty for doing so—and then also resentful that there seems no way to have some solitude.

"Privacy," say Lasswell and Lobsenz, "extends to thoughts and feelings, too. To ask, 'What are you thinking about?' can sometimes be an intrusion. When it produces the usual response—'Oh, nothing'—the questioner feels rebuffed, left out. The person who insists on sharing everything runs the risk of alienating a partner, rather than drawing him or her closer.

"Giving each other private time and space means respecting your partner's needs and trusting his or her motives. Couples who do not understand this may find their relationship studded with problems."

So don't be surprised if your spouse habitually locks the bathroom door. Some people, especially those in large families, have been raised that way. And don't be surprised if your partner chooses to take a vacation alone. That may be no reflection on you. Many people, long before getting married, became used to solitary travel and much prefer it to joint travel. Many individuals love solitary hobbies—in fact, many think that the very definition of a hobby is a personal project done alone. It is difficult for two people together to arrange delicate butterflies or to read a worthwhile book.

Some tasks simply can't be done with others—like contemplation. Many a partner is more interesting company if he or she has had an opportunity alone to gather thoughts, contemplate the past or the future.

Because each of us has been raised to respect the sanctity of the mails, don't be surprised when your spouse gets irritated if you read his or her mail. Your partner has nothing to hide. It's just a shock to some people's systems to discover someone else reading their mail. Every person—especially every married person—has an inalienable right to see his or her mail first. Not to prevent disclosure of something embarrassing. But just because it's right.

The important thing to remember is that each person craves privacy. We crave it in varying degrees, to be sure, and in varying forms, but each of us wants some kind of privacy. We should remind ourselves of this often so that our feelings are not hurt when we discover this basic human trait in a loved one. It may come at times of illness or at family gatherings or in leisure hours or in personal hygiene or in discussing personal facts or in recreation or in travel or at what appear to be peculiar times. But it comes.

There is nothing to hide. A person simply wants a sense of autonomy, a sense of one's own personhood. What could be more basic? We want to choose for ourselves when information about us or a view of ourselves is released. Don't equate privacy with solitude or loneliness. Gregarious people seek privacy. They like to be with other people, but they like also to control what those other people know about them. Don't equate privacy with secretiveness or concealment. People who honestly and candidly disclose everything about themselves seek privacy. They want to make sure their personal freedom, their autonomy, is not restricted by what they have revealed about themselves.

Some people do not care at all about common notions of privacy. We come to know who those people are. The important thing to remember is that not everybody else is like that.

Children crave privacy. A British author of children's books, Maria Edgeworth, observed as far back as 1822, in *Essays on Practical Education* (quoted in Carl D. Schneider's *Shame, Exposure and Privacy*):

> Nothing hurts young people more than to be watched continually about their feelings, to have their sensibility measured by the surveying eye of the unmerciful spectator. Under the constraint of such examinations they can think of nothing but that they are looked at, and feel nothing but shame or apprehension.

Even the very youngest crave privacy. They want either a chance to be—or act—alone, a physical space that is under their control, or a chance to keep personal secrets. My son, when he was eight, said, "Privacy is having your own room." He's right, but it's not always possible for each child to have his or her own room. Still, it is possible for each child to have a private preserve of space—whether a bureau drawer, a cardboard box, or a corner of the back yard. Youngsters like to have a place where they can keep "my things"—whether collected rocks or bottle caps or pressed flowers or snapshots or loose change or secret notes. That space should be inviolable against snoopers, whether grownups or others.

Each parent will have occasion to empty the pockets of the kids' soiled clothing. But what's found there is the kids' business, and it may be embarrassing, or just downright annoying, to have the contents of that personal space announced to others (regardless of how "cute" it may be). A child's performance at school can be extremely embarrassing if it is talked about to others, even if the chatter is complimentary. Most kids probably don't care, but for the kid who does care the invasion of privacy hurts. Some kids are sensitive about undressing in front of others, and many other kids are sensitive only during brief periods of their adolescence. Many other kids are minor-league exhibitionists. Whatever the characteristic, basic rules of privacy in the home would say that the child's wishes be respected.

For what it's worth, researchers do know that humans are adversely affected by crowding. We don't know exactly why this is true. A couple of studies described in 1975 in *Environment and Behavior* showed that preschool children became less aggressive when the available space decreased and the size of the group remained the same. On the other hand, they showed increased aggression and decreased play together when the group size *increased* and the amount of space *remained the same*. One study showed that boys were slightly more affected by crowding than girls (although another study said that grown men perform better in high density and women perform less well).

One environmental researcher recommends that institutions housing children should use more private rooms (but not so large that their scale frightens a child) and that bedrooms for two children should provide more space than simply double what one child would need. Here's another finding: walls painted blue minimize one's perception of noise; red walls have the opposite effect.

Elderly persons seem not to mind crowded surroundings so much. They feel less afraid, according to experiments. If other tests bear this out, researchers suggest that housing for the elderly include numerous small and cozy rooms, as opposed to one-room efficiencies. It's true that solitude can be deadly for older persons, but so can a lack of privacy. Elderly persons who live with relatives or in nursing homes need physical privacy at times—for contemplation, confidential conversation, embracing, and, yes, sexual activities. Most institutions provide absolutely no opportunity for physical or emotional contact.

A WORD ABOUT NOISE

Sharp, loud noises increase a person's blood pressure, no doubt about it.

One 1970–72 study of families who live directly under the noisy landing patterns of the Los Angeles International Airport found that children born there have far greater chances of birth defects than those born to the rest of the population.

The family home is becoming louder and louder, as we add mechanical devices and are forced to live closer to heavily traveled arteries. We seemingly accommodate to these noises, but they affect us subtly. They make us tired, irritable, depressed, tense, sick, or forgetful—or all of these at the same time. Sound control, and privacy, have not been major considerations in the design of family homes, and so families must adapt their living quarters accordingly. We spend a lot of time in the parts of the house where there are the most noisy appliances, the kitchen and bathroom. And these are the places in the home where the most accidents occur.

Koss Corporation, a manufacturer of stereo sound equipment, lists the following home appliances in order of their sound levels:

More than 100 decibels, beyond the point where efficiency decreases and approaching the threshold of human pain: doorbell and furnace blower.

More than 70 decibels, the point at which the nervous system is activated, blood pressure rises, and supply of blood to the heart lessens: electric blender, electric can opener, electric fan, garbage disposer, hair dryer, knife sharpener, electric mixer, radio, stove fan, electric shaver, shower, sink drain, telephone ring, and (especially) vacuum cleaner.

After several weeks, I know that the sound of an electric typewriter has significant effects on the mind and body. I have had solitude in writing this book, but not peace and quiet.

Here are some suggestions: Spend most of your time in rooms away from traffic noises. Try to separate the eating area from the clatter of the kitchen (pots and pans produce seventy-three decibels). Choose appliances that make the least noise. Cushion appliances and plumbing. Use carpeting, tiling, and upholstery to absorb noise. Use double windows and weather stripping. Arrange traffic flow in the house to preserve quiet spaces. Use earphones for home entertainment units. Use intercommunication devices to eliminate shouted messages. Cushion slamming doors. If you must use power lawn and garden equipment, arrange with your neighbors to use them all at the same hour. Use landscaping to screen out noise. Close books gently.

PART V

Psychological Aspects of Privacy

28

In Mind and Body

Control. That's what we have been talking about in this book. Privacy is the right to control your own body, as in the right to an abortion or the right to whatever sexual activities you choose. Privacy is the right to control your own living space, as in the right to be free from unreasonable searches and seizures. Privacy is the right to control your own identity, as in the right to be known by a name of your choice and not a number, the right to choose your own hair and dress styles, the right to personality. Privacy is the right to control information about yourself, as in the right to prevent disclosure of private facts or the right to know which information is kept on you and how it is used.

Privacy encompasses all of these rights. The challenge for each of us in a crowded, complex, and computerized era is to maintain some sense of this control. It may be only a psychological sense of control, but that is adequate. The benefits that flow from privacy, after all, are psychological.

Privacy is often thought to be synonymous with one of the following terms, but it is not:

Confidentiality. This is the status of information we wish not to be disclosed. As we have seen, the right to informational privacy includes far more than confidentiality. It includes the right to inspect information about yourself and to correct it and the right to withhold information that is either irrelevant or needlessly embarrassing.

Anonymity. Many people seek both fame and privacy. Privacy, in fact, includes the right to one's own identity. It is not at all the right to be unknown.

Concealment. Some people seek privacy in order to camouflage facts about themselves, it is true. But this is not the primary motivation. Privacy is a self-imposed state, not a coerced one. We seek privacy when in prayer, not because we have something to hide—for surely no one would draw negative connotations from that—but because we are preoccupied and vulnerable. It is unfair for strangers to be prying at that time.

Isolation. The nation's largest consumer investigating company thinks that modern men and women need to live in a mountaintop cave to enjoy full privacy. But privacy is not withdrawal from others. Those who are most alone in this world are those with the least privacy, no control over their own destinies, no identity to others, no control over what is known about them—for very little is said about them in their presence.

Shame. If people sought privacy out of a sense of shame, they wouldn't assert, as they do, that the right to privacy includes the right to swim in the nude or to wear outrageous clothing. Privacy is not modesty. Nor is shame a negative characteristic. (How strange it is that we condemn persons who are shameful *and* those who are shameless.) Shame, in fact, might be a natural feeling that protects us when we are growing, changing, and learning—when we are not ready to face the rest of the world.

Solitude. This may be one component of privacy, but it is not synonymous with privacy. Someone whose privacy has been destroyed among a certain circle of acquaintances does not covet solitude, he or she covets a new circle of friends to begin afresh.

Secrecy. Many government officials will tell you all about the government's right to privacy. There is no such right, of course. Privacy is uniquely a right for individuals. What those government officials are talking about is the government's perceived right to secrecy. Those who think that the right to privacy is no more than the right to keep secrets are unaware of the Supreme Court decisions on contraception and abortion. A woman argued once that her right to privacy included the right to breast-feed her baby at her place of employment. A man argued that his right to privacy included the right to pose nude for a magazine photographer without jeopardizing his job. Surely neither was trying to keep a secret. They were trying to preserve their freedom of choice.

Freedom. Privacy is freedom, but it includes more than that. It includes the prerequisites and the environment in which freedom may be exercised. Freedom is often thought to be the right to do great things—to fight for one's country, to speak one's mind, to defy authority. The late J. Braxton Craven, Jr., a judge in the Fourth U. S. Circuit, said of privacy: "To the average man, who may not wish to make a speech or print a newspaper, it may be the greatest freedom of all. The right to be let alone is the only non-political protection for that vast array of human activities which, considered separately, may seem trivial, but together make up what most individuals think of as freedom. I am thinking of little things, mostly taken for granted, such as the right to attend a football game, to refrain from attending a political rally, to wear a hat, or to ride a bicycle to work through city traffic." This he called *personhood*.

Intimacy. Privacy provides the setting for intimacy. When persons are intimate with each other, they sacrifice their ultimate privacy to achieve interdependence with each other. Their needs for privacy, then, are protection against the rest of the world, not against each other.

Separation. Privacy, as we have seen, is not limited to physical isolation. The person with a strong sense of privacy often seeks *more* active participation in society, not less.

In this book, we have discussed the *objective* aspects of privacy. We have described the information-gathering and the surveillance technology that exists today. Our aim is to help each of us, as individuals, to master the surveillance before it masters us. We have suggested steps each of us can take to make sure we remain in control. When we think about the capacity of technology and of large institutions, the suggestions for protection that we have listed may seem distressingly inadequate.

And so they are. In the end the *subjective* aspects of privacy are what will save us. How each of us perceives the psychological aspects of privacy will determine our survival in the machine age.

Stage actors maintain a psychological sense of privacy even when they are exposed before the eyes of hundreds, or millions, of other persons.

"For me being on stage is an exhilarating experience," an aspiring actor named Roy Haller told me. "To be the focus of hundreds of eyes imparts electric shockwaves to my brain; my energy flow is quadrupled as my fingers and toes tingle, my genitals and anus throb and my heart pounds." Most of the rest of us would call that stage fright, but for an actor the experience is exhilarating. But how to preserve a sense of privacy when exposed to the world? "My secrets have become the character's secrets," says Haller. "I can maintain my privacy and my identity by concentrating not on hiding myself but on revealing character." This paradox of "public solitude" envelops the stage actor in a protective shield when he appears most vulnerable. "I maintain my own identity while on stage, thus freeing my creative powers to create the identity of the character. My secrets are safe with me. I reveal what I wish; I hide what I must for my own sake. I can trust the other actors and the audience. I am public and private at the same time. In my imagination I find my private space from which I can extend, freely drawing from the storehouse of my own experience."

Jeanne Moreau, the actress, says (in *The New Yorker*, March 13, 1978), "Art is not autobiographical. . . .

"What's good about stage fright," she says, "is that it's transformed into concentration as soon as you're working. Maybe the longing to see the naked body [on stage and in films] is a longing to know everything about someone. But you find then that the body itself is a cover."

To appear nude, to cry, to kiss. Accomplished actors and actresses do this without sacrificing privacy.

The same is true of the oppressed residents of tyrannical regimes. In such states, personal privacy is the enemy of the state. The government diminishes privacy.

"Throughout the Soviet empire today the rulers do have that power—and use it," says Erazim Kohak, a philosopher from Czechoslovakia now at Boston University. "As long as a person retains the privacy of his soul, he can resist; absolute rulers cannot tolerate that."

To prove his point, Kohak asks men to recall the deprivation of privacy required on induction into the armed forces. The recruit is stripped of his hair style, his personal effects, his full name (and given a "serial number"), his individuality, and his clothing. (The same is true of prisoners.) Each serviceman is dressed like every other one, sleeping on identical bunks, using identical foot lockers and latrines with no partitions. "There is precious little objective privacy here, and yet how deeply, intensely private can be the thoughts and experiences of each of those men! If you ever were a sergeant shouting orders to a private who was a poet in his civilian life, you know how impenetrably *private* his experience remains to you—and yours to him."

And still, Kohak points out, there are plenty of examples of the opposite. "There are people who have little to call their own in their soul. To them you can give objective privacy, their own room, perhaps even their own desert island—and yet they will remain incapable of privacy because they bear nothing private within themselves. Surely you have met them; you can tell them by the blaring transistor radios they bring into the woods to fill their emptiness."

In the end, we must realize that it is the trivial aspects of our personhood that are recorded by the government and by business. There is nothing quite so trivial as an FBI report on an individual. An Equifax "investigation" is full of meaningless gossip. Our bank may know how we spend our money, but it couldn't begin to know how our spending affects our growth as human beings.

The stuff they gather on us hurts sometimes, but it does not stifle the most genuine individuals among us.

The crucial facts about our beings remain our own. When the privacy of that sphere is breached, we still have remedies. We still have our private places—whether physical or mental.

> In that zone [the individual] can think his own thoughts, have his own secrets, live his own life, reveal only what he wants to the outside world. The right of privacy, in short, establishes an area excluded from the collective life, not governed by the rules of collective living.

So says Thomas I. Emerson, the eminent constitutional scholar at Yale University (*The System of Freedom of Expression* [New York: Random House]).

Emerson the lawyer sees the need for a zone of privacy to ensure political freedom. The late Sidney M. Jourard, the psychologist, saw the need for a sanctuary of privacy to ensure public mental health ("Some Psychological Aspects of Privacy," *Law and Contemporary Problems*, Spring 1966):

> The experience of psychotherapists and of students of personality growth has shown that people maintain themselves in physical health and in psychological and spiritual well-being when they have a "private place," some locus that is inviolable by others except at the person's express invitation. This "private place" may be a physical location, such as a room, a cabin, a "pad," or a monastic cell. It may be a place for solitude, or it may be an ambience peopled by individuals who share the values and ideals held by the person in question. There, he can do or be as he likes and feels. He can utter, express, and act in ways that disclose his being-for-himself. And he does not need to fear external sanctions. Nor does he feel guilt for the discrep-

ancy between the way he appears in public and the way he *is* in private.

We must create this "private place," this "zone of privacy," in our own way, whether it be physical space or psychological space. As Emerson and Jourard tell us, this is essential for political freedom and for mental health.

Privacy is not an end in itself. It is the creation of an environment for creativity, thought, sharing, happiness, experimentation, and growth. If an individual can achieve these without "privacy," there is no need to seek more. If a person is not able to achieve these with privacy, then what good is privacy?

Jourard said, in "Some Psychological Aspects of Privacy":

> In short, privacy is experienced as "room to grow in," as freedom from interference, and as freedom to explore, to pursue experimental projects in science, art, work, play, and living. In the name of the *status quo* and other, even more attractive goals, privacy may be eroded. But without privacy and its concomitant, freedom, the cost to be paid for the ends achieved—in terms of lost health, weak commitment to society, and social stagnation—may be too great.

Using laws where they exist and common sense and determination where they do not, we must preserve this right to privacy for ourselves, our neighbors, and those still to come.

Notes

1. *The Information Economy*, by Marc Uri Porat (Washington, D.C.: U. S. Government Printing Office, 1977).
2. *The Right to Privacy*, by Samuel D. Warren and Louis D. Brandeis, 4 HARVARD LAW REVIEW at 195–6 (1890).
3. Galella v. Onassis, 487 F. 2d 986 (2d Cir. 1973). The legal cases listed in this book can be found at the law library in your county courthouse, a law school, a public defender's office, or a private law firm. The reference after the case name is to the volume, legal reporter, page number, court, and year of decision, in that order. In this case, the court was the U. S. Second Circuit Court of Appeals.
4. Nader v. General Motors Corp., 25 N.Y. 2d 560, 307 N.Y.S. 2d 647, 255 N.E. 2d 765 (Ct. App. N.Y. 1970).
5. *A Treatise on Constitutional Limitations*, by Thomas McIntyre Cooley (8th ed., Boston: Little, Brown, 1927), I, 611.
6. Paul v. Davis, 424 U.S. 693 (1976).
7. California Bankers Association v. Shultz, 416 U.S. 21 (1974).
8. U.S. v. Miller, 425 U.S. 435 (1976).
9. The Bank Secrecy Act is found at 31 U.S.C. 1051. This means Title 31, U. S. Code, section 1051, which can be found in any law library. The U. S. Code, which is published in different collections, includes all of the federal laws of the nation classified by general subject matter. The regulations under the Bank Secrecy Act are found at 31 C.F.R. 103.11. This refers to Title 31, Code of Federal Regulations, part 103.11. The Code of Federal Regulations includes all of the regulations written by federal agencies to implement laws in the code. The numbering system in the C.F.R. is not related to that of the U.S.C. Proposed and final regulations drafted by federal agencies are first published in a daily compilation called the *Federal Register*, available in large city and university libraries and most federal buildings.
10. 26 U.S.C. 7609.
11. Gregory v. Litton Systems, Inc., 316 F. Supp. 401 (C.D. Calif. 1970).
12. 42 U.S.C. 1983.
13. 42 U.S.C. 3771(b).
14. 28 C.F.R. 20.1.
15. 15 U.S.C. 1643.
16. 15 U.S.C. 1681.
17. 15 U.S.C. 1691.

18. 15 U.S.C. 1666.
19. *Ford,* by Allan Nevins (New York: Arno Press, 1976).
20. "Job Hunting," by Tom Nadeau, *The New Republic* (April 28, 1973), p. 13.
21. 15 U.S.C. 1681.
22. *Computers and Invasion of Privacy,* July 26, 1966, 89th Cong., 2nd Sess., pp. 2–11, House Committee on Government Operations.
23. 5 U.S.C 552a.
24. 5 U.S.C. 552.
25. Department of the Air Force v. Rose, 425 U.S. 352 (1976).
26. 13 U.S.C. 221.
27. 2 U.S.C. 438, 11 C.F.R 104.13.
28. 39 U.S.C. 3008.
29. 39 U.S.C. 3010.
30. 39 C.F.R. 265.6(d).
31. 16 C.F.R. 435.
32. Whalen v. Roe, 429 U.S. 589 (1977).
33. 20 U.S.C 1232g, 45 C.F.R. 99.
34. Doe v. McMillian, 412 U.S. 306 (1973).
35. Privacy Act of 1974, 5 U.S.C. 552a, and Tax Reform Act of 1976, 26 U.S.C. 6109.
36. GM Leasing Corp., et al. v. U.S. et al., 429 U.S. 338 (1977).
37. 26 U.S.C. 6334.
38. 26 C.F.R. 301.7216, issued under 26 U.S.C. 7216(a).
39. 47 C.F.R. 42.9.
40. 15 U.S.C. 1692c.
41. 18 U.S.C. 2510, sometimes called "Title III," because this was Title III of the Omnibus Crime Control Act of 1968.
42. Frye v. U.S., 293 F. 1013 (1923).
43. Paul v. Davis, 424 U.S. 693 (1976).
44. 19 U.S.C. 482.
45. U.S. v. Ramsay, 431 U.S. 606 (1977).
46. 42 U.S.C. 2702.
47. Birnbaum v. U.S., 436 F. Supp. 967 (E.D. N.Y., 1977).
48. 16 C.F.R. 429.
49. Forbush v. Wallace, 341 F. Supp. 217 (M.D. Ala., 1971), aff'd *per curiam,* 405 U.S. 970 (1972).
50. Virgil v. Time, Inc., 527 F. 2d 1122 (9th Cir., 1975).

Index

About the Author

Robert Ellis Smith is the publisher of *Privacy Journal*, a monthly Washington newsletter that *The New Yorker* called "the most interesting publication to come out of the capital since I. F. Stone's walloping *Weekly*." After graduating from Harvard in 1962, Mr. Smith worked as a news reporter in Alabama, Long Island, and Detroit, and then as an assistant director of the Office for Civil Rights in the Department of Health, Education, and Welfare. A graduate of Georgetown University Law Center and an attorney, he was associate director of the privacy project of the American Civil Liberties Union. In 1974 he began his own newsletter out of an office in the carriage house behind his Capitol Hill home. He has become a leading authority on the right to privacy and has been called the "Ralph Nader of privacy."